The Businessman in
American Literature

The

BUSINESSMAN

in American Literature

Emily Stipes Watts

The University of Georgia Press   Athens

Set in 10 on 12 Times Roman

Designed by Richard Hendel

The paper in this book meets the guidelines
for permanence and durability of the Committee
on Production Guidelines for Book Longevity
of the Council on Library Resources.

Printed in the United States of America

Library of Congress Cataloging in Publication Data

Watts, Emily Stipes.
The businessman in American literature.

Bibliography: p.
Includes index.
1. American literature—History and criticism.
2. Businessmen in literature.   3. Capitalism in
literature.   I. Title.
PS173.B87W3   810'.9'352338   81-21977
ISBN 0-8203-0616-9   AACR2

For Robert Allan Watts

CONTENTS

Acknowledgments
IX

Introduction: The Scrooge Syndrome
I

1 Capitalism Is God's Way for Fallen Man
8

2 The Problems of Liberty
22

3 The Yankee Peddler and the Con Man
34

4 "The American" and the Artist
45

5 Crooked Money and Easy Money
55

6 The Generation Trap
64

7 "The Hog-Squeal of the Universe"
72

Contents

8 The Boobus Americanus and the Artist
81

9 "Is Money Money or Isn't Money Money?"
91

10 The Businessman and the Corporate Capitalist
103

11 "The Great American Tradition of Tinkers"
114

12 "Hello Babies. Welcome to Earth"
125

13 The Businessman as Hero
136

14 The Values of Capitalism
150

Notes
161

Bibliography
171

Index
179

ACKNOWLEDGMENTS

I am grateful to my colleagues and students at the University of Illinois at Urbana-Champaign for the complex and challenging intellectual environment in which this book was written; to John T. Flanagan for his careful reading of the manuscript; to our sons, Ben, Ned, and Tom, for their interest in this topic and in my work; and to my husband for his vigorous criticism and his expansive perspective.

Grateful acknowledgment is also made to those who hold copyright on poems quoted in this volume and have given permission for their use. Charles Scribner's Sons, for "Richard Cory" by Edwin Arlington Robinson, from *The Children of the Night*, copyright under the Berne Convention (New York: Charles Scribner's Sons, 1897). Harcourt Brace Jovanovich, for "The Age Demanded" from *88 Poems* by Ernest Hemingway, edited by Nicholas Georgionnis, copyright © 1979 by The Ernest Hemingway Foundation and Nicholas Georgionnis. Harcourt Brace Jovanovich, for "economic secu" by E. E. Cummings, from *Poems, 1923–1954*, copyright 1938 by E. E. Cummings, renewed 1966 by Marion Morehouse Cummings, reprinted from *Complete Poems, 1913–1962* by E. E. Cummings. Harcourt Brace Jovanovich, for "of all the blessings which to man," by E. E. Cummings, published in *Poems, 1923–1954*, copyright 1944 by E. E. Cummings, renewed 1972 by Nancy T. Andrews, reprinted from *Complete Poems, 1913–1962* by E. E. Cummings. Harper and Row, for *Conversation at Midnight* by Edna St. Vincent Millay, copyright 1937, 1964 by Edna St. Vincent Millay and Norma Millay Ellis. Harper and Row, for "Daddy" by Sylvia Plath, from *Ariel*, copyright © 1965 by Ted Hughes. New Directions, for "Hugh Selwyn Mauberley" by Ezra Pound, from *Per-*

The Businessman in
American Literature

INTRODUCTION

The Scrooge Syndrome

As I looked through a catalogue of books recently, I noted a new edition of William Dean Howells's *The Rise of Silas Lapham*, a novel first published in 1885. The advertising blurb read, "The first major novel to center on the American businessman and to treat this theme with a realism that was to foreshadow the work of modern writers." The copy writer had echoed a question familiar to literary Ph.D. candidates in contemporary academia. Question: "What was the first American business novel?" Answer: *The Rise of Silas Lapham*. Some of us who were educated in the high schools of the 1950s remember reading this moral piece in our junior year, although Howells's novel is generally reserved today for college-level students.

Silas Lapham is an American cousin of Ebenezer Scrooge, that star of American yuletide television specials who was created by the English novelist Charles Dickens in 1843. "A Christmas Carol" has been an "American classic" ever since it crossed the Atlantic the year of its publication. The image of the businessman advanced by Dickens and developed by Howells is one of greed and grasping miserliness, of unethical business dealings somewhere on the way to financial success, of insensitivity to the needs of employees, of emotional atrophy, and of exploitation. Both Lapham and Scrooge repent, with Scrooge undergoing a miraculous transformation into benevolence and generosity. Scrooge helps the Cratchit family, and Silas is morally cleansed by the failure of his business, which was in large part the result of Silas's unethical treatment of a former business partner. However, it is the selfish, unregenerate Scrooge to whom Americans refer when someone is described as a "Scrooge." And it is "Bah, humbug" which is printed in red on green ties for sale at Christmas time. Indeed, so pervasive is this negative image of the businessman, especially in American literature, that it can be labeled a syndrome, "a group of signs and symptoms that occur together and characterize a particular abnormality."

It is not difficult to discover this general image of the businessman in "the work of modern writers," as the advertising writer tells us, although, in this Age of Anxiety and this time of Existential Despair, the modern Scrooge's repentance is not often effected, as was Silas Lapham's. Critics who have taken the trouble to account for and examine such a pervasively negative image of the businessman in American literature have analyzed this situation from different perspectives.

In the first post-World War II excursion into the subject, John Chamberlain attempted in a retrospective to account for the negative image of the businessman in two ways, beginning with *The Rise of Silas Lapham*. First, Chamberlain admitted that "U.S. business enterprise has not always been carried out within the scope of the ethics that must apply to it as a functional system."[1] The robber barons and their exploitative excesses seem to have been exposed just before and contemporaneously with the appearance of antibusiness novels. In fact, Chamberlain suggests that muckraking novelists like Upton Sinclair had a positive effect in the passage of reform legislation; the Pure Food and Drug Act was "Sinclair-inspired." Chamberlain argues that the novelists had quite responsibly exposed unethical businessmen and business practices. The problem, however, is that authors like Sinclair "[go] on writing about businessmen as though they were impervious to suggestion. Thus Mr. Sinclair writes off the solid accomplishments of his own long and busy life."

The second reason Chamberlain cites for the antibusiness theme in novels is the presence of "two alien [literary] traditions" in America. Our native tradition, according to Chamberlain, is "critical realism"— a tradition that "developed as a part of westward expansion; it was a response to frontier conditions that demand a hearty and commonsensical way of looking at things." Juxtaposed to critical realism are two traditions that are "implacably hostile to 'trade' and the 'bourgeois.'" "The first tradition was bound up with the aristocrat's point of view, and it may be found in the novels of Edith Wharton, in Henry Adams's *Democracy*, and in the works of Henry James that have got away from James's own view of the American businessman as the great 'innocent.'

The second tradition, which invaded the later novels of Howells and ultimately reached noisy fruition in the books of the 'proletarian' 1930's, was that of literary socialism."

Chamberlain harshly criticizes the exponents of literary socialism whose businessmen characters are only caricatures and whose plots have no originality. "Since the modern anti-business novelist has never paused to make a comparative audit of systems, he tends to contrast the world of free capitalism with a perfect socialized order that has no existence outside of his own head. Naturally the anti-business novelist wins easy victories; no mere human businessman can stand up against a perfect figure of the idealist's mind." [2] Chamberlain's attack has recently been echoed in the *Saturday Review* by novelist John Gardner, who deplores those contemporary writers who preach a "tyrannical Marxism and a whining hatred of 'American business.'" [3]

However, that other "alien" tradition which Chamberlain cites—that of the "aristocrat"—has more significant implications than simply a nondemocratic class consciousness of tradition and elitism. This tradition has its roots in New England intellectualism and is today largely defended in such works as Richard Hofstadter's *Anti-Intellectualism in American Life*, a Pulitzer prizewinner in 1964 and a book in which the author assumes that "traditional capitalism" had collapsed before 1941. Hofstadter castigates the businessman for his "widely shared contempt of the past" and his "ethos of self-help and personal advancement in which even religious faith becomes merely an agency of practicality." The businessman is "anti-cultural" and "utilitarian." [4]

A similar standard of judgment was established by Henry Nash Smith in his 1964 essay "The Search for a Capitalist Hero." As Smith explores the image of the businessman, he finds that hostility arose in the 1880s against the financier or "stock market operator," men like Jay Gould. Opposed to this "almost universally considered reprehensible" type was the character with a New England background. "New England figured as the innocent bystander among the regions, the passive custodian of a moral and cultural tradition that provided the only basis for rendering judgment upon the post-Civil War chaos." Smith sees the first evidence of this dichotomy in Mark Twain's and Charles Dudley Warner's *The Gilded Age* (1873). [5]

In such novels of the late nineteenth century, Smith observes that there was "an inchoate sense of guilt somehow related to the rapid economic expansion of the period."

> [The businessman] was a candidate for the role of scapegoat be-
> cause he was an alien intruder into the fictive world. In contrast
> with the familiar protagonists of sentimental love stories, he
> seemed both crude and immoral. Yet he was acknowledged to be
> immensely powerful. He controlled the energies of economic, so-
> cial, and political change; the future belonged to him; and no
> matter how many times the novelists might condemn the busi-
> nessman to social rebuffs, rejection by the heroine, bankruptcy,
> public exposure for his crimes, or even suicide, they recognized
> at bottom that traditional manners and morals were doomed by
> the growing dominance of the business system. (p. 55)

Soon, even New England values disappeared from these novels and, as
Smith comments, "It was difficult to find the elements of an acceptable
code of values within the [capitalistic] system" (p. 86). Moreover, as
Smith observes, the economic naiveté of many novelists indicated that
newspaper headlines were the source of their knowledge of capitalism
and of its technology. Later antibusiness novelists, such as Jack London
and Robert Herrick, depict businessmen as a kind of superman, but a
superman who must "abandon his role [in business] before he becomes
an acceptable husband and receives the fictional good-conduct medal of
a wife's devotion" (p. 99). On the other hand, Smith sees Theodore
Dreiser's Frank Cowperwood (*The Financier* [1912], *The Titan* [1914],
and *The Stoic* [unfinished, begun in the 1920s]) as a Nietzschean superman whose virtues were considered vices in the earlier novels. Yet here
again, Smith concludes, no positive moral values have sprung from
capitalism to replace the traditional aristocratic and intellectual values
of New England.

Since Dreiser's novels, the "emergent type" is Babbitt of Sinclair
Lewis's 1920 novel, who is a "buffoon" (pp. 102–3). The novelist's
own perspective thus becomes the moral standard—a perspective of
"the artist, of emancipated intellectual, a Bohemianism more vividly
impressed by the businessman's philistinism and his ineptitude as a
lover than by his power or wickedness" (pp. 102–3). However, the perspective of such novelists is "rickety," Smith continues, and in fact,
"the only significant effort to discover a source of value and hence a
vantage point from which to pass judgment on the business system in
the 1920s and 1930s was that of the radical left" (p. 103). After charac-
terizing John Galt of Ayn Rand's *Atlas Shrugged* (1957) as revealing

"the fantasy life of an unusually disturbed businessman" (p. 110), Smith concludes that his search for a capitalist hero has had "no viable results." "For the stereotypes used by the popular novelists cannot sustain a character of real imaginative substance, and serious writers seem unable to take an interest in a system of values based on economic assumptions" (p. 112).

The antibusiness bias is most certainly a larger and more complex issue than that raised by Dickens in his moral tale of Scrooge, especially as it concerns American literature. Clearly, it involves cultural and literary traditions, economic systems, democratic and aristocratic tendencies, and systems of morality. One obvious difficulty in our understanding of this complex problem is the lack of historical perspective. When the advertising copywriter and the professors and scholars assume that *The Rise of Silas Lapham* represents the earliest realistic businessman's novel, they are able to isolate the theoretical and moral problems exemplified by the robber barons and "the rise of capitalism" in the post–Civil War period. The assumption is that before this period the businessman was treated sympathetically, if he was treated at all, and that literary hostility toward the businessman arose and was justified because of the excesses of the post–Civil War period. The truth of the matter is that American writers produced works with anticapitalistic tendencies from the very beginning, despite our current clichés about the Puritan work ethic and the economic motives of our Founding Fathers. The capitalist has been attacked for any number of reasons throughout our literary history, and Silas Lapham (and even the English Scrooge) are rather late manifestations of this image.

Our critical silence regarding this pre-Silas Lapham hostility has made it necessary for me through the course of this book to examine the image of the businessman as it developed. I have attempted to draw examples from our most universally recognized major writers, citing the so-called popular writers when their work reflected, enhanced, or even precipitated tendencies in our major authors. By examining a broad scope of writers and their varying concerns, I hope to suggest positive values of American society, a significant proportion of which is composed of capitalists. Unlike Henry Nash Smith, I have found "viable" businessmen heroes in the work of several major authors as well as a growing tendency among our recent writers to treat the businessman with compassion, understanding, and even admiration.

Notwithstanding our current assumptions about the American Puritans and their work ethic, Puritan poets, ministers, and governmental leaders were largely hostile to businessmen. Puritan ministers sent them off to the hellfire and brimstone of eternal damnation, while Puritan leaders imposed a variety of controls to limit capitalism. To be sure, the Puritans were capitalists, but, as Richard Hofstadter and others have observed, they were also the founders of the New England intellectual tradition which has historically opposed what was and is interpreted to be the materialistic impulse of the businessman. How the Puritans themselves rationalized what is apparently an inherent contradiction is the topic of the first chapter.

The American writer mounted direct attacks on capitalism as an economic system during and shortly after the War of Independence. Even this early, the artists who had stayed in the new United States (many had already fled to Canada or New England) felt themselves isolated from the dominant economic system, for any number of reasons. Some reasons were most basic: the dichotomy between those who wish to live a life of the mind or heart and those who pursue a merchant's career, the lack of financial support for the artist in a capitalistic society, and the fundamental distrust of a system that appeared to many to be based only on economic self-interest.

Concurrently, in the late eighteenth and early nineteenth centuries, novelists and playwrights developed the largely hostile literary character of the American businessman from two already established literary types—the native image of the Yankee Peddler and the imported image of the English Rogue. For the American Romantic writer such as Nathaniel Hawthorne, Ralph Waldo Emerson, or Walt Whitman, non-materialistic ideals nearly precluded any positive characterization of the businessman.

In the post–Civil War period, when Chamberlain and Smith date the beginning of antibusiness literary sentiment, as business scandals became widely known and workers began to organize into unions, businessmen became literary villains, either major or peripheral, in a number of novels. Writers also began to examine the families of wealthy businessmen as well as the society in which the wealthy moved and to which the newly wealthy aspired. By the early twentieth century, muckrakers like Upton Sinclair were exposing fraudulent and unethical business practices in novels and in plays. Soon, the radical and leftist writers were preaching outright anticapitalism, while openly advocating socialism or Marxism.

As the radical writers reached their zenith in the 1930s, some American writers began finally to reexamine the businessman as well as to consider the merits of capitalism. Even before the Russo-German pact of 1939, important writers like Gertrude Stein and E. E. Cummings had begun to publish essays and poems defending capitalism. By the post-1945 period, the American writer was distinguishing between corporate and private capitalism and was at the same time suggesting that the businessman was not the sole, or perhaps even the primary, source of suffering in society, as the radical writers had been charging for half a century.

Although many contemporary novelists, for example, William Gaddis and Kurt Vonnegut, Jr., continue to attack the capitalist, others, such as Ken Kesey and Stanley Elkin, have been able to characterize the businessman in a more favorable, even an heroic, image. At the same time, these writers have posed paradoxes in the relationship of the businessman and society. Contemporary works that have dealt with the businessman tend to suggest broad social and cultural issues in American society, as the fictional businessman must act in a context that evokes a variety of ethical and historical issues. Of course, opposition between capitalists and employees is a constant theme, but the context has often been expanded to encompass the opposition of artist and society, the social milieu, the conflict of idealism and materialism, even philosophical speculations upon the more theoretical issues.

CHAPTER 1

Capitalism Is God's Way
for Fallen Man

When the Cabots—John and Sebastian, father and son—ventured into the New World in 1497, they found only the foggy forests of Nova Scotia, Labrador, and Newfoundland. Disappointed that they, like Columbus, had not found Cathay, they turned around and went back home to England. No possibility of lucrative trade in a land occupied by squirrels, they concluded.

When Englishmen finally decided that North America might offer a site for colonial capitalistic enterprise, Spain had already established colonies in Florida, so Englishmen in the 1580s settled farther north in what today is North Carolina. The motive was economic, the establishment of a colony that would turn an abundant profit for private investors who stayed in England. Eventually, the colony completely disappeared, and its fate is still a mystery. Englishmen like Sir Walter Raleigh lost fortunes in their attempts to plant colonies in the New World. At least until 1600, attempts to establish capitalism—private ownership of property and free enterprise—in the New World failed, largely because of disorganization and undercapitalization.[1]

Nevertheless, one of Raleigh's men, Captain Arthur Barlowe, who had sailed to the coast of Virginia in 1584, reported to English readers that the New World was a land of plenty, a veritable Garden of Eden. Captain John Smith soon urged Englishmen to colonize the New World. Although his motives were mixed (the threatening papist Spaniards were gradually moving up the coast), his appeal to his countrymen was largely economic.

And here are no hard Landlords to racke vs with high rents, or
extorting fines, nor tedious pleas in Law to consume vs with their
many yeeres disputations for Iustice; no multitudes to occasion
such impediments to good orders as in popular States: so freely
hath God and his Maiestie bestowed those blessings, on them that
will attempt to obtaine them, as here euery man may be master of
his owne labour and land, or the greatest part . . . and if hee
haue nothing but his hands, he may set vp his Trade; and by
industry quickly grow rich, spending but halfe that time well,
which in *England* we abuse in idleness, worse or as ill.

Indeed, Smith elaborated, "if a man worke but three daies in seuen, hee
may get more than hee can spend vnlesse he will be exceedingly
excessive."[2]

Smith had helped to establish the first permanent English colony at
the mouth of the James River in 1609. The colony had been financed by
the London Company, a group of English speculators, who stayed in
London. The colonists themselves were not allowed to own land until
1619—an important year for the Jamestown group, the same year during which the Virginia House of Burgesses was established and the par-
ent London Company sent a boatload of young females to help colonize
and propagate. The colonists themselves prospered, but the capitalists
in London lost their charter in 1624 when James I declared Virginia a
royal colony.

At the same time, another group in London established a company
that sent the Pilgrims to New England in 1620. Although the economic
basis of the Pilgrims' venture was initially capitalistic, the Pilgrims
themselves were not interested in private profit; rather, they sought religious freedom. When they arrived in the New World, they immediately
established an economic system which, they felt, was in accordance
with ancient principles—communal ownership of property.[3] After several tragic years of crop failure and unrest among the group, the communal system was abandoned in 1623, and William Bradford, a member of the Mayflower Pilgrim group and a governor of the colony,
attempted to explain just why this ideal system had collapsed. Bradford
recognized that a communal system had been recommended by "Plato
and other ancients" and had been "applauded by some of the later
times." Such people who proposed "the taking away of propertie"
thought themselves "wiser then God," according to Bradford.

> For this communitie . . . was found to breed much confusion and
> discontent, and retard much imployment that would have been to
> their benefite and comfort. For the yong-men, that were most
> able and fitte for labour and service did repine that they should
> spend their time and streingth to work for other mens wives and
> children, with out any recompense. The strong, or man of parts,
> had no more in divission of victails and cloaths, then he that was
> weake and not able to doe a quarter the other could; this was
> thought injuestice. The aged and graver men to be ranked and
> equalised in labours, and victails, cloaths, etc., with the meaner
> and yonger sort, thought it some indignite and disrespect unto
> them. And for mens wives to be commanded to doe servise for
> other men, as dressing their meate, washing their cloaths, etc.,
> they deemd it a kind of slaverie, neither could many husbands
> well brooke it. Upon the poynte all being to have alike, and all
> to doe alike, they thought them selves in the like condition, and
> one as good as another; and so, if it did not cut of those relations
> God hath set amongst men, yet it did at least much diminish and
> take of the mutuall respects that should be preserved amongst
> them.

Indeed, Bradford continued, had the Pilgrims been of "another condition," the situation would have been worse. As Bradford reasoned,
corrupt men could not live under such a system. Thus, "seeing all men
have this corruption in them, God in his wisdome saw another course
fiter for them." [4]

Objectively, Bradford understood that the Pilgrim experiment failed
for a variety of reasons: the conflict of lazy men and hardworkers; the
refusal of the wife to "serve" men other than those in her family; the
loss of respect which older men sensed in this system; the problems of
adequate rewards for talents and achievements. Subjectively, however,
Bradford could only reason that the communal experiment had failed
because of man's sinful nature. A system of private property among the
Pilgrims, although a course chosen by God, was a system for sinful and
corrupt men. Private property and free enterprise were, after all, values
rejected by those higher authorities—Plato and the Bible.

With the failure of their communal system, the Pilgrim fathers established a limited system of private property, and Bradford's words describe what was apparently to him the startling result.

At length, after much debate of things, the Govr (with the advise of the cheefest amongst them) gave way that they should set corne every man for his owne particular, and in that regard trust to them selves. . . . And so assigned to every family a parcell of land, according to the proportion of their number for that end, only for present use (but make no division for inheritance), and ranged all boys and youth under some familie. This had very good success; for it made all hands very industrious, so as much more corne was planted then other waise would have bene by any means. . . . The women now wente willingly into the fielde, and tooke their litle-ons with them to set corne, which before would aledg weaknes, and inabilitie; whom to have compelled would have bene thought great tiranic and oppression.[5]

Ten years later, the Puritans followed the Pilgrims to Massachusetts. Better educated and of the middle class, the original Puritans had not allowed London speculators to own and control their company but, rather, had invested their own capital in their enterprise. The Puritans established a commonwealth in which large tracts of land, carefully organized within village areas, were owned in common by the "proprietors," or original settlers. Some few tracts of land were assigned to private owners. After the first generation of Puritans, however, with the waves of land-hungry immigrants from England, as well as the equally land-hungry second-generation sons of the Puritans, the people pushed into the woods, toward the west, to settle and clear their own farms. With individual, privately owned farms established, the commonwealth—and ecclesiastical control of the people through the village system—soon collapsed. The theocracy was doomed.

For the Puritans had not come to the New World as capitalists. They came to settle God's new Eden, to form a City on the Hill for all humanity. The commonwealth concept, a village organization controlled by the ministers and the civil authorities, was intended to minimize worldly achievements for the sake of communal and heavenly rewards. Indeed, those same people who were to give us Harvard College in 1636 had already in 1633 established mandatory wage and price controls in their commonwealth, as John Winthrop recorded in his *Journal*.

[1633] The scarcity of workmen had caused them to raise their wages to an excessive rate, so as a carpenter would have three shillings the day, a laborer two shillings and sixpence, etc.; and accordingly those who had commodities to sell advanced their prices sometime double to that they cost in England, so as it grew to a general complaint, which the court, taking knowledge of, as also of some further evils, which were springing out of the excessive rates of wages, they made an order, that carpenters, masons, etc. should take but two shillings the day, and laborers but eighteen pence, and that no commodity should be sold at above four pence in the shilling more than it cost for ready money in England; oil, wine, etc. and cheese, in regard of the hazards of bringing, etc., [excepted]. The evils which were springing, etc. were: 1. Many spent much time idly, etc. because they would get as much in four days as would keep them a week. 2. They spent much in tobacco and strong waters, etc. which was a great waste to the commonwealth, which, by reason of so much foreign commodities expended, could not have subsisted to this time, but that it was supplied by the cattle and corn, which were sold to new comers at very dear rates, viz., corn at six shillings the bushel, a cow at £20,—yea, some at £24, some £26—a mare at £35, an ewe goat at 3 or £4; and yet many cattle were every year brought out of England, and some from Virginia. Soon after order was taken for prices of commodities, viz., not to exceed the rate of four pence in the shilling above the price in England, except cheese and liquors, etc.[6]

For Winthrop, idle hands were the devil's tools, but the so-called Puritan work ethic was not for a capitalistic end. Idle hands created communal problems within the holy commonwealth, as well as, of course, corrupting the soul of the individual pilgrim on his way to heaven. In 1639, Robert Keayne, Boston's wealthiest merchant, was actually called to court for what the Puritan fathers considered "excessive rates" and was castigated in a public sermon by John Cotton.[7]

The leaders of the Puritan oligarchy were, in fact, fearful of capitalistic success, of private property, and of free enterprise. They groaned as the common land of the villages, within which ecclesiastical leaders and the aligned civil officers could control the populace, gave way to the large tracts of privately owned farms. They feared a merchant aristocracy that would challenge their authority.

Businessmen, especially, were held suspect by the Puritans. Even honest businessmen were condemned to the fires of hell in the first American bestseller, Michael Wigglesworth's "The Day of Doom"

(1662). Here businessmen are characterized as antinomians, as do-gooders, who believe that by their own achievements and "blameless lives" they can pass God's right hand to heaven on Judgment Day. However, Wigglesworth, himself a Puritan minister, let the dread Judge Himself respond to the self-justifying and pleading businessmen in terms presumably understandable to the misguided capitalists.

> Then answered upon their dread,
>   the Judge: "True Piety
> God doth desire and eke require,
>   no less than honesty.
> Justice demands at all your hands
>   perfect Obedience;
> If but in part you have come short,
>   that is a just offence.
>
> On Earth below, where men did ow
>   a thousand pounds and more,
> Could twenty pence it recompence?
>   Could that have cleared the score?
> Think you to buy felicity
>   with part of what's due debt?
> Or for desert of one small part,
>   the whole should off be set?"

The great Judge builds his case steadily against these "Civil honest [business] Men" whose "dealing [was] square," and, in the end, they are sent to eternal damnation.

> Your Gold is brass, your silver dross,
>   your righteousness is sin:
> And think you by such honesty
>   eternal life to win?
> You much mistake, if for its sake
>   you dream of acceptation;
> Whereas the same deservest shame
>   and meriteth Damnation.[8]

However, within the system of wage and price controls and under condemnation from his spiritual leaders, the Puritan capitalist, whether businessman or farmer, thrived in the New World but was careful to reserve a large portion of his profits for God. Such wealthy Puritans as

John Hull, Philip English, and William Browne devoted their money and time to the Puritan establishment. Business records of the Puritans abound with thanks to God, amen, for success, in the same words of thanks extended to the Deity for children, a chastening religious experience, a wife, a drought-ending rain, or New England. Diaries of businessmen such as John Hull reflect the spiritual crisis that for a Puritan was involved in commercial success: "more and more [I] affect and embrace opportunity of getting out rather than running into the business of this world, specifically foreign traffic, as desirous to be more thoughtful of launching into that vast ocean of eternity whither we must all shortly be carried that so I might be in a posture for my Lord's coming." [9]

In the latter half of the seventeenth century in Boston emerged the "progenitor of a practical race that was to spread the gospel of economic individualism across the continent," as Vernon L. Parrington labeled Samuel Sewall (1652–1730).[10] Sewall is the symbolic link between Puritanism and capitalism; he is the symbolic representative of a race of businessmen who advocated the "Puritan work ethic" (the inevitable epithet) and created the American capitalistic system. Samuel Sewall, the progenitor of Jay Gould as well as of Jay Gatsby: a theory forged by cultural historians like Max Weber, whose *The Protestant Ethic and the Spirit of Capitalism* appeared in 1905 and set the tone for such studies as Parrington's *Main Currents in American Thought* (1927, 1930) and, more recently, Hofstadter's *Anti-Intellectualism in American Life* (1963). In such studies, the businessman with his Protestant or Puritan work ethic is viewed as materialistic, vulgar, philistine, greedy, opposed to liberal and intellectual values.

The Puritan-capitalist connection has dominated the consciousness even of procapitalist Americans to the extent that today *Time* can invoke the image with assurance that its readers will understand the negative connotations. It is a theory which, simply by juxtaposing a religious system with an economic system, implies that the economic system has in fact become a religious system and that, correspondingly, whatever transcendent and cultural values the religious system once had have been subsumed under an economic system. Such values, the argument runs, soon disappeared as the economic system became dominant and created a race of unregenerate Scrooges. It was a theory concocted by cultural historians, many of whom were not capitalists themselves, and at least until recently was a theory advocated by much of America's intellectual establishment. It lies at the basis of Henry Nash Smith's statement that it is "difficult to find the elements of an acceptable code of values within the [capitalistic] system";[11] it is no wonder that Smith could find no "viable" capitalist hero in his 1964 article "The Search for a Capitalist Hero: Businessmen in American Fiction."

Max Weber, a German sociologist and historian, postulated the Puritan-capitalist unholy alliance at the turn of the century in his *Protestant Ethic and the Spirit of Capitalism.* Weber actually began his discussion with Ben Franklin as the proto–modern capitalist (the emergence of Sewall was to come later) and traced capitalism to the Puritan's search for a "calling" (work became that "calling") and to the Puritan's need for "assurance of grace": could God allow His saint to suffer and starve in poverty? Thus, according to Weber, the hard-working, successful capitalist thought himself blessed by God. Along the way, Weber pointed out that the Puritans did not like elaborate clothes or the theater; hence the rise of cultural philistinism among capitalists.

Weber wrongheadedly argued that the Puritans held it an "absolute duty to consider oneself chosen" because lack of such confidence was a sign of "imperfect grace."[12] Furthermore, Weber argued, a Puritan was obliged to fulfill his proper secular "calling" as a way of attaining certainty of his or her own election. By such reasoning, Weber theorized, "In the place of the humble sinners to whom Luther promises grace if they trust themselves to God in penitent faith are bred those self-confident saints whom we can rediscover in the hard Puritan merchants of the heroic age of capitalism" (pp. 111–12).

The concept of a "fixed calling" led, Weber contended, to "an ethical justification of the modern specialized division of labor" (p. 163). Profit-making became a providential activity for the Puritan whose calling was business. As a result, because of "the [Puritan's] religious valuation of restless, continuous, systematic work in a worldly calling," the spirit of capitalism quickly spread, but soon separated itself from any religious or ethical basis (p. 172). Hence the socialist Weber could triumphantly conclude:

> In the field of its [capitalism's] highest development, in the United States, the pursuit of wealth, stripped of its religious and ethical meaning, tends to become associated with purely mundane passions, which often actually give it the character of sport.
>
> No one knows who will live in this cage in the future, or whether at the end of this tremendous development entirely new

prophets will arise, or there will be a great rebirth of old ideas and ideals, or if neither, mechanized petrification, embellished with a sort of convulsive self-importance. For in the last stage of this cultural development, it might well be truly said: "Specialists without spirit, sensualists without heart; this nullity imagines that it has attained a level of civilization never before achieved." (p. 182)

In Weber's Land of Nullity the argument was quickly expanded, in works such as Waldo Frank's *Our America* (1919) and Harvey O'Higgins's *The American Mind in Action* (1920), which, as Frederick J. Hoffman has so succinctly commented, "read like lengthy case histories of the Puritan as the archetype of all neurotics." [13] In case anyone had missed the connection, the English historian R. H. Tawney even more specifically linked *Religion and the Rise of Capitalism* in 1926 for the American audience. Although Charles Beard in an article in the *New Republic* in 1920 attempted to point out the historical fallacies of the Puritan-capitalist alliance, nobody listened. D. H. Lawrence repeated Weber's arguments and even his metaphors in the still influential *Studies in Classic American Literature* (first published in America in 1923 and used as a classroom text in many universities today) and viciously attacked Franklin as a "snuff-colored little man."

> Now if Mr. Andrew Carnegie, or any other millionaire, had wished to invent a God to suit his ends, he could not have done better. Benjamin did it for him in the eighteenth century. God is the supreme servant of men who want to get on, to *produce*. Providence. The provider. The heavenly store-keeper. The everlasting Wanamaker.
>
> And this is all the God of the grandsons of the Pilgrim Fathers had left. Aloft on a pillar of dollars. [14]

In 1925, with a deft show of academic one-upmanship, Vernon L. Parrington substituted Samuel Sewall in Weber's thesis for the later Franklin and thus forged a solid link in the chain between Puritanism and capitalism. The academic and intellectual establishment bought it all—at least until recently. Weber's Puritan-capitalistic alliance was in effect only another attempt to discredit the American capitalist, but this time with all the intellectual trappings and footnotes. The argument fell on fertile ground, land already prepared by generations of anticapitalist literature and theories, extending, despite Weber's concepts, even to the

Puritan Fathers. Capitalism was, after all, according to William Bradford, God's system for fallen man.

Recent historians, such as Michael Walzer in "Puritanism as a Revolutionary Ideology," have punctured the arguments of Weber and his followers in a variety of ways, the most potent of which is by recourse to examination of historical evidence.[15]

> [Weber's] argument breaks down. If there is in fact a peculiar and irrational quality to the capitalists' lust of gain, its sources must be sought elsewhere than among the saints. For Puritanism was hardly an ideology that encouraged continuous or unrestrained accumulation. Instead, the saints tended to be narrow and conservative in their economic views, urging men to seek no more wealth than they needed for a modest life, or, alternatively, to use up their surplus in charitable giving. The anxiety of the Puritans led to a fearful demand for economic restriction (and political control) rather than to entrepreneurial activity as Weber has described it. Unremitting and relatively unremunerative work was the greatest help toward saintliness and virtue. . . .
>
> There is also another defect in Weber's argument, and it also stems from a failure to ask historical questions about the saints. Neither Weber nor any of his followers have ever demonstrated that the men who actually became Puritans, for whatever reasons—who really believed in predestination and lived through the salvation panic—went on, presumably for the same reasons, to become capitalists. They have not immersed themselves in the history of the period. . . . There is, for example, considerable evidence to show that many of the most sensitive of the saints went on, after the crisis of their conversion, to become ministers, and very little evidence that many went on to become capitalist businessmen. Among lay Puritans, the weight of the diaries, letters and memoirs clearly suggests that the most significant expression of their new faith was cultural and political rather than economic.[16]

One of the most prominent of these diarists was Samuel Sewall, "the progenitor of modern capitalists." A reading of his diary and an assessment of his life will substantiate Walzer's assertions. Sewall was born into a financially substantial family, was educated at Harvard, and married a woman from a very wealthy family. Thereafter, Sewall managed the family money and estates and added to this wealth by banking, moneylending, and printing. And yet his diary and his public activities clearly reveal that his chief interests in life were his religion, Harvard College (which he served as an overseer), his family, and his culture. An amateur theologian, Sewall was the author of *The Selling of Joseph* (1700), credited with being the first antislavery tract written in America. As a judge, he condemned witches to death in the oyer and terminer court in Salem in 1692—a judgment he later recanted in public.

Sewall's diary is a remarkable journal covering his life from 1674 to 1729 (with a gap from 1677 to 1685). The diary is a record of his daily life, an accounting of his successes and failures in just about everything other than finances and business, as well as a record of his wonderment at God's visible world, from the destructive Boston fire in 1676 and the sound of the British Tattoo ("Dūrrera dum") to the reasons why his son Sam is several times involved in boating accidents but is saved by God's pleasure. Indeed, his "economic individualism" is most evident when, in 1720, he courts another "economic individualist," the Widow Winthrop. She proves as hard a bargainer for her own financial status within the proposed marriage as Sewall was for his. Their final meetings center upon money and finances and in the end come to naught. As Sewall leaves the widow's presence for the last time, he notes that "Her Dress was not so clean as sometime it had been." [17]

Sewall's chief concern was simply not money, nor greedy accumulation of wealth, but rather the state of his own soul, the building of churches, the reading of theological tracts, the abolition of slavery in Massachusetts, his friendship with the Mathers, his children, and his courtship of various women. His hands and mind were not idle, but they were not confined to capitalistic enterprise either.

Sewall's diary, as well as the *Personal Narrative* of the most important Puritan of the next generation, Jonathan Edwards, clearly indicates that the Puritan layman and minister were not "economic individualists" with a lust for systematic accumulation of wealth, or "self-made men," or even self-seeking individuals. What many of the Puritan-capitalist analogies ultimately imply is that the Puritan emphasis upon the sense of "calling" and the hope of salvation for the individual soul led ultimately to the entrepreneur, the businessman as self-seeking individual, or, as Hofstadter terms this phenomenon, "an ethos of self-help and personal advancement in which even religious faith becomes merely an agency of practicality." [18] Reviving Weber's own arguments and suggesting an inevitability of historical tendencies in Chapter X, "Self-Help and Spiritual Technology," of *Anti-Intellectualism in American Life*, Hofstadter associates self-help with "Puritan preachings" and the "Puritan doctrine of the calling." But here again, the cultural historians have refused to acknowledge the historical evidence and have misunderstood the soul of the American Puritan saint.

In a recent study, Sacvan Bercovitch has convincingly exposed the superficiality with which Weber, Parrington, and Hofstadter have approached the Puritan saint's sense of his own individuality. In a directly counter argument, Bercovitch argues that the Puritan's sense of self ultimately involved a sense of otherness.

> The basis of Puritan psychology lies in this contrast between personal responsibility and individualism. We can say, with William Haller, that they believed "man's chief concern should be with the welfare of his own soul," [19] only if we bear in mind their horror at the "very name of Own," their determination "to *Hate* our *selves* and *ours*," their opposing view of *soul* and *self*. The way of the soul, they maintained, starts "with a holy despair in ourselves" and proceeds "with a holy kind of violence" back to Christ; it means acknowledging the primacy of that which is Another's, and *receiving* the ability to respond. Hence the advantage of self-knowledge: the terror it brings may exorcise our individuality. It may drive us to "desire to be found, not in ourselves." It may teach us that to love our neighbors as ourselves is to realize how drastically "self is against the good of our neighbours"; that at best the saint had "no more feeling or relishing . . . himself, than if he were not at all"; and that what Augustine meant by our two opposing wills was the conflict between "our own proper Will" and "the Divine Will": that is, between a private, inherent, discrete identity, and an imposed, Christ-centered exemplariness that results in "self-nothingnesse." [20]

Bercovitch's Puritan bears little or no resemblance to the self-centered, accumulating capitalist of Weber, Parrington, or Hofstadter. No, the Puritans would and did condemn the self-seeking businessman who sought only to accumulate wealth. If the Puritan Fathers have left us any image of the capitalist or the "economic individualist," it is a negative representation. Calvinistic Puritanism emphasized otherworldliness of the soul in a universe directed by an all-powerful God. Puritanism sought to establish a community of faithful brethren in the New World who would establish a New Israel. At least for the first generation of saints, state and church were united, and control was maintained by the oligarchy through the commonwealth and village system. Puritan ministers preached regularly on such themes as the vanity of worldly wealth; Puritan poets dutifully reiterated such themes and, like Wigglesworth, sent the businessmen off to hell. Capitalism—private ownership and private enterprise—was, at least in Bradford's eyes, God's system for fallen man. The so-called Puritan work ethic, if it ever existed, was directed to community ends as well as to the ultimate heavenly goal of the selfless soul.

The confusion of Puritanism and capitalism has made it difficult for Americans in the twentieth century to separate the two and hence to understand private capitalism without the inherently negative connotations of a failed religious movement. Scholars such as Walzer and Bercovitch have not provided us with answers to the problem of the origins of capitalism, nor have they elaborated upon the positive or negative values of capitalism. They have, however, begun to clear the intellectual arena of Weber's theories, which have dominated the American intellectual scene since 1905. Walzer and Bercovitch have at the same time suggested that American Puritanism was antithetical to capitalism and that, even from the nation's beginnings, the businessman has been denigrated.

Thus, what seems to be a contradiction in post-Weberian scholars— that Puritanism spawned capitalism, but at the same time, as Hofstadter for example claims, "The Puritan clergy founded the tradition of New England intellectualism" [21]—is no real contradiction. The tradition of New England intellectualism has been anticapitalist and antibusiness from its origins. The eminent New England intellectual Ralph Waldo Emerson proclaimed in 1850 that "Napoleon; or, The Man of the World" is representative of a combination of the conservative, or old, established capitalist, and the democrat, or the young, entrepreneurial capitalist on the make. Although Emerson admires Napoleon's common sense, his "self-made" success, and his will to power, in the end Emerson calls him "singularly destitute of generous sentiments . . . unjust . . . egotistic and monopolizing . . . a boundless liar . . . unscrupulous . . . perfidious" and so on. As Emerson summarized his analysis of this "representative man"—Napoleon—who symbolizes the capitalist (but who, Emerson somehow overlooked, was no capitalist): "As long as our civilization is essentially one of property, of fences, of exclusiveness, it will be mocked by delusions. Our riches will leave us sick; there will be bitterness in our laughter, and our wine will burn in our mouth. Only that good profits which we can taste with all doors open, and which serves all men." [22]

CHAPTER 2

The Problems of Liberty

In 1721 young Benjamin Franklin fled Samuel Sewall's Boston and journeyed to Philadelphia, the city of the Quakers, where he eventually made his fortune. As an old man, Franklin recorded his life, at least to 1757, in his *Autobiography*, a work that was not completely published until 1868, although parts of it appeared in France as early as the 1790s. The appearance of the complete text in the late nineteenth century corresponded with the rise of business and the appearance of the robber barons in the post–Civil War period and, of course, made the text available to Max Weber, who used Franklin to advance his anticapitalist theories in *The Protestant Ethic and The Spirit of Capitalism*.

Franklin's *Autobiography* appears to be a rags-to-riches story, a moral tale of a poor boy who makes good, a paradigm for the American businessman. Indeed, it is clear that at least through the first portion of his *Autobiography*, written at Twyford, England, in 1771 and dedicated to his bastard son William, Franklin was attempting to define how he was able "to secure my credit and character as a tradesman" in Philadelphia. Having run away from an apprenticeship with his brother in Boston, Franklin arrived in Philadelphia dirty and poor, and found work with a printer. He spent a year in England, returned to Philadelphia, and opened his own stationer's shop. His method for success is clearly described for his son.

> I began now gradually to pay off the Debt I was under for the Printing-House. In order to secure my Credit and Character as a Tradesman, I took care not only to be in *Reality* Industrious and frugal, but to avoid all *Appearances* of the Contrary. I drest

plainly; I was seen at no Places of idle Diversion; I never went out a-fishing or shooting; a Book, indeed, sometimes debauch'd me from my Work, but that was seldom, snug, and gave no Scandal; and, to show that I was not above my Business, I sometimes brought home the Paper I purchas'd at the Stores, thro' the Streets on a Wheelbarrow. Thus being esteem'd an industrious, thriving young Man, and paying duly for what I bought, the Merchants who imported Stationary solicited my Custom; others propos'd supplying me with Books, I went on swimmingly.[1]

Franklin's admonitions owe something to that popular English genre of his time, the moral letter, best represented by Lord Chesterfield's letters to his son. However entertaining, the genre is often shallow and tends to moral platitudes. Nevertheless, it is clear from this passage that Franklin was not hypocritical in his directions to William: Franklin was in *reality* an industrious and honest businessman; his attention to *appearance* was for the purposes of public relations. He was his own walking advertisement.

In the same years that Franklin was pushing his wheelbarrow through the streets of Philadelphia, he was writing essays that explained his desire for financial success as well as his means to success. Sometime, perhaps back in his brother's shop in Boston, Franklin had made the discovery that private property and free enterprise are directly related to the freedom of the individual. Franklin perceived that economic self-sufficiency necessarily corresponded to personal liberty and freedom. Within and among the homilies of *Poor Richard's Almanack* ("Lost Time is never found" and "The Cat in Gloves catches no mice"), the careful reader can see a theory emerging. In "The Way to Wealth," the preface to his 1758 edition of the *Almanack*, Franklin, in the voice of Richard Saunders, urges his reader not to go into debt.

But, ah, think what you do when you run in Debt; *You give to another Power over your Liberty.* . . . What would you think of that Prince, or that Government, who should issue an Edict forbidding you to dress like a Gentleman or a Gentlewoman, on Pain of Imprisonment or Servitude? Would you not say, that you were free, have a Right to dress as you please, and that such an Edict would be a Breach of your Privileges, and such a Government tyrannical? And yet you are about to put yourself under that Tyr-

> anny when you run in Debt for such a Dress: Your Creditor has
> Authority at his Pleasure to deprive you of your Liberty, by con-
> fining you in Gaol for Life, or sell you for a Servant, if you
> should not be able to repay him! . . . Then since as [Poor
> Richard] says, *The Borrower is a Slave to the Lender, and the
> Debtor to the Creditor*, disdain the Chain, preserve your Free-
> dom; and maintain your Independency: Be *industrious* and *free*;
> be *frugal* and *free*.[2]

Economic self-sufficiency and individual liberty are inextricably involved in Franklin's writings. Indeed, in Franklin's curious "Speech of
Polly Baker" (1747), even an unwed mother of five children can be admired for her economic self-sufficiency. Franklin assumed a free capitalistic market as the basis for economic opportunity and further associated a free economy with personal freedom. In his understanding of
the relationship between free enterprise and personal freedom, he had
undoubtedly been influenced by the French physiocrats and later by the
classical economist Adam Smith, whose *Inquiry into the Nature and
Causes of the Wealth of Nations* appeared in 1776.

Like Smith, Franklin advocated a laissez faire economy. In international trading, his farmer capitalist "Arator" argues for a free world
grain and wool market in "On the Price of Corn, and the Management
of the Poor" (1766). Objecting to governmental restrictions that favor
manufacturers, Arator reasons, "My wool would produce me a better
price if it were suffer'd to go to foreign markets. But that, Messieurs the
Public, your law would not permit. It must be kept all at home, that our
dear Manufacturers may have it the cheaper. And then, having your-
selves thus lessened our encouragement for raising sheep, you curse us
for the scarcity of mutton!"[3] Moreover, as Arator observes, the manufacturers' prices remain high because they are allowed to export their
goods. Furthermore, with government regulations restricting a free
market price for corn, Arator protests that the farmers alone are being
forced to support the poor.

Later, in "Information for Those Who Would Remove to America,"
written in 1782, Franklin noted that the American government was re-
fusing to support and encourage manufacture, that "it may be carried
out by private Persons to Advantage; and if not, it is a Folly to think of
forcing Nature." Franklin asserted that "Artisans generally live better
and more easily in America than in Europe," primarily because of a

competitive market. "If the Merchant demands too much Profit on imported Shoes, they buy of the Shoemaker; and if he asks too high a
Price, they take them of the Merchant; thus the two Professions are
checks on each other." [4]

Franklin favored "Free Trade" and, like Smith, objected to mercantilism.[5] Eighteenth-century mercantilism emphasized the wealth and
power of the state and has been defined by some historians as "the economic and political manifestation of statism, wherein doctrines are less
important than the major goal of state-building." [6] By means of taxation
and by trade restrictions, governments controlled the economy in just
such ways as Arator describes, presumably for the common national
good. Franklin had had enough of English mercantilism—a policy that
had contributed largely to the revolutionary notions of the Americans.

And so, as his *Autobiography* tells us, Franklin made a small fortune
and, for all practical purposes, retired from business, as he established
managers in his own print shop and invested in other print shops. It was
at this point, with his finances secure, that Franklin began his full-time
career of public service. In the third part of his *Autobiography*, written
at Philadelphia in 1788, Franklin records his public activities—the for-
mation of a fire company, the invention of the Franklin stove (for which
he himself quite intentionally took no patent and hence no profits), the
creation of a public library, and so forth. Even D. H. Lawrence, who
otherwise viciously condemned Franklin in his *Studies in Classic American Literature* (1923), had to admit his admiration of the public-
spirited and sagacious Franklin: "All the qualities of a great man, and
never more than a great citizen" (p. 19). However, at least in Franklin's
scheme of things, his public good works could only have followed his
personal economic self-sufficiency and personal freedom.

Business success, therefore, was not an end for Franklin, but rather a
means. When he proposed a university in Philadelphia, he suggested
that the students pursue the usual course of humanities and science, but
he also added a business curriculum: "The History of *Commerce*, of the
Invention of Arts, Rise of Manufactures, Progress of Trade, Change of
its Seats, with Reasons, Causes, &." "The Education of Youth" (1749),
however, concludes with this paragraph: "The Idea of what is *true
Merit*, should also be often presented to Youth, explain'd and impress'd
on their Minds, as consisting in an *Inclination* join'd with an *Ability*
to serve Mankind, one's Country, Friends and Family; which *Ability*
is (with the Blessing of God) to be acquir'd or greatly encreas'd by

true Learning; and should indeed be the great *Aim* and *End* of all Learning."[7]

Sandwiched between the first part of the *Autobiography* which concerns Franklin's business success, and the third part, which concerns his public works, is a comparatively short middle section, written at Passy, France, in 1784. This middle section records his own introspective, spiritual self-examination as well as his search for a God. Although post-Weberian scholars like to use this middle section to indicate further elements of Puritanism in Franklin, the virtues he describes are fairly standard in nearly any Western culture and derive from traditional classical virtues: Temperance, Silence, Order, Resolution, Frugality, Industry, Sincerity, Justice, Moderation, Cleanliness, Tranquility, Chastity, and Humility.[8] Franklin had separated his own spiritual beliefs from those of the Puritans with his rejection of original sin and eternal damnation. With his own definition of God and man's relationship to Him, Franklin believed that he had discovered a faith that most men held in common. "I never doubted, for instance, the Existance of the Deity, that he made the World, and govern'd it by his Providence; that the most acceptable Service of God was the doing Good to Man; that our Souls are immortal; and that all Crime will be punished and Virtue rewarded either here or hereafter; these I esteem'd the Essentials of every Religion."[9] In Franklin's rejection of Puritanism came a release, a hopefulness that man could achieve "moral perfection." Franklin himself made a list of his thirteen virtues and a schedule for each day. He claimed that he had "most Trouble" with his third virtue, "Order."[10]

Franklin's emphasis in the *Autobiography* is thus not really upon the rags-to-riches story, but rather upon the ultimate goal of "doing good." For Franklin himself, the time to do good, the time for public service could come only after his own economic self-sufficiency had released him from personal financial concerns. It is in fact difficult to understand the negative image of Franklin that has permeated our literature and the writings of our social historians in the post-Weberian period. Franklin was certainly no monopolist nor shady speculator; he did not spend his life in a quest for personal wealth. He was, however, an advocate of private capitalism and a free market and believed that both were crucial to the political, personal, intellectual, and hence religious freedom of men and women.

On the other hand, Franklin's doctrine of economic self-sufficiency and the sociological implications of the American Revolution created a fundamental and crucial shift in artistic milieu—a shift American artists understood almost immediately and with which they are still attempting to deal. I am not speaking here of the problem of subject matter in a classless society, bewailed early by James Fenimore Cooper in his *Notions of the Americans* (1828) and later by Henry James, whose best novels place Americans in a European setting (where there were still social classes). Nor am I speaking here of the imperative to create an American literature—a literature identifiably national, commensurate with our achievements, a hopeful prediction most notably uttered by Ralph Waldo Emerson in his "American Scholar" (1837), our "Intellectual Declaration of Independence."

I am speaking here of the new situation of the artist within the new American society created after the War of Independence. With no aristocratic classes and with no established artistic Academy in America after 1776, the American artist was suddenly without any means of financial support from such traditional forms of patronage.[11] Among the 75,000 Loyalists who fled the country either before or during the war were a number of artists: the painter John Singleton Copley, the historians Cadwallader Colden and William Smith, the poets Joseph Stansbury and Jonathan Odell, and the pamphleteers Samuel Seabury and Daniel Leonard. Other writers, having donated their pens to the cause before the Revolution and to the establishment of the Republic after the Revolution, suddenly found the need for some sort of financial support, since there would be no government subsidy, no patronage from an aristocracy, and no support from an Academy in the new country. Economic self-sufficiency for an American writer, therefore, could only mean "popularity" of his work or "moonlighting" that would limit his time for creative projects.

In his journey through America in the 1830s, the Frenchman Alexis de Tocqueville had noted such a situation and predicted a bleak future for American artists: "among democratic nations, a writer may flatter himself that he will obtain at a cheap rate a meagre reputation and a large fortune. For this purpose he need not be admired; it is enough that he is liked. . . . Democratic literature is always infested with a tribe of writers who look upon letters as a mere trade; and for some few great authors who adorn it you may reckon thousands of idea-mongers."[12]

For the "few great writers," the capitalist system offered no financial shelter. Authors in the later eighteenth century often supported themselves through journalism or were doctors and lawyers. In the early nineteenth century, Nathaniel Hawthorne accepted government service, and Ralph Waldo Emerson traveled the lyceum circuit, while each deplored the condition of popular literature produced by Tocqueville's idea-mongers. In a letter to his publisher, Hawthorne condemned the "d——d mob of scribbling women" and their "trash," which dominated the popular market of his day. And he added, "[I] should be ashamed of myself if I did succeed" in competition with the women's trash.[13]

Moreover, in the later eighteenth and early nineteenth centuries, the situation of the American writer was further complicated by the lack of an international copyright law. Books already popular in England and thus tested in the market could simply be reprinted by American publishers. New works by American authors were regarded as a risky enterprise for a publisher. Even a preeminent postrevolutionary author, the Connecticut Wit Timothy Dwight, acknowledged that, with the English books "already written to our hands . . . book-making is a business, less necessary to us than to any nation in the world."[14] The image of the starving artist in a cold-water flat has been a constant American image, from Philip Freneau's "Advice to Authors" (1788) to Kurt Vonnegut's Kilgore Trout.

Furthermore, the American artist found an atmosphere in the young nation which was simply not conducive to the creation of art. Although another of the Connecticut Wits, Joel Barlow, filled his poems with visions of future artists and poets blossoming in America, he admitted in "Prospectus of a National Institution to be Established in the United States" (1806) that "What are called the fine arts, in distinction from what are called the useful, have been little cultivated in America. Indeed, few of them have yet arrived, in modern times, to that degree of splendor which they had acquired among the ancients. Here we must examine an opinion, entertained by some persons, that the encouragement of the fine arts savors too much of luxury, and is unfavorable to republican principles."[15] Barlow refuted that opinion but could find only his projected "National Institution" a possible solution for encouraging the arts in a republic.

Franklin, who himself had reprinted Samuel Richardson's *Pamela* in 1744, believed that postrevolutionary America was not yet ready for a flourishing of the arts. "To America, one schoolmaster is worth a dozen poets, and the invention of a machine or the improvement of an implement is of more importance than a masterpiece of Raphael. . . .

Nothing is good or beautiful but in the measure that it is useful; yet all things have a utility under particular circumstances. Thus poetry, painting, music (and the stage as their embodiment) are all necessary and proper gratifications of a refined society but objectionable at an earlier period, since their cultivation would make a taste for their enjoyment precede its means." [16] As Benjamin T. Spencer pointed out, "the man of letters was neither honored nor respected by the majority of his compatriots. Hence belletristic writing faltered because it lacked motivating power of social approval." [17]

As a result, in the context of the new American society, the artist felt the need to justify his existence, his reason for being. He reexamined his art not just because he wanted to create an *American* literature, or, as Hugh Kenner calls it, a "Homemade World," but also because in his new and precarious existence, he felt the need to redefine art and to examine its relationship to this new society. For a writer such as Joel Barlow, the object of his epic *The Columbiad*, that is, the object of the new American art, is both poetical and moral, but primarily moral: "to inculcate the love of rational liberty, and . . . to show that on the basis of the republican principle all good morals, as well as good government and hopes of permanent peace, must be founded." [18] The new American poet will not have to write of "vengeful chiefs and furious gods," nor Olympic gods, nor heavenly rebellions, as Barlow tells his reader in Book VIII of "The Vision of Columbia" (1787). [19]

Barlow, however, was a man with visions of the future, one who seemed unable to recognize—or at least was unwilling to record—the current situation. His contemporary, a Revolutionary propagandist turned postwar journalist, Philip Freneau, recognized the dangers for the artist at this time and addressed a warning to his fellow citizens.

TO THE AMERICANS OF THE UNITED STATES

First published November, 1797

Men of this passing age!—whose noble deeds
Honour will bear above the *scum* of Time;
Ere this eventful century expire,
Once more we greet you with our humble rhyme:
Pleased, if we meet your smiles, but—if denied,
Yet with YOUR sentence, we are satisfied.

Catching our objects from the varying scene
Of human things; a mingled work we draw,
Chequered with fancies odd, and figures strange,
Such as no *courtly* poet ever saw;
Who writ, beneath some GREAT MAN'S cieling [*sic*] placed;
Travelled no lands, nor rove the watery waste.

To seize some *features* from the faithless past;
Be this our care—before the century close:
The colours strong!—for, if we deem aright,
The *coming shall be an age of prose*:
When *sordid cares* will break the muses' dream,
And COMMON SENSE be ranked in seat supreme,

Go now, dear book; once more expand your wings:
Still to the cause of Man *severely true*:
Untaught to flatter *pride*, or fawn on kings;—
Trojan or Tyrian,—*give them both their due. —*
When they are right, the cause of both we plead,
And both will please us well,—if both will read.[20]

Freneau told his compatriots that the events of the century were unique
and worth poetic consideration—that the American poet had witnessed
life as had no "*courtly* poet," sheltered under "some GREAT MAN'S cieling." Freneau wanted to record poetically the events of the American
experience—"To seize some *features* from the faithless past." He
feared that the "*coming shall be an age of prose*," dominated by "COM-
MON SENSE," a quality which is antithetical to poetry or to "the muses'
dream." In "To an Author," Freneau complained that "few critics will
be found [in America] / To sift your works" and that there is no fellow-
ship of poets such as "Thrice happy Dryden" had experienced in England.[21] For Freneau, "lovely *Fancy*" has no chance in a country
"where rigid *Reason* reigns alone" and in a time when the people are
"employed in edging steel."

Such a sense of disaffection led, on one hand, to artistic introspection
and, on the other hand, to a certain hostility to America's economic and
governmental structures. From the introspective tendency, for example,
have come the many American poems that are simply about poetry, as
the artist attempted to justify his own nonutilitarian existence, from
Emerson's "Merlin" (1847), who "Must smite the chords rudely and

hard," [22] to Marianne Moore's disarming confession in "Poetry" (1921): "I, too, dislike it: there are things that are beyond all this fiddle. / Reading it, however, with a perfect contempt for it, one discovers in / it after all, a place for the genuine." [23] From the artists' tendency toward hostility came, for example, the various experiments in communal and cooperative living in the early nineteenth century by the Transcendentalists at Brook Farm and Bronson Alcott and his friends at Fruitlands to the outright advocacy of socialism and communism by many of our artists in the twentieth century. Another kind of hostility emerged in Freneau's "Advice to Authors," which prefigures a common theme in later American literature: that businessmen are stupid and that a fortune is easy for such men to acquire. As Freneau suggested in 1788 to American authors who "are at present considered as the dregs of the community": "If you are so poor that you are compelled to live in some miserable garret or cottage; do not repine. . . . Fortune most commonly bestows wealth and abundance upon fools and idiots; and men of the dullest natural parts are, notwithstanding, generally best calculated to acquire large estates, and hoard up immense sums from small beginnings." [24]

The American artist had been placed in a new situation and assumed tremendous responsibilities. As Joel Barlow observed, "Republican principles have never been organized or understood, so as to form a government, in any country but our own. It is therefore from theory, rather than example, that we must reason on this subject [the need for and encouragement of the fine arts in a republic]." [25] And so, looking to his own country for a topic, a poet such as Barlow celebrated his vision of a glorious future in *The Columbiad*, while other poets, such as his fellow Connecticut Wit Timothy Dwight, wrote of the revolution itself and of the near-idyllic life led by the country folk following the war. *Greenfield Hill*, published by Dwight in 1794, is a poetic history of this rural Connecticut area and the neighboring town of Fairfield. Dwight celebrates the small farmer, who, not bound by the law of primogeniture, leaves his land in equal shares to his children, with the result, of course, that there are no large landholders: "See the wide realm in equal shares possess'd! / How few the rich, or poor! how many bless'd! / . . . No nuisant drones purloin the earner's food; / But each man's labour swells the common good." [26]

Indeed, as the American writer looked about him, it would not be the businessman he would extoll. The American artist of the Federal period was guided by the same noncommercial, nonurban, and nontechnological impetus that one of the Founding Fathers had also expressed. Fearful of urban mobs and factories, Thomas Jefferson had hoped that the new nation would be one of rural husbandmen. In respect to the economic development of the nation, Jefferson had, in *Notes on the State of Virginia* (1784–85), argued that America should remain a land of farmers. Economically, America has an abundance of land, Jefferson reasoned, so it should be a nation of husbandmen. Morally, Jefferson contends that "those who labour in the earth are the chosen people of God"—people who have historically been virtuous.[27] In contrast to this independent and virtuous farmer, the businessman is dependent upon his customers—not on the soil and heaven; and such dependence, Jefferson observed, "begets subservience and venality, suffocates the germ of virtue, and prepares fit tools for the designs of ambition" (p. 164). Thus Jefferson called for a nation based on agrarianism: "for the general operations of manufacture, let our work-shops remain in Europe. . . . The mobs of great cities add just so much to the support of pure government, as sores do to the strength of the human body" (p. 165).

For Jefferson, man's right to private property was a given, whether that property was a farm or a factory. However, Jefferson believed that the small farmer, or the family farmer, working his own fields could best achieve a contented and virtuous life and thus provide stability for the new country. Jefferson's agrarianism, however, was both a moral and an economic statement. The urban mobs are "sores" in humanity's body. Let Europe suffer the plague of the Industrial Revolution.

When Jefferson became president of the United States, however, he urged mercantilist protectionist measures for manufacturers, and, in 1816, he summarized the shift in his position from that expressed in *Notes on Virginia* in 1785.

> You tell me I am quoted by those who wish to continue our dependence on England for manufactures. There was a time when I might have been so quoted with more candor, but within the thirty years which have since elapsed, how are circumstances changed! . . . who in 1785 could foresee the rapid depravity which was to render the close of that century the disgrace of the history of man? Who could have imagined that the two most distinguished in the rank of nations, for science and civilization, would have suddenly descended from that honorable eminence.

. . . We have experienced what we did not then believe, that there exists both profligacy and power enough to exclude us from the field of interchange with other nations: that to be independent for the comforts of life we must fabricate them ourselves. We must now place the manufacturer by the side of the agriculturist.[28]

It was, however, that earlier image of the family farmer which caught the poet's imagination. As Leo Marx has pointed out in *The Machine in the Garden: Technology and the Pastoral Ideal in America*, Jefferson's 1785 farmer lived in a kind of Arcadia, an ideal world situated somewhere between a primitive natural state and an urban culture. In the late eighteenth and early nineteenth centuries, this farmer was a veritable ideal, as Dwight depicted him in *Greenfield Hill*.

> Not long since liv'd a Farmer plain,
> Intent to gather honest gain,
> Laborious, prudent, thrifty, neat,
> Of judgment strong, experience great,
> In solid homespun clad, and tidy,
> And with no coxcomb learning giddy.[29]

A lasting, but minor image in American literature, this farmer still survives, for example, in the yeoman farmers created by William Faulkner.

Moreover, while the poet remembered Jefferson's idyllic Corydon, the family farmer, he also remembered Jefferson's early mistrust of the urban businessman who tends toward "venality" and whose career may be governed by the "designs of ambition." In the early nineteenth century, while poets such as William Cullen Bryant sought relief from the cares of commerce by walks in the country, other writers were creating fictional city businessmen who would cheat and con the country Corydon, as we will see in the next chapter.

CHAPTER 3

The Yankee Peddler and
the Con Man

The terrible "tribe of writers," the "idea-mongers," whom de Tocqueville juxtaposed to the "few great authors," increased and prospered in the late eighteenth and early nineteenth centuries. Indeed, it is to the popular literature of the time that we must next look for the developing image of the American businessman. More serious writers, such as the city-dweller William Cullen Bryant, spiritually and poetically fled to the country from the trials of industry and the city, as in this passage from "Inscription for the Entrance to a Wood" (1821), a poem whose sentiments extended beyond Thomas Jefferson's celebration of a rural Arcadia.

> Stranger, if thou has learned a truth which needs
> No school of long experience, that the [urban] world
> Is full of guilt and misery, and hast seen
> Enough of all its sorrows, crimes, and cares,
> To tire thee of it, enter this wild wood
> And view the haunts of Nature.[1]

In the first of the Leather-Stocking Tales, *The Pioneers* (1823), James Fenimore Cooper's frontiersman, Natty Bumppo, flees to the woods, unable to adjust even to the little pioneer village of Templeton. In the 1830s, Ralph Waldo Emerson was preaching an antimaterialism that was denying any value to private property, a contention best expressed in "Hamatreya."

> Bulkeley, Hunt, Willard, Hosmer, Meriam, Flint,
> Possessed the land which rendered to their toil

Hay, corn, roots, hemp, flax, apples, wool, and wood.
Each of these landlords walked amidst his farm,
Saying, " 'Tis mine, my children's and my name's.
How sweet the west wind sounds in my own trees!
How graceful climb those shadows on my hill!
I fancy these pure waters and the flags
Know me, as does my dog: we sympathize;
And, I affirm, my actions smack of the soil."
Where are these men? Asleep beneath their grounds:
And strangers, fond as they, their furrows plough.
Earth laughs in flowers, to see her boastful boys
Earth-proud, proud of the earth which is not theirs;
Who steer the plough, but cannot steer their feet
Clear of the grave.[2]

It was a broad kind of anticapitalist and antibusiness sentiment floating
along at the intellectual and creative top of our literature.

The image embodying this sentiment was to spring in large part from
the popular literature, the stage, the jokebook, and the frontier tales first
published in popular journals. The Yankee Jonathan, a kind of country
bumpkin, first appeared in Royall Tyler's comedy *The Contrast* (1787).
He was of course modeled on that famous Yankee Doodle, a name of
derision applied to soldiers from Connecticut by the English redcoats
during the French and Indian War.

Yankee Doodle went to town
Riding on a pony.
He stuck a feather in his cap
And called it macaroni.

Unsophisticated and comic, the Yankee was a stock character in postrevolutionary drama—one who, nevertheless, could help fool and destroy a foppish English dandy.

By 1808 the country bumpkin had matured. In the work of our one
serious writer of the time who attempted to deal in specifics, the Yankee
had become a restless and virile "improver"—a jack-of-all-trades, still
unsophisticated but no longer foolish. As Washington Irving humor-
ously traced the development of the Yankee in *Knickerbocker's History
of New York*, he points out that the Yankees, "a certain shrewd race of
men," had originally fled Europe because of their love of "the liberty of

conscience" and, its corollary, the "*liberty of speech.*"[3] In fact, the Yankee is a person who "always thinks aloud, [who] rides a cock-a-hoop on the tongue." This garrulous and freedom-loving soul emigrated to Connecticut, where the Indians bestowed upon him the name "Yanokies," ironically meaning "*silent man*" (p. 119). The Yankees, who came to the New World for freedom of conscience, were soon busy persecuting members of other religious sects, Irving's narrator Knickerbocker waggishly tells his readers. Moreover, the Yankees began to practice zealously a "singular custom"—bundling, a custom which Knickerbocker describes as corresponding to the economic shrewdness of the Yankee. "This ceremony [bundling] was likewise, in those primitive times, considered as an indispensable preliminary to matrimony, their courtships commencing where ours usually finish. . . . Thus early did this cunning and ingenious people display a shrewdness of making a bargain which has since distinguished them, and a strict adherance to the good old vulgar maxim about 'buying a pig in a poke'" (p. 119). The living results of this Yankee union—that is, the children—"grew up a long-sided, raw-boned, hardy race of whoreson whalers, wood-cutters, fishermen, and peddlers, and strapping corn-fed wenches" (p. 121).

The Yankee is a "rambler," says Knickerbocker, who first provides himself with a buxom wife and then, "having thus provided himself, like a peddler with a heavy napsack, . . . he literally sets out on his peregrination. His whole family, household furniture, and farming-utensils are hoisted into a covered cart, his own and his wife's wardrobe packed up in a firkin, which done, he shoulders his axe, takes staff in hand, whistles 'Yankee Doodle,' and trudges off to the woods" (p. 122). So the Yankee clears his land and breeds children and, when he has "improved" his land enough—or is prosperous, he abandons his log cabin and builds himself an "air castle," "a huge palace of pine boards" (p. 123). Surprisingly, however, the Yankee is not satisfied. He abandons his "air-castle," packs up his family and goods, and heads west. Knickerbocker complains that the Yankee disturbed the stolid Dutch burghers of New York; that the Yankee, a fast-talking "varlet," seduced the Dutch girls; that the noise of fiddles and children disturbed the Dutchmen's peace; that the Yankee asked too many questions; and that, most odiously, the Yankees "squatted" on "*new lands*" (p. 125).

The Yankee has thus become clever and shrewd, a fast talker, an "improver," a "varlet" with women, a squatter who could outwit "great landholders." Clearly a shrewd bargainer, he is a small-time capitalist, sometimes a peddler, sometimes a whaler. He is the Yankee who soon was to be found in every corner of the earth, as Knickerbocker remarked with wonder.

After Irving, the Yankee took on different aspects. For example, he became Major Jack Downing, the creation of Seba Smith, a Down-East commentator on current events. No longer a countryman, Downing lives in a small town but travels to larger cities, such as New York and Washington. More sophisticated and still shrewd, Downing was the literary father for a number of commenting Yankees. But Downing is not a businessman. The businessman Yankee became the Yankee Peddler, mentioned by Irving.

As Daniel Hoffman has pointed out in *Form and Fable in American Fiction*, the Yankee Peddler permeated our jokebooks and popular literature in the early nineteenth century, but he never seemed to be a totally honest peddler. And, of course, with his background in Irving's Yankee, such a situation should be no surprise. His sexual proclivities and attractiveness have survived today in our traveling salesman jokes.

The image of the Yankee Peddler is that of a traveling peddler who strolls over the mountain with a pack on his back. When he is first seen, his prospective customers hurry to hide. However, the peddler, by his gift of gab, soon has sold the villagers or farmers items they neither want nor need. Sometimes the peddler is even dishonest, a wheeler-dealer, who cheats and runs. On the other hand, the peddler brings news from other areas, even from the "world." In the early almanacs and jokebooks, the Yankee Peddler is not so much condemned for his duping of the rural folk but is, rather, celebrated for his shrewdness and cleverness. The laughter is at the expense of the villagers or farmers, not at the peddler. He was a character "newly minted," as Constance Rourke has observed.[4]

At the same time that the Yankee Peddler was developing as an image of the native American, American writers were borrowing, most immediately from England, another kind of character, rich in folk background. This character came to be called the Confidence Man.[5] Based upon the rogue of English fiction, the Confidence Man developed from stories of thieves, gamblers, and other practitioners of confidence games. More often than not, he preyed upon the poor and incompetent. He attempts to trick with malicious intent toward his victim and often with disastrous personal results for his victim. His ploy is based upon gaining the confidence of the victim—to violate, ultimately, the very human need for trust. In contrast to the victims of the Confidence Man, those people who bought items from the Yankee Peddler, at least in the early stories, were well aware that they were quite possibly buying useless items (thus they hid, when he first appeared), and the items which were sold by the peddler were small and of little consequence.

Furthermore, the Confidence Man was a man of masks, a trickster who donned clothes and a lingo to fit his assumed character or his con game. He was a man of constantly dissolving character and, therefore, a man of no real character. He might on occasion be a city man or, with a change of clothes and dialect, a backwoodsman. If he came upon a church revival meeting, he might suddenly become a missionary. In short, he could change clothes, language, and character to comply with the necessities of the con game. The early Yankee Peddler had none of this devious and maliciously destructive contrivance in his character. He was what he was—a Yankee Peddler—and only the buyer need beware.

An early example of the Confidence Man in America is Yaller Blossom, the horsetrader in Augustus B. Longstreet's short story "The Horse Swap" (1835). Yaller Blossom appears in a Georgia county seat with an apparently superior horse he wishes to trade. He intends to con the country folk, who have gathered in town for a session of the court. Yaller Blossom finally enters into negotiations with Peter Ketch, a countryman, and the horses are swapped. Of course, Yaller Blossom's horse Bullet is soon revealed to have a hideous sore on his back, and it appears that Ketch has been conned. However, as Yaller Blossom discovers, the horse he has gained, Ketch's Kit, is both deaf and blind. The con man has been conned. On the other hand, the con man usually did not lose, as many young virgins in the moralistic women's novels of the time discovered. The sexual con man was a different kind of con man, but a con man, nevertheless.

The two characters—the Confidence Man and the Yankee Peddler—have, in some works, remained separate in American literature. The Confidence Man sometimes became a kind of supernatural spirit, Philip Traum of Mark Twain's *The Mysterious Stranger* (posthumously published in 1916), or he was the dissolving characters of the Duke and Dauphin in Twain's *Adventures of Huckleberry Finn* (1884). More recently, the Confidence Man has appeared as Burlingame in John Barth's *The Sot-Weed Factor* (1960) and as Rinehart in Ralph Ellison's *Invisible Man* (1952). The Yankee Peddler has survived in our traveling salesman jokes but has also become a pathetic and fumbling Willy Loman in Arthur Miller's *Death of a Salesman* (1949). However, in another variation, V. K. Ratliff, a sewing machine salesman, is juxtaposed to Flem Snopes, a master Confidence Man–businessman, in William Faulkner's *The Hamlet* (1940).

However, and perhaps inevitably, in other works, the Confidence Man and the Yankee Peddler merged in American tales of the early nineteenth century. This new character, the Confidence Man as peddler, first appeared as Thomas Chandler Haliburton's Sam Slick, who was in the 1830s the subject of a number of brief sketches, but who soon became the protagonist of his own book, *The Clockmaker, or Sayings and Doings of Samuel Slick* (1837). Although Sam Slick is at first associated with the Yankee Peddler,[6] he assumes disguises as the con game changes. He travels from east to west and changes opinions, clothes, and lingo as he travels. His bursting ego and his obvious greed led James Russell Lowell to protest against this corruption of the native, regional image. Sam Slick thus emerged as the con man–peddler, and a literary image of the American businessman, even the simple salesman, had been created.

Sam Slick's con man qualities are most obviously evident in the next decade in Johnson J. Hooper's *Adventures of Captain Simon Suggs*, a series of short tales reprinted in book form in 1845. Suggs's motto, "IT IS GOOD TO BE SHIFTY IN A NEW COUNTRY," typifies his amoralistic approach to life and is, as Hooper tells his reader, "his whole ethical system." Further, Hooper observes, "The shifty Captain Suggs is a miracle of shrewdness. He possesses in an eminent degree, that tact which enables man to detect the *soft spots* in his fellow, and to assimilate himself to whatever company he may fall in with." Coldly calculating, Suggs proves he can out-con another master conman, the revivalist minister, in a sketch entitled "The Captain Attends a Camp Meeting."[7]

At the same time Captain Suggs was being shifty in the New World, a character from the Old World appeared in a Christmas giftbook and proved amazingly popular. Charles Dickens sent Ebenezer Scrooge from England to America in "A Christmas Carol" in 1843. Scrooge is, of course, neither con man nor Yankee Peddler; he is a greedy and selfish old businessman who pays his employee Bob Cratchit slave wages. Scrooge, however, is transformed; that is, he becomes more generous with his employee because of a series of apparitions, the Ghosts of Christmas Past, Christmas Future, and Christmas Present. It is an allegorical tale: the evil and greedy businessman reformed by *dei ex machina*.

Dickens himself had toured America in 1842. A most popular writer in the New World, he had been mobbed at each stop with admirers. However, he intensely disliked Americans—their manners, their customs, but especially their con men, as he revealed most clearly in *The Life and Adventures of Martin Chuzzlewit* (1844). The young Englishman Martin himself is transformed into a Confidence Man when he journeys to America, as he becomes involved in the Eden Land Corporation, a fraudulent land speculating company. However, Martin is no match for all the other American con men, and he returns to England an altered and chastened young man. Dickens was amazingly sensitive to the emerging image of the American businessman as a con man, but American readers were angry with his negative characterizations of "the American" in his novel. Greed is the driving force of the American businessman–con man in Dickens's novel—the same greed displayed by Ebenezer Scrooge, who has at least the virtue of reforming and who, unlike the native American con man, is not so treacherous, devious, or amoral.

Greed, too, is the driving force of that Scrooge-like con man Bildad of Herman Melville's *Moby-Dick* (1851). Ironically a Quaker, Bildad has behind him a lifetime of whaling (much like Irving's earlier Yankee whalers) and is presently a capitalist, one of the chief owners of the *Pequod*, upon which Ishmael has decided to ship. Bildad's greed and devious dealings have been unaffected by his Quaker faith; as Ishmael surmises, Bildad must have long ago concluded that "a man's religion is one thing, and this practical world quite another. This world pays dividends." Bildad is a cruel and menacing character, "a bitter, hard taskmaster"; when he was an active officer aboard ship, he was "hardhearted." Now, as Ishmael observes, "His own person was the exact embodiment of his utilitarian character. On his long, gaunt body he carried no spare flesh, no superfluous beard, his chin having a soft, economical nap to it, like the worn nap of his broad-brimmed hat." Bildad plans to give Ishmael only a tiny "lay" (a percentage of the profits) as salary; however, with the help of Bildad's partner Peleg, Ishmael signs aboard the ship with a larger lay than Bildad had first offered, but a lay that is still pitifully small.[8]

Bildad the businessman–con man is ultimately fooled by the captain of his ship, Ahab. Ahab has no intention of catching whales for the profit his ship will bring his employers; he is out to kill the White Whale, Moby Dick. On the surface, Ahab bears no resemblance to the American capitalist con man: he himself has no money invested in the ship; he is not even greedy for money. No matter in what light we interpret Ahab's quest to kill the whale, he does not appear to fit the Confidence Man – Yankee Peddler mold. However, if we look closely, Ahab's story suggests another aspect of the developing image of the American businessman, that man who, once involved in manufacturing, becomes, as Thomas Jefferson had contended, "venal" and potentially the victim of the "designs of ambition."

The whaling ship, as Ishmael describes it, is a factory, not for textiles, as had been springing up in America for some time, but a factory for killing and processing whales. In a chapter such as "Cutting In," the process of butchering the whale is described as a kind of assembly line. In *White Jacket*, a novel published just the year before *Moby Dick*, Melville had described the American frigate as "a system of cruel cogs and wheels, systematically grinding up in one common hopper all that might minister to the moral well-being of the crew." [9] The captain of that machine in *Moby-Dick* is Ahab, who sacrifices both machine and conned crew to his metaphysical monomania.

Melville was soon to elaborate more fully upon the evils of machine technology, which enslaved the workers to both machine and master, in "The Paradise of Bachelors and the Tartarus of Maids" (1855). "The Tartarus of Maids" begins with a description of a Dantean Inferno, a bit of American landscape, a hollow called Devil's Dungeon. "Not far from the bottom of the Dungeon stands a large whitewashed building, relieved, like some great whited sepulchre, against the sullen background of mountainside firs, and other hardy evergreens, inaccessibly rising in grim terraces for some two thousand feet. The building is a paper mill." The reader hardly needs to proceed further to know that in the first room the narrator enters he sees the workers as "the blank-looking girls." [10] At the same time, Thoreau complained in *Walden* (1854) that the American man "has no time to be anything but a machine" and that "the mass of men lead lives of quiet desperation." [11] Thoreau and Melville were both responding to the smoky factories springing up at this time throughout New England. Each believed that the humanity of the workers was destroyed by the machines and the factory environment, a theme to be reiterated by American writers in the twentieth century.

However, Melville was not quite through with the con man–business-man and his increasing association with the factory system and the evils of technology. In "The Lightning Rod Man" (1853), the Yankee Peddler peddles the steel product of modern technology. In effect, he is an advo-cate of the Devil, or perhaps the Devil himself. "A lean, gloomy figure. Hair dank and lank, mattedly streaked over his brow. His sunken pitfalls of eyes were ringed by indigo halos, and played with an innocuous sort of lightning: the gleam without the bolt." [12] In this story, however, the con man fails because of the honesty and simple values of the prospec-tive pigeon.

Certainly, Melville's most despairing work is *The Confidence-Man: His Masquerade* (1857), in the course of which the reader is introduced to a master con man who assumes a number of forms in the close quar-ters of the ironically named steamboat *Fidèle*, bound for New Orleans from St. Louis. A master of disguises, the Confidence Man is variously transformed into several different characters, among them, a herb doc-tor (who, as a peddler of patent medicine, springs from the tradition of the Yankee Peddler), an agent of the Black Rapids Coal Company, a representative of the Philosophical Intelligence Office, a philanthropist, and the cosmopolitan, ironically named Frank Goodman, who is the last metamorphosis of the Confidence Man. The cluster of con men, nearly all involved in some perverted capitalistic scheme, may not present "swindle on a grand scale," as Newton Arvin observed,[13] but does in-corporate a nihilistic portrait of the American people, especially the subspecies "capitalist." It is perhaps no coincidence that Melville began writing *The Confidence-Man* in 1855, the year P. T. Barnum published his *Autobiography*.[14]

The masquerades of the herb peddler and the cosmopolitan Frank Goodman perhaps best delineate the two separate traditions of the Yankee Peddler and the rogue–Confidence Man. The herb doctor, also a bone-setter, sells his Samaritan Pain Dissuader at various prices, de-pending on the pigeon. Prospective buyers are suspicious of him imme-diately (as buyers always are of the Yankee Peddler), but through clever manipulations and a line of convincing patter, he manages to sell a num-ber of bottles of medicine. When one person in a crowd is convinced enough to buy a bottle, others respond also. However, when one person objects, others refuse to buy and "Those who had purchased looked sheepish or ashamed." [15] As the herb doctor describes himself, " 'How different we herb-doctors! who claim nothing, invent nothing; but staff in hand, in glades, and upon hillsides, go about in nature, humbly seeking her cures.' " [16]

The cosmopolitan, the final mask of the Confidence Man in the novel, does not so much intend to gain money as to gain "confidence" and trust. His actual cons are for pittances, a free shave from the barber, for example. He preaches a philosophy of benevolence, a Christian theology of faith in one's fellow man. " 'Charity, charity!' exclaimed the cosmopolitan, 'never a sound judgment without charity.' " [17] He urges upon others "a generous confidence" in himself. His goal is the deception itself as much as his possible financial gain. Early in the book, a one-legged skeptic observes that " 'Money, you think, is the sole motive to pain and hazard, deception and deviltry, in this world. How much money did the devil make by gulling Eve?' " [18] The one-legged man wisely understands that the motive of the cosmopolitan is devilish, far more vicious than the herb doctor's marginal profits from the sale of the medicine.

On the other hand, the coupling of the peddler and the rogue is presented in several characters in Melville's novel. One masquerade of the Confidence Man is the agent of the Black Rapids Coal Company, who is able to sell shares in his fraudulent business to several people aboard the *Fidèle*. A more interesting manifestation is Egbert, a businessman who is a disciple of the transcendental philosopher Mark Winsome (Ralph Waldo Emerson). Egbert, who "is first among mankind to reduce to practice the principles of Mark Winsome," is not "any soft Utopian," but rather "a thriving young merchant," who applies "a business-like view" to all circumstances. [19] Although he asserts that he will give away money, he will never loan it, especially to a friend, for that puts friendship on a "pecuniary basis"; friendship, according to Egbert, is "social and intellectual." [20] Indeed, only Egbert is finally able to confound the Confidence Man. And yet Egbert himself is a Confidence Man, in this case a businessman, who, as Daniel G. Hoffman has observed, is also an offspring of "the traditional type of the Yankee peddler." [21] His noble transcendental sentiments are the sugary surface of a hardhearted master of money. He represents the Confidence Man – Yankee Peddler blend in a particularly vicious form.

Perhaps most interesting is Melville's suggestion that an Egbert could have developed from the philosophy of that eminent New England intellectual Ralph Waldo Emerson, who, as Mark Winsome, is described by Melville as a "metaphysical merman," "a kind of cross between a

Yankee peddler and a Tarter priest." [22] It is, of course, the New England intellectual tradition which contemporary cultural historians such as Richard Hofstadter celebrate in opposition to the American capitalist. In *Anti-Intellectualism in American Life*, Hofstadter contends that Emerson's New England "tradition, exported wherever New Englanders settled in large numbers, was responsible for a remarkably large portion of the country's dynamic intellectual life throughout the nineteenth century and into the twentieth." [23] Melville has suggested, however, that it was this same New England tradition, the tradition of Emerson and Thoreau, which, when applied in practical life experiences, led to the viciousness of Egbert.

Egbert is only one of several characters in the American pre–Civil War period who embody the coupling of the native image of the Yankee Peddler and the imported character of the rogue–Confidence Man. He is a businessman of a heartless sort who will proliferate throughout American literature for the next century.

CHAPTER 4

"The American" and the Artist

The American businessman, distrusted even from the beginnings of the American nation by the Pilgrim and Puritan Fathers, emerged in the imaginative literature of the early nineteenth century as a con man–businessman, an exploiter both through devious schemes as well as through the terrors of technology. However, the American artist of this Romantic generation was not quite through with the American businessman.

Nathaniel Hawthorne was one of those "few great authors," who, as Tocqueville had pointed out, must suffer at the hands of the "idea-mongers." [1] In letters to his publishers, he raged at the "d——d mob of scribbling women" and their "trash." [2] Hawthorne, we can only surmise, did not have a high regard for popular literature or for its readers. To express his frustrations, Hawthorne created a struggling artist, Owen Warland in "The Artist of the Beautiful" (1845), whose conflicts are primarily with a representative of the American bourgeoisie, a businessman, in this case a retired clockmaker named Peter Hovenden. Also contrasted to the American artist is Robert Danforth, the village blacksmith, who embodies hard, physical violence and the virtues of hard work. Both Owen the artist and Robert the blacksmith ("the worker in iron," as old Peter describes him [3]) are rivals for the hand of Peter's lovely daughter Annie. Of course, Robert wins Annie, while Owen is struggling to create the Beautiful.

Peter has sold his shop to Owen, who was his apprentice, and is now dismayed at what appears to be Owen's lack of commercial industry. Owen, however, is using his craft to create the Beautiful. Ironically, although a watchmaker, Owen hates watches and all machinery. (The pocket watch came into wide use at about this time, when factory workers were given specific work hours.) As the narrator tells us, Owen looks "with singular distaste at the stiff and regular process of ordinary machinery" (p. 507). As a child, he had been sickened by the sight of a steam engine. Owen cares nothing about the watchmaker's business or "the measurement of time."

When old Peter rebukes Owen for his apparently time-wasting attempts to create the Beautiful, Owen responds to him, " 'You are my evil spirit . . . you and the hard, coarse world! The leaden thoughts and the despondency that you fling upon me are my clogs, else I should long ago have achieved the task that I was created for.' " Peter leaves "with an uplifted finger and a sneer" (p. 515). The conflict in this story is clear; the artist is isolated from American society, but most especially from Peter Hovenden, the proto-Rotarian. The conclusion of the story is, however, curious and provocative.

Owen does finally create the Beautiful—a mechanical butterfly—and presents it as a belated wedding gift to Annie and Robert, who by now have a baby son. The butterfly, into which Owen has placed his soul, flies first to Annie (who, like all Hawthorne's female characters, has something of the "aesthetic" in her). Then Annie hands the butterfly to Robert, who admires it as a toy but wonders what use it has. When the butterfly is about to be passed to Peter, the butterfly appears to die. Next passed to the baby, the butterfly recovers and responds to the innocence of the little boy. The baby, however, is the grandson of Peter, and he crunches the butterfly in his hand.

Is Owen disturbed? No, he placidly watches the remains of his beautiful butterfly fall from the baby's hand, and the narrator of the story concludes, "When the artist rose high enough to achieve the beautiful, the symbol by which he made it perceptible to mortal senses became of little value in his eyes while his spirit possessed itself in the enjoyment of the reality" (pp. 535–36). The artist, therefore, is satisfied; his creation of beauty is only a kind of symbol for the Beauty which is in his soul. The public? The public's response to the Beautiful has been symbolized in the characters of Annie, the baby, Robert, and Peter, in a descending scale of sensitivity and appreciation. The question, however, hinges upon the responsibility of the artist to communicate the beauty he sees, to teach others to appreciate great beauty. Owen has not been successful in creating any permanent work of art, nor is it clear that he has "communicated" his sense of beauty to anyone other than, perhaps,

Annie. It is a question not finally answered in this short story, but it is an American problem, raised again in the twentieth century when, for example, Gertrude Stein warned Ernest Hemingway that he was too "Rotarian" to write great art.

Living in a small town, with the ease of visiting Nature, which was the source of the Beautiful, Owen could succeed in embodying the Beautiful in the butterfly, even though Peter and Robert could not appreciate or even understand his creation. The artist in American society, therefore, could create, only at the risk of personal loss and isolation and, in the end, even at the risk of noncommunication and condemnation. The artist in a large city, however, has no chance whatever, as Herman Melville's "Bartleby the Scrivener: A Story of Wall-Street" (1853) implies. Bartleby is a mysterious, sour man who is employed as a legal copyist in New York's Wall Street by an elderly lawyer. On the surface, the story appears to have little to do with the businessman. The lawyer, despite so many crooked ones throughout our literature, has always been treated with more respect than has the businessman. And Bartleby's employer is a kind man, with compassion and an amazing patience for his employee. Although the situation is that of Scrooge and Cratchit (employer and employee), the Americanization of the situation is crucial and the results are far different.

Bartleby's employer is a servant of capitalists. He does, in his own words, "a snug business among rich men's bonds, and mortgages, and title-deeds. All who know me, consider me an eminently *safe* man." The lawyer loves to "repeat" the name John Jacob Astor, "for it hath a rounded and orbicular sound to it, and rings like unto bullion." With a rush of business, the lawyer needs another clerk and hires Bartleby, a former employee of the Dead Letter Office in Washington.[4]

On the third day of his employment, the lawyer asks Bartleby to "examine a small paper," but Bartleby responds, "I would prefer not to" (p. 29). And this is to be nearly the whole of Bartleby's speeches throughout the rest of the story: "I would prefer not to." Although Bartleby does complete certain assignments for the lawyer, at other times he simply "prefers not to." Finally, Bartleby "prefers" to cease copying entirely. The lawyer quite naturally fires Bartleby, but Bartleby prefers "*not* to quit." The lawyer, by now at the point of questioning his own sanity but having no doubts as to the insanity of Bartleby, reads two treatises concerning predestination and natural determinism and concludes that it is his fate to allow Bartleby to stay. However, the lawyer finally decides to change his chambers to another building and says good-bye to Bartleby, who of course prefers "not to leave" the old chambers. The new tenants force Bartleby out of the rooms, but he will not leave the building. Eventually, Bartleby is jailed and dies. A tale of insanity to be sure, but also, perhaps, a tale of "passive resistance," as the lawyer tells us (pp. 33–34).

Because Bartleby's profession involves writing, because he has apparently lost faith in man's ability to communicate, and because, further, Bartleby is placed on Wall Street, the center of American capitalism, his tale might well be a parable of the American artist in a capitalistic society, as Newton Arvin observed, "a parable of the frustrated relations between the man of letters and the man of affairs, between the artist's world and the world of practice."[5] On another level, however, it might also be a parable of Bartleby's wrongheaded self-isolation, his refusal to attempt to communicate, a refusal, a "preference," which can only be self-destructive and suicidal.

At the same time that Bartleby "preferred not to," Walt Whitman felt that perhaps he could communicate with the American people. Whitman set out to be the Great Democratic Poet. He could "embrace" nearly all Americans both past and present. He could embrace the American land; he could embrace himself and even embrace God, the "great Camerado," as he tells us in "Song of Myself" (1855). The poem is composed of overwhelmingly lovely lyrical passages, interspersed with long catalogues of people, places, and things—all American and all embraceable. What Whitman could *not* embrace, however, is the American capitalist: the "jour printer," the mechanic, the butcher-boy, yes, but not the employer, the factory owner, the capitalist. The drover, the peddler, even the gentleman, the farmer, and the lawyer he can embrace, but not the businessman. Whitman does acknowledge that he is "part" of the businessman, but it is not a very attractive part.

> This is the city and I am one of the citizens,
> Whatever interests the rest interests me, politics, wars,
>   markets, newspapers, schools,
> The mayor and councils, banks, tariffs, steamships, factories,
>   stocks, stores, real estate and personal estate.
>
> The little plentiful manikins skipping around in collars
>   and tail'd coats,
> I am aware who they are, (they are positively not worms or
>   fleas,)

I acknowledge the duplicates of myself, the weakest and
   shallowest is deathless with me,
What I do and say the same awaits for them,
Every thought that flounders in me the same flounders in them.

I know perfectly well my own egotism,
Know my omnivorous lines and must not write any less,
And would fetch you whoever you are flush with myself.[6]

The curious parenthetical phrase was apparently meant to offset the image of the little capitalistic dolls, full of egotism and floundering thoughts.

However, the American people—even the Annie Hovendens—did not respond to Whitman, although Emerson praised *Leaves of Grass* and in September 1855, the popular journal *United States Magazine* welcomed Whitman as a great American bard ("At last!"). After the Civil War, Whitman, depressed about the state of the country and Lincoln's death, as well as aware of the fact that he would not be the Great Democratic Poet at least for his own age, wrote *Democratic Vistas* (1871), a summation of his views concerning art and society. It is a generally damning view of America, as one might have expected, although it is hopeful for the future. However, Whitman is willing to give the businessman a more important role in his scheme of things than he was willing to grant those same "manikins" in 1855. As he reviews the historical development of the New World, he defines the "First stage" as political: the establishment of national independence and the political forms for independent men.

He continues: "The Second stage relates to material prosperity, wealth, produce, labor-saving machines, iron, cotton, local, State and continental railways, intercommunication and trade with all lands, steamships, mining, general employment, organization of great cities, cheap appliances for comfort, numberless technical schools, books, newspapers, a currency for money circulation, &c."[7] Even in his younger days, Whitman had not shunned the cities and the laborers, as had many other American Romantic writers, nor had he rejected technology. And although, in 1855, he had depicted businessmen as "manikins," they were not "worms or fleas." In his old age, the good gray poet was willing to include both the businessman and his technology as a vital part of America.

Moreover, "The Third stage," that is, the hoped-for development toward which *Democratic Vistas* points, will arise "out of the previous ones, to make them and all illustrious" (p. 427). Whitman predicts that "original" American poets will sing of American achievements, both political and technical, which will form the basis of a "true revolution" of the "interior life." However, these achievements are only the basis. "I hail with joy the oceanic, variegated, intense practical energy, the demand for facts, even the business materialism of the current age, our States. But wo to the age and land in which these things, movements, stopping at themselves, do not tend to ideas" (p. 436). At this point, Whitman's sentiments to some extent echo those of Benjamin Franklin; Franklin's projection of the moral and individual businessman, who establishes private and economic self-sufficiency and then participates in public good works, is enlarged by Whitman to a vision of the nation: political independence, economic sufficiency, and then the higher act, in Whitman's case, a call for a new and original revolution "of the interior life, and of the arts."

So that everyone would understand just how material progress and capitalistic enterprise become "idea," Whitman wrote "Passage to India" (1871), in which technological achievement—the transcontinental railroad, the steamship, the Suez Canal—becomes a means for universal brotherhood and, through the agency of a true poet, a new universal, God-inspired peace. First, however, the physical or technological unity:

> Passage to India!
> Lo, soul, seest thou not God's purpose from the first?
> The earth to be spann'd, connected by network,
> The races, neighbors, to marry and be given in marriage,
> The oceans to be cross'd, the distant brought near,
> The lands to be welded together.
>
> A worship new I sing
> You captains, voyagers, explorers, yours,
> You engineers, you architects, machinists, yours,
> You, not for trade or transportation only,
> But in God's name, and for thy sake O soul.

Then, after the physical union, a true poet shall come who will spiritually unify mankind:

> All these separations and gaps shall be taken up and hook'd
>   and link'd together,
> The whole earth, this cold, impassive, voiceless earth, shall
>   be completely justified,

Trinitas divine shall be gloriously accomplish'd and compacted
   by the true son of God, the poet,
(He shall indeed pass the straits and conquer the mountains,
He shall double the cape of Good Hope to some purpose,)
Nature and Man shall be disjoin'd and diffused no more,
The true son of God shall absolutely fuse them.[8]

Thus far Whitman believed that the capitalist, the "materialist," had
a place in American society. Indeed, he was to prepare the way for the
new revolution and the true poet. Capitalism was, however, not an end
in itself, but was only a means to the new revolution, which was the
ultimate objective. It should be no surprise that the radical left writers
of America in the early twentieth century misinterpreted Whitman's vision as an early expression of their own ideology.

Whitman was, of course, correct about the traveling, the world-
wandering of the American. Anyway, the Yankee had always been a
traveler, as Washington Irving's Knickerbocker had observed in 1808.
After the interruption of the Civil War, the American began wandering
again. This time, however, it was wealthy Americans traveling to Europe. Strangely enough, these democratic sons and daughters of America began to marry the sons and daughters of European aristocracy. The
American seemed to want a noble name, an ancient family; the European wanted the American dollar. So Jenny Jerome married Lord Randolph Churchill, a trend that continued through Wally Simpson's marriage to the Duke of Windsor and Grace Kelly's marriage to her Prince.
(The trend was reversed, perhaps, when American aristocracy, Jackie
Kennedy, married European money.) In the post–Civil War period,
other Americans, even without the benefit of an aristocratic marriage,
became patrons of European art, and the Ryersons and the Palmers, for
example, formed a significant basis for the Art Institute of Chicago.

With all this, it is no surprise that an American novelist sent an American businessman off to Europe. Henry James's Christopher Newman of
The American (1877) was the first of many American fictional characters to return to the Old World. "The American," by his very name
Christopher Newman, suggests an explorer—a Christopher Columbus—as well as a "new man." He is not a Yankee Peddler, except perhaps in the sense that he is selling himself, nor is he a con man. He is an
open, unsophisticated, almost innocent soul who, in the end, is conned
by the old and corrupt French nobility.

We learn little of Newman's background except that he grew up in the
West and that he has had an amazingly successful career on the stock

market. Extremely wealthy, Newman travels to Europe to absorb some culture (which is apparently nonexistent in America) and to find a perfect wife. It is important to note that nineteenth-century America suffered from a cultural inferiority complex. Emerson's call for an American literature in "The American Scholar" (1837) and Whitman's call for a revolution are really admissions that America was "without art," or, as Whitman proclaimed in *Democratic Vistas*, "America has yet morally and artistically originated nothing" (p. 411). American artists themselves have had difficulty recognizing "art" in their own native land. Even Hemingway, the "Rotarian," has Jackson, Colonel Cantwell's driver in *Across the River and into the Trees* (1950), denigrate American art with his description of an American regional museum. " 'All they got in the local museum is arrow heads, war bonnets, scalping knives, different scalps, petrified fish, pipes of peace, photographs of Liver Eating Johnson, and the skin of some bad man that they hanged him and some doctor skinned him out. One of those woman pictures [an Italian madonna] would be out of place there.' " [9] Newman readily admits his desire to find culture in Europe. " 'I am not cultivated, I am not even educated; I know nothing about history, or art, or foreign tongues, or any other learned matter. But I am not a fool, either, and I shall undertake to know something about Europe by the time I have done with it. I feel something under my ribs here . . . that I can't explain—a sort of mighty hankering, a desire to stretch out and have in.' " [10]

When Newman finally does believe that he has found culture, he realizes that it is a culture not produced by businessmen and their technology. Indeed, as Newman tours Europe, he reflects a thoughtful American attitude toward business and art, in which a feeling of ambiguity toward business is clearly evident.

> A thousand forgotten episodes [of his life in "enterprise"] came trooping back into his memory. Some of them he looked complacently enough in the face; from some he averted his head. They were old efforts, old exploits, antiquated examples of "smartness" and sharpness. Some of them, as he looked at them, he felt decidedly proud of; he admired himself as if he had been looking at another man. And, in fact, many of the qualities that made a great deed were there: the decision, the resolution, the courage, the celerity, the clear eye, and the strong hand. Of certain other achievements it would be going too far to say that he was ashamed of them, for Newman had never had a stomach for dirty

work. He was blessed with a natural impulse to disfigure with a direct, unreasoning blow the comely visage of temptation. And certainly, in no man could a want of integrity have been less excusable. Newman knew the crooked from the straight at a glance, and the former had cost him, first and last, a great many moments of lively disgust. But none the less some of his memories seemed to wear at present a rather graceless and sordid mien, and it struck him that if he had never done anything very ugly, he had never, on the other hand, done anything particularly beautiful. He had spent his years in the unremitting effort to add thousands to thousands, and, now that he stood well outside of it, the business of money-getting appeared tolerably dry and sterile. It is very well to sneer at money-getting after you have filled your pockets, and Newman, it may be said, should have begun somewhat earlier to moralise thus delicately. To this it may be answered that he might have made another fortune, if he chose; and we ought to add that he was not exactly moralising. It had come back to him simply that what he had been looking at all the summer [in Europe] was a very rich and beautiful world, and that it had not all been made by sharp railroad men and stock-brokers. (p. 72)

The businessman is thus seen as cultureless, unless, like Newman, he is willing to give up "money-getting" and admit the limitations of his life in "enterprise." Newman is transformed into Samuel Dodsworth by Sinclair Lewis in his 1929 novel *Dodsworth*; fortunately, Dodsworth has enough sense not to challenge the European aristocracy, as Newman did, and finds an American widow, Edith Cortwright, to help him appreciate European culture.

Newman's quest for culture succeeded, but his search for the perfect wife of European nobility failed. It is important to note that, at least until the twentieth century, American writers were unable to create great love stories because such tales ultimately involve conflicts and insurmountable difficulties for the lovers. As in *Romeo and Juliet*, these conflicts arise in societies with class and family distinctions. In democratic, nineteenth-century America, James was thus forced to send Newman to Europe where class lines were tightly drawn.

One of Newman's problems is that he does want a perfect mate, a woman of beauty, culture, and tradition to complement and counterbalance his own wealth, energy, and ambition. Newman has calculated that it is time for him to seek a wife and that he wants a beautiful wife. As Newman admits, " 'I want to possess, in a word, the best article in the market' " (p. 35). His wife, therefore, is to be chosen much as he would have chosen a possession like a Rolls-Royce today.

Newman is, in many ways, an admirable character, generous and good natured, loyal to his French friend Valentin, the brother of the "perfect woman," Madame de Cintre. He is a gentleman despite the machinations of Madame's family—machinations which rob Newman of his perfect wife and send Madame to a nunnery. He even refuses to avenge himself on Madame's family when its terrible secret comes into his possession. In the end, he proves himself at least the moral superior of the European.

Henry James, one of the most respected American writers, thus sent his American to Europe to gain culture. James himself became an ex-patriate and died in England as a naturalized Englishman. Moreover, Newman is not Hawthorne's Peter Hovenden; he is at least open to art and, although Newman occasionally suffers "an aesthetic headache" (p. 1), as James tells us, we might have expected Newman to import European art to America beyond the book's conclusion, as Henry Edwards Huntington was soon to do in California and John Pierpont Morgan in New York. Because of his European experience, however, Newman becomes different from other American businessmen. Indeed, at the end of the novel, Newman returns to Europe. His old occupation in America "appeared unreal" to him; his friends on the stock exchange are puzzled at his "indifference" (p. 361). He had "nothing to do" in America. In short, James implies that the cultured American businessman is no longer a businessman.

CHAPTER 5

Crooked Money and
Easy Money

After *The American*, a rush of books appeared with the negative image of the businessman enlarged. Throughout the next eighty years, that is, generally until 1945, American artists developed the image in a variety of ways, in novels, short stories, plays, and poems. Problems already raised before 1870 were explored and examined. This negative image of the businessman dominated our literature, however, during the late nineteenth century even at a time when the books of Horatio Alger, Jr., were flooding the market and the newspapers and journals were presenting to the public heroic images of John Jacob Astor and Cornelius Vanderbilt. In this chapter, I am going to discuss works in which the businessman is viewed as a crook and also examine that strange attitude adopted by certain American authors that a fortune is easy to make.

The justification of the first charge is clear: alongside the heroic images of the Astors and Vanderbilts in the popular press were the tales of scandals and bribery. The writers, however, extended these tales of corruption to include nearly every wealthy businessman depicted in our literature. The justification for the second charge is less certain. In part, such a charge undoubtedly reflects the unfortunate separation of the artistic world and the mercantile world in America. Perhaps the American artist actually believed those tales of money-making described in the popular press as relatively smooth and uncomplicated. On the other hand, such a charge might also reflect the artist's sense that the life of the mind is far more difficult— and more significant—than that of materialistic, mercantile pursuits.

First, the crooks. This section could be a book in itself. With the Crédit Mobilier scandal hovering in the background, business money became dirty and wealthy businessmen were generally assumed to be corrupt. However, the theme was not new, even in the late nineteenth century; the Confidence Man – Yankee Peddler was a heartless exploiter. Throughout the late nineteenth and early twentieth centuries, in most of the novels in which money is crooked, the businessman has out-maneuvered another businessman or has cheated his partner in one way or another. A theme implicit in *The American*, it is perhaps first explicit in William Dean Howells's *The Rise of Silas Lapham* (1885). Lapham is "a fine type of the successful American," a man of humble origins, who was taught as a child "the simple virtues of the Old Testament and Poor Richard's Almanac." [1] He had traveled to the West as a young man but eventually returned to Vermont, where he worked in the mills and bought a stage line and then married the village schoolteacher. Soon, however, he realized the value of the "paint-mine," which his father had discovered years earlier on the family farm. With a little chemistry and ingenuity, Lapham had become a prosperous paint manufacturer. How-ever, the business had suffered badly during the war, and Lapham had been forced to take a partner with capital. Eventually, Lapham forced his partner out of the business and became a millionaire during the post – Civil War period. All this is told in the form of an interview with a journalist, Bartley, in the first chapter of the book. The chapter con-cludes later in the day with Bartley's telling his wife about "the old fool" Lapham (p. 29).

The Laphams are building a new home in an exclusive neighborhood of Boston as a way for the ladies of the family (mother and two daugh-ters) to approach society. As nouveaux riches, the Laphams had been snubbed by the residents of "The Hill" and "New Land." Howells's de-scriptions of the Laphams' plan for the house—and the architect's "sug-gestion"—can only remind the reader of those air castles that Knicker-bocker's Yankees had built (and then abandoned).

By the end of Chapter III, Rogers, Lapham's old partner, has turned up, and Lapham's rise becomes a fall. Mrs. Lapham reminds her hus-band that it was with Rogers's capital that Lapham had made his millions.

> [Lapham] "What do you want I should own up about a thing for when I don't feel wrong? I tell you Rogers hain't got anything to complain of, and that's what I told you from the start. It's a thing that's done every day. I was loaded up with a partner that didn't know anything, and couldn't do anything, and I unloaded; that's

all." [Mrs. Lapham] "You unloaded just at the time when you
knew that your paint was going to be worth about twice what it
had ever been; and you wanted all the advantage for yourself."

"I had a right to it. I made the success."

"Yes, you made it with Rogers's money; and when you'd made
it you took his share of it. I guess you thought of that when you
saw him, and that's why you couldn't look him in the face."

At these words Lapham lost his temper. (pp. 64–65)

Lapham does loan money to Rogers in an attempt to compensate for
the earlier conning. Moreover, Lapham has a chance to act honestly in
another business situation. At the same time, however, Lapham's business gets into financial trouble. To conclude Lapham's problems, the
still-unfinished new house burns to the ground. Lapham is financially
ruined but is now an honorable man. As Lapham describes the loss of
his fortune, "Seems sometimes as if it was a hole opened for me, and I
crept out of it" (p. 515). This final image suggests that his money was a
kind of box or trap from which his bankruptcy brought release.

It is clear that Lapham might have become a millionaire even if he
had not conned Rogers. It is equally clear that, before his bankruptcy,
Lapham would not have been in such a difficult financial situation had
he not loaned so much money to Rogers in an attempt to make repara-
tions for his earlier swindle. Lapham's rise and fall is a moral tale, told
by a man who had been raised on Benjamin Franklin's "Poor Richard's
Almanac."

For Lapham's daughters, who had not been involved in the conning
and had no knowlege of it, it is evident that money cannot bring happiness. Restless and ill at ease in society, the girls Penelope and Irene are
early examples of just what happens to millionaire's children in American literature. Penelope is allowed to marry a socially desirable young
man, but only after her father's bankruptcy and only after the young man
has convinced his family, who are of course originally opposed to the
marriage.

Silas Lapham lacks the qualities of "natural aristocracy" inherent in
Henry James's Christopher Newman. Barely educated, he shows no interest in culture, and his ideas of a proper house are pretentious and
ridiculous. He does love his wife and children and wants very much to
make them happy. His only talent is in becoming a millionaire—and at
that, too, he finally fails. In the end, however, he has his honesty and

self-respect, but he had had a mighty brush with that venality and ambition which Thomas Jefferson so feared as the husbandman moved to the city and mingled with other businessmen.

The Rise of Silas Lapham was soon followed by a flood of similar novels, such as Robert Herrick's *The Memoirs of an American Citizen* (1905) and Frank Norris's *The Pit* (1903), in which tainted money is a necessity for the protagonist's success. The novelists seemed unable to accept the possibility that a millionaire's money might have been made in a legal and honorable way. Indeed, the novelists indicated little insight into the ways that money was actually made and, as a result, the fictional millionaires are not fully delineated characters.

For our poets in the late nineteenth century, the businessman remained a creature of mystery, but he was certainly not happy. Edwin Arlington Robinson's "Richard Cory" was written in 1895 (and was adapted to music by Simon and Garfunkel in the 1960s).

> Whenever Richard Cory went down town,
> We people on the pavement looked at him:
> He was a gentleman from soul to crown,
> Clean favored, and imperially slim.
>
> And he was always quietly arrayed,
> And he was always human when he talked;
> But still he fluttered pulses when he said,
> "Good morning," and he glittered when he walked.
>
> And he was rich—yes, richer than a king—
> And admirably schooled in every grace:
> In fine, we thought that he was everything
> To make us wish that we were in his place.
>
> So on we worked, and waited for the light,
> And went without the meat, and cursed the bread;
> And Richard Cory, one calm, summer night,
> Went home and put a bullet through his head.[2]

So much for the hopes and dreams of the frugal and hardworking "people on the pavement."

In the years following *The Rise of Silas Lapham*, a number of novelists imitated both the image and the social realism. The most important is Theodore Dreiser, who in 1912 published *The Financier*, the first part of the trilogy of novels concerning Frank Cowperwood. In *The Financier*, Cowperwood, who emerged from a modest home, has become a respected and wealthy financier and broker in Philadelphia. Cowperwood is married and has a family, but he is not particularly interested in either wife or children and keeps a mistress, Aileen Butler. However, Cowperwood has housed his family in an elaborate home and has bought *objets d'art* and fine paintings. Although quite wealthy, Cowperwood is continually in need of capital and, with the complicity of the city treasurer, "borrows" monies from the city to invest in Chicago. With the Great Fire, however, Cowperwood's finances are precarious, and local reform groups in Philadelphia are preparing for the next election. Eventually, Cowperwood goes to jail for his misuse of city monies but is released after only thirteen months. As the book ends, Cowperwood has already made another fortune, divorces his wife, and moves with Aileen to Chicago—the site of the second novel of the trilogy, *The Titan* (1914).

Cowperwood's story advances the crooked money motif in several new and significant ways. First, unlike Silas Lapham, Cowperwood does not repent his evil ways. He seems to be an amoral creature, a wheeler-dealer, who is defeated time and again in the course of the trilogy, who makes fortunes and loses them with no scruples. Amazingly resilient, Cowperwood tends to recover more quickly than do his colleagues. He has, it seems, no sins to repent; he is the con man–businessman extraordinaire.

Second, dirty business is now involved in dirty politics in effective ways. In Mark Twain and Charles Dudley Warner's *The Gilded Age* (1873), corrupt Washington politicians connive with private speculators, but with few results. Cowperwood successfully schemes with corruptible and corrupted politicians. In *The Financier*, Cowperwood and the city treasurer had successfully used city monies for personal investments. In *The Titan*, Cowperwood gains control of the Chicago city council and even manages to get a bill through the Illinois state legislature that is favorable to his enterprises. The governor, however, vetoes the bill.

Third, Cowperwood has a seemingly endless variety of wives and mistresses. He provides for each to live in luxury, and it is a rare year in Cowperwood's life when he is not sexually active with at least two women at the same time. At fifty-two, he has a seventeen-year-old mistress. When, in *The Titan*, he plans to leave Chicago for New York, he moves both wife and mistress to lavish but separate New York residences. Needless to say, Cowperwood has no real concern for children or family.

Virility and business acumen in the American businessman hereafter diverge, and opposite types emerge. The Cowperwood type, for example, reappears in the character of an unnamed sixty-year-old grain broker in Ernest Hemingway's *To Have and Have Not* (1937). The broker's sexual vitality is linked to his business success. As he appears in the novel, he is an old sick man who has run into trouble with the IRS. When he was younger, "he had possessed extraordinary sexual vitality which gave him the confidence to gamble [on the market] well." However, as he thinks about "his now useless and disproportionately large equipment that had once been his pride," his "remorse" is not because of the many men he had ruined financially nor even that IRS is investigating him.[3] He is sorry because he has been caught. Significantly, he had begun his financial career as a peddler, a door-to-door salesman. It was Irving's Knickerbocker who first noted that the Yankee was a "varmint" with the women.

On the other hand, a lack of sexual vitality or a tendency toward sexual perversity is also associated with the successful American businessman. In William Faulkner's trilogy about the rise of Flem Snopes, Flem is sexually impotent and yet is able to marry the most sexually desirable of women, Eula Varner. Flem represents in Faulkner's novels the frightening and evil success of the amoral manipulator in modern society—a manipulator who destroys whatever values remain in the Old South, either aristocratic or folk. In *The Hamlet* (1940), Flem's conning of the community with his spotted horses represents to Cleanth Brooks "an account of the world of advertising and Madison Avenue." Moreover, Brooks adds, "like finance-capitalism itself, Flem works inside the law."[4] Needless to say, however, he is just "inside the law." Flem becomes successful and respected—a banker who viciously forecloses on the poor. He is a monster of evil, sexually impotent, whose wife commits suicide.

A fourth quality which Dreiser's Cowperwood introduces to the crooked-money novels is that the public itself, the people who are conned by Cowperwood, are themselves greedy, selfish, and foolish. This is not quite the same as to admit, with P. T. Barnum, that there is a sucker born every minute. Rather, in Dreiser's naturalistic world, Cowperwood and the public seem to deserve each other. As H. L. Mencken remarked concerning Dreiser's later *American Tragedy* (1925), Dreiser was "content to think of the agonies of mankind as essentially irremediable, and to lay them, not to the sin of economic royalists, but to the blind blundering of the God responsible for complexes, suppressions, hormones and vain dreams." [5]

Finally, it should be noted that Cowperwood is a man of limited culture, a patron of the arts. In fact, in *The Titan*, he plans his New York mansion so that he can best display his extensive collection of art. What James's Christopher Newman set out to learn in Europe in 1877, Cowperwood already has a sense of. Furthermore, an appreciation of art is shown in Cowperwood's case to have nothing to do with scruples and character. Moreover, even Cowperwood's great wealth and taste in art do not allow him entree into the circles of the socially elite in either Chicago or New York. The social register set is depicted as having adopted prejudicial attitudes against commercialism.

The best known of the crooked-money novels is F. Scott Fitzgerald's *The Great Gatsby* (1925). The source of Gatsby's wealth is mysterious until, midway in the novel, Nick is introduced to Mr. Wolfsheim, Gatsby's business partner, who had, among other ventures, fixed the 1919 World Series.

> It never occurred to me [Nick] that one man could start to play with the faith of fifty million people with the single-mindedness of a burglar blowing a safe.
> "How did he happen to do that?" I asked after a minute.
> [Gatsby] "He just saw the opportunity."
> "Why isn't he in jail?"
> "They can't get him, old sport. He's a smart man." [6]

Wolfsheim is obviously a master con man who sees in Gatsby's "Oggsford" sophistication a counterbalance to himself in the world of business. As Tom announces later in the story, Gatsby's and Wolfsheim's "drug store" business is bootlegging and other kinds of New York racketeering. It was quick, crooked money for Gatsby, the young man of poor parents from the Midwest who could hope to win Daisy only by reaching her financial status.

Gatsby's crooked money lies at the core of his rottenness and of his "corruption," of the "foul dust," that floated among his dreams (p. 2). It is, however, Nick who makes these judgments, the son of a respectable hardware store family in Minnesota—a family business to which

Nick will return at the end of the novel. Despite his condemnation of Gatsby and his past, Nick admires Gatsby and his dream—the "American dream"—the dream of success, of association with the "best," of Daisy, who can sob over a stack of Gatsby's "beautiful shirts" (p. 93). Nick admires "the colossal vitality of his illusion," and, in the end, Nick associates Gatsby's dreams with those of the seventeenth-century Dutch sailors who first discovered East Egg. Gatsby, Nick concludes, had the qualities of hope and wonder; he "believed in the green light, the orgiastic future" (p. 182). He was, nevertheless, a millionaire whose money was based in corruption. His tale is not a morality piece like Lapham's; nor is the reader expected to withhold judgment, as in the case of Frank Cowperwood; rather, Gatsby, the crooked businessman, has become a sentimental hero.

Gatsby might well have made millions through legal schemes, but it would have taken him too long. However, throughout American literature a number of wealthy businessmen make money in a seemingly effortless manner. As the popular song of the 1920s—a song played in the *The Great Gatsby*—has it, "The rich get rich and the poor get. . . ." It is again to William Dean Howells that we can trace this theme; in *A Hazard of New Fortunes* (1890), the angel for a new magazine is old Jacob Dryfoos, a millionaire to whom money simply flows. When natural gas is discovered on his farm in the Midwest, Dryfoos sells his land for $100,000. Dryfoos had not wanted to sell, but his family urged him to do so. With the farm sold, Dryfoos moves to town and begins to invest his capital. The old farmer turns out to be a King Midas. " 'He was making money, hand over hand, then; and he never stopped speculating and improving till he'd scraped together three or four hundred thousand dollars; they said a million . . . and I guess half a million would lay over it comfortably and leave a few thousand to spare, probably. Then he came on to New York.' " [7] The farm family is hopelessly out of place in the big city, and the children immediately turn from the simple values of their farm background. Dryfoos himself has "been all broke up since he came to New York" and has stopped attending church. The money that just "pours in and *pours* in" has corrupted Dryfoos (p. 399).

As Basil March, Howells's spokesman, comments, " 'He must have undergone a moral deterioration, an atrophy of the generous instincts, and I don't see why it shouldn't have reached his mental make-up. He has sharpened, but he has narrowed; his sagacity has turned into suspicion, his caution to meanness, his courage to ferocity. That's the way I philosophize a man of Dryfoos's experience, and I am not very proud when I realize that such a man and his experience are the ideal and ambition of most Americans'" (p. 190). Unlike Howells's other millionaire, Silas Lapham, Dryfoos does not repent and return to the farm. In the final pages of the book, March tells us that the Dryfooses have gone to Europe, where they have met the social success "denied them in New York" (p. 428). Christine, old Dryfoos's daughter, even manages to marry "a nobleman full of present debts and of duels in the past" (p. 429).

The curious quality about the easy-money novels is that money, usually honest money, simply accumulates. In the short story "Winter Dreams" (1922), Fitzgerald created his proto-Gatsby, a young man named Dexter Green. Green is actually a character embodying the virtues of both Gatsby and Nick: an honest businessman like Nick who also has the dreams of Gatsby. From a middle-class home, Green has been attracted by a wealthy girl and sets out to make his fortune in order to win her. Although he eventually ends up on Wall Street, his fortune is based on a string of laundries, which are successful because he knows how to launder clothes of the "best quality." Despite the title of the story, he does work in the winter, but his fortune is made with ease and honesty.

Perhaps the most unbelievable easy money in American literature is that earned by Billy Pilgrim, the optometrist of *Slaughter-House Five, or The Children's Crusade* (1969) by Kurt Vonnegut, Jr. Billy is not a millionaire, but his income is substantial. He had married an optometrist's daughter, and, under Billy, the business thrives and grows. It is incredible that this space-wandering, passive, and meek man—the exact opposite of the powerful and shrewd Cowperwood—should have had such business success. The novel is a fantasy, and the theme of easy money is certainly more appropriate in a fantasy than in novels of social realism.

The most recent—and perhaps the dead end—of the easy-money novels is William Gaddis's *JR: A Novel* (1975). The innocent and inept Billy Pilgrim of Vonnegut's novel has become a young teenage boy who corners the stock market with a paper empire that he directs from a public telephone booth. He is finally found out, but the story of a child who can capture the stock market can only be a tale which denigrates the intelligence and abilities of the businessman.

CHAPTER 6

The Generation Trap

Along with their lack of ethics and their amazing ease in making money, the fictional businessmen of the late nineteenth and early twentieth centuries were also accused of neglecting or destroying their wives and children. The families of these businessmen suffer terribly. Some fathers, such as Frank Cowperwood, are bored with their children and family life. Although they provide lavishly for their family's financial needs, these fathers ignore their children or desert them emotionally. Other fathers, such as Silas Lapham or old Jacob Dryfoos, find that their children are not socially acceptable to the social register families. So much for the children of the new millionaires. What of the children of the old millionaires? Two roads seem open to them, at least as reflected in our literature: in the late nineteenth and early twentieth centuries, either they become snobbish loafers, or they reject capitalistic business to become social workers.

Tom Corey, the son of a prestigious Boston family, is able to talk his family into letting him court and then marry Silas Lapham's daughter. He is a generous and intelligent young man, quite unusual for the children of old-family America. His sisters, however, are not unusual. They cuttingly criticize the Lapham girls and are in despair that their brother should even consider such a match. It is not Tom Corey, but rather his sisters who will typify the children of the old rich, at least until the post–World War II period in our literature. These children are, ironically, the very same ones whom the children of the new rich admire and emulate.

Some are simply loafers, harmless time-wasters, who busy themselves with the trivia of social fun and gossip. In Theodore Dreiser's *American Tragedy* (1925), the rich young set to which Clyde Griffith aspires is represented by Sondra Finchley, who leads the group in a round of parties. Sondra speaks to Clyde in babytalk. Sondra's set is, however, only foolish, only socially vicious. Useless, but not really evil. Clyde is a cousin to the wealthy Griffith family and, although socially snubbed by the family, he is given a job at the Griffith factory. Clyde's tragedy is that, faced with having to choose between Sondra or Roberta, his pregnant working-class girlfriend, Clyde kills Roberta and then is himself executed for her murder.

The "Sondra set" is, however, a more vicious group in *The Great Gatsby*. Daisy and Tom Buchanan are also rich loafers, enjoying a life of sports and parties. Although they are parents, their daughter appears only briefly in the book, and Tom seems to have a continual string of mistresses. Daisy, the object of Gatsby's quest, is a lovely creature, of course, and is at least able to admit that life is a boring and senseless round of inaction. " 'What'll we do with ourselves this afternoon?' cried Daisy, 'and the day after that, and the next thirty years?' " (p. 118). To Nick, however, Tom and Daisy represent something else. "They were careless people, Tom and Daisy—they smashed up things and creatures and then retreated back into their money or their vast carelessness, or whatever it was that kept them together, and let other people clean up the mess they had made" (pp. 180–81).

In the wake of such messy lives, some of the second- and third-generation rich turn to homosexuality or sexual perversions. In Ernest Hemingway's *To Have and Have Not* (1937), both Harry Carpenter and Wallace Johnson, a homosexual couple whose yacht is sitting in Key West harbor, are from wealthy families, although Carpenter's family inheritance is dwindling. On Key West, wealthy Tommy Bradley finds pleasure in observing his wife Helène make love with her string of young men.

Such a view of the rich and their children is the foundation for a number of chronicles of wealthy families, as in John P. Marquand's *The Late George Apley* (1937) or Philip Barry's play *Holiday: A Comedy in Three Acts* (1929). In *The Late George Apley*, George Apley becomes a lawyer, on the advice of his Uncle William, who feels that George has no talent for business.

> I have seen George and I do not think that he is a businessman. If he succeeds me here at Apley Falls I am convinced the Mills' earnings will show a corresponding drop. He is popular with the men but he is too easy-going. As a cotton buyer he has not the

shrewdness of soul, and when he sells he lacks pliability, so necessary. He lacks also the capability of understanding the other
party's intentions. I regret to say besides that there is an erratic
streak in George. It is my experience that when someone "goes
off the handle" once he may very well repeat the process. I am
much afraid that in him the Apley stock is running wild. It is my
belief that he should be set up in a law office without too much
responsibility, where he can eventually become a trustee with the
advice of effective junior clerks. I am very sure that George
would be a successful guardian of other people's money, but not
of his own. What little he may inherit I strongly advise should be
put in trust, rather than under his own management.[1]

However, within this satiric novel, written in the midst of the Depression, the old Boston aristocracy can be seen as generous supporters of
charitable organizations, such as the Boston Waif Society, patrons of
the arts, and, despite their wealth, people with a certain sense of frugality. Marquand's George Apley is perhaps a transitional figure between the Daisy and Tom Buchanans and those rich young people in
more recent American literature, a group who will be discussed in a
later chapter.

Some of the second- and third-generation children of wealthy families busy themselves with other kinds of projects. In *A Hazard of New
Fortunes* (1890), old Jacob Dryfoos's son Conrad rebels against his father's desire to involve him in the world of finance. He is a religious
young man whose sympathies turn to the plight of striking New York
transportation workers. In fact, it is over the issue of the strike that Conrad, who has generally been an obedient son, confronts his father. Conrad argues that the strikers have a "righteous cause" and that, in fact,
his "whole heart is with those poor men" (p. 362). Old Dryfoos hits his
son. Conrad then takes a walk and, without realizing it, becomes involved with the mob of strikers. When he notices that a friend of his is
among the strikers and is being beaten by a policeman, he intervenes.
"The policeman stood there; [Conrad] saw his face; it was not bad, not
cruel; it was like the face of a statue, fixed, perdurable—a mere image
of irresponsible and involuntary authority. Then Conrad fell forward,
pierced through the heart" (p. 366). Conrad's death is viewed as a tragedy. March, Howells's fictional spokesman, believes that the workers
are justified in their strike and that Conrad has died valiantly.

Not so pure in motive nor so noble in deed are other children of the rich who enter into social causes. Probably the most devastating portrayal of such a person is Eugene O'Neill's Mildred Douglas in *The Hairy Ape* (1922). Accompanied by her aunt, Mildred is a passenger on a transatlantic steamer. Her aunt is very cynical about Mildred's interests in social welfare: "After exhausting the morbid thrills of social service work on New York's East Side—how they must have hated you, by the way, the poor that you made so much poorer in their own eyes!— you are now bent on making your slumming international. Well, I hope Whitechapel will provide the needed nerve tonic." [2] Mildred is only two generations from her grandfather, the family's millionaire, and she is proud of her great-grandmother, a woman who smoked a clay pipe. Although she believes that her social welfare motives are sincere, Mildred nevertheless recognizes that she is the enervated and debilitated child of wealth. " 'But I'm afraid I have neither vitality nor integrity. All that was burnt out in our stock before I was born. Grandfather's blast furnaces, flaming to the sky, melting steel, making millions—then father keeping those home fires burning, making more millions—and little me at the tailend of it all. I'm a waste product in the Bessemer process—like the millions. Or rather, I inherit the acquired trait of the by-product, wealth, but none of the energy, none of the strength of the steel that made it. I am sired by gold and damned by it, as they say at the race track— damned in more ways than one' " (pp. 203–4).

By bullying the ship's officers, Mildred gets them to take her on a tour of the ship's boiler room. She insists upon wearing a white dress for her Dantean descent to the boiler room, where she sees Yank, the "hairy ape" of the title. Mildred turns pale at the sight of this strong, gorilla-like man, and he is shocked at the sight of this pale apparition in the hell-like boiler room. Mildred crumbles and whimpers, "Take me away! Oh, the filthy beast!" In anger and bewilderment, Yank yells, "God damn yuh!" (p. 214). Mildred disappears from the play (Did she give up her plans to "do good" at Whitehall?), but Yank wants to avenge himself, to destroy the Mildreds of the world, who, he comes to realize, have enslaved him. Yank ultimately dies at the hands of a gorilla that he has loosed from its cage at the City zoo. Mildred's act of "social purpose" has revealed to Yank the depths to which the Yankee has slipped in a society based upon materialistic capitalism. For neither Mildred nor Yank has the result been good. Mildred should have been content with donations to charity, as had the late George Apley.

In Barry's *Holiday*, the three children of wealthy financier Edward Seton represent a symbolic spectrum of despair among the socially prominent. Son Ned is an alcoholic who works for his father and reacts passively to a life he hates. Daughter Julia, who is engaged to self-made man Johnny Case as the play begins, is Seton's only child who advocates her father's belief that "There's no such thrill in the world as making money." [3] Daughter Linda is the rebel, not yet involved in social work but condemning her father's values and, in the final scene, running after Johnny, who has broken his engagement to Julia and is leaving for Europe in order to discover "who I am and what I am" (p. 123). Johnny claims that he does not "want to be identified with any one class of people" (p. 124).

The children of the newly rich also have problems, but they at least have an immediate objective—acceptance into the Sondra set of the rich children of the old wealthy families. Some of the problems are alleviated if their father—the new millionaire—has been able to marry a woman with connections in the desired social circle. Thus, in John Dos Passos's *The Big Money* (1936), Charlie Anderson has married Gladys Wheatley, the daughter of a Detroit financial power. Unlike some of the old-money parents, the Wheatleys do not object to the upstart Charlie. In fact, Mr. Wheatley proudly tells his wife, " 'Mr. Anderson, Mother, was one of our most prominent war aces, he won his spurs fightin' for the flag, Mother, an' his whole career seems to me to be an example . . . of how American democracy works at its very best pushin' forward to success the most intelligent and bestfitted and weedin' out the weaklin's . . . Mr. Anderson, there's one thing I'm goin' to ask you to do right now. I'm goin' to ask you to come to church with us next Sunday an' address ma Sundayschool class. I'm sure you won't mind sayin' a few words of inspiration and guidance to the youngsters there.' " [4]

Gladys and Charlie settle into "the prettiest little old English house. . . . Half-timbered Tudor they call it" (p. 302), a gift from Gladys's father. When Charlie is caught in adultery by Gladys's private detectives and is divorced, the children stay in Detroit and presumably enjoy the kind of life Gladys had always led—country clubs, charity balls, and so on. Although, at one point later in the book, Charlie drunkenly complains about the loss of his children and claims that he is "out to get the kids back" (p. 346), he does not even try.

On the other hand, even when the newly rich man manages to marry into an older family, happiness is certainly not guaranteed for the children. In William Faulkner's *Absalom, Absalom!* (1936), the newly rich Thomas Sutpen builds an antebellum plantation from the Mississippi swamps and manages to marry Ellen Coldfield, the daughter of an old but impoverished family from nearby Jefferson. As Rosa, Ellen's sister, complains, Thomas Sutpen was "not even a gentleman."[5] In fact, as Rosa reasons, " 'And the very fact that he had had to choose respectability to hide behind was proof enough (if anyone needed further proof) that what he fled from must have been some opposite of respectability too dark to talk about' " (p. 17).

But Sutpen courted and won Ellen, and they planned a "big wedding," which Sutpen especially wanted. " 'He wanted, not the anonymous wife and the anonymous children, but the two names, the stainless wife, the unimpeachable father-in-law, on the license, the patent' " (p. 51). As Sutpen becomes the wealthiest plantation owner in the county, he and Ellen have two children, Henry and Judith. Ellen is "the chatelaine to the largest, wife to the wealthiest, mother of the most fortunate" (p. 69). Henry goes off to college, and Judith and her mother regularly call on the ladies in town.

Eventually, the empire crumbles, because of a character from Sutpen's past—Sutpen's mulatto son, ironically named Charles Bon. Driven by his desire for wealth and respectability, Sutpen had discarded Charles's mother before he came to Jefferson. After a number of years, the grand plantation house burns to the ground, and the only survivor of Sutpen is an idiot mulatto grandson, also called Charles Bon, who disappears. Although the events of Faulkner's novel take place in the nineteenth and early twentieth centuries, the story can certainly be assumed to reflect Faulkner's own 1930s milieu, when the novel was written.

Most of the children of the newly wealthy have parents who rose to their millions together. The couple married and had children, as the father was making his fortune. Because the father is financially established only when he is in his early forties, the children are in their late teens or early twenties and thus just the proper age for the parties of the Sondra set. In this situation, the wives and daughters find themselves particularly vulnerable. The husband can at least handle himself in the business world, and the son is always more independent than the socially inept and inexperienced wife and daughters. The wife, however, is often cast as a woman who does not like her daughter's social ambitions, who in fact would rather return to the farm, but who, in the end, falls prey to her daughter's social ambitions and thus becomes involved in the search for social respectability. Mrs. Dryfoos and Mrs. Lapham are the prototypes of this kind of mother.

The situation of Mrs. Dryfoos and Mrs. Lapham, country women come to the city, is not so very different from that of a woman who was born in the city but whose family was outside the elite social set. Eliza Marshall of Henry Blake Fuller's *With the Procession* (1895) grew up in Chicago, a town which was an Arcadia to her, even in the midst of the bustling commercial growth of the 1890s. Her husband David has made a fortune based in the wholesale grocery business. David and Eliza have five children: Alice, already married and living in the suburbs, "a confirmed and condemned suburbanite"; Jane, who is upwardly mobile; Truesdale, a dilettante son with artistic inclinations, who is returning from Europe as the novel opens; Roger, a lawyer, "tough and technical and litigious; his was the hand to seize, not to soothe"; and Rosy, who has been allowed to spend a year at "the New York school." [6]

Alice, the suburban housewife, insists that she is already "with the procession," but Jane describes her life in a passage which presents the essence of suburbia seventy years before the many suburban novels, such as John Cheever's *Bullet Park* (1967), appeared. Here is Chicago suburbia, "Riverdale Park," in the late nineteenth century:

> "There isn't any river; there isn't any dale; there isn't any park. Nothing but a lot of wooden houses scattered over a flat prairie, and a few trees no bigger than a broomstick, and no more leaves on them either. In the morning the men all rush for the train, and the rest of the day the nurse-girls trundle the babies along the plank walks, while 'society' amuses itself. Society consists of Mrs. Smith, Mrs. Brown, Mrs. Jones, and Mrs. Alice Robinson. On Wednesday, Mrs. Smith gives a lunch to Mrs. Brown, Mrs. Jones, and Mrs. Robinson. On Thursday, Mrs. Brown gives a tea to Mrs. Smith, Mrs. Jones, and Mrs. Robinson. On Friday, Mrs. Rob—(no, Mrs. Jones, I'm losing the place) gives a card-party to Mrs. Smith, Mrs. Brown, and Mrs. Robinson—in the daytime, too, mind you. And on Saturday. . . . Then Mrs. Jones—but you've all played the game: for breakfast I had this and that and the other. That is society in Riverdale Park. It would be too rich for *me*!" (pp. 35–36).

Me is Jane, who wants, not suburbia, but old Chicago city society. Jane insists that the family has been "falling"—"an old [but not old within Chicago society] family, with position and plenty of means and everything to make an impression"—and it is the "impression" she wants (p. 40). The first step is to plot Rosy's debut, and the next step is to build a grand new house, an "air castle" of Irving's Yankee.

Moreover, Mrs. Bates, an old girlfriend of Mr. Marshall and a woman

safely established within Chicago society, takes the family in tow and
helps them move into "the procession." Her advice to David Marshall:
" 'But doesn't it seem to you,' she proceeded, carefully, 'that things are
beginning to be different?—that the man who enjoys the best position
and the most consideration is not the man who is making money, but the
man who is giving it away—not the man who is benefiting himself, but
the man who is benefiting the community' " (p. 114). Mrs. Bates announces that she has donated a dormitory, which will of course bear her
name, to the university. By such means, the children thus have a better
chance to make an impression and to gain acceptance.

As it turns out, however, the family's plans eventually fail, and most
of David Marshall's fortune is lost because of an earlier, shady business
deal, a "card shuffling, so to speak—which was quite outside the lines
of mercantile morality, and barely inside the lines of legality itself"
(p. 120). Marshall dies, and the family is pleased that his obituaries are
tributes.

With the Procession presents the problems of the younger generation
as they try to join the Sondra set. However, the scenes which involve
parties, teas, and social conversation are not so interesting as those in-
volving the business world, Truesdale's interest in art, or the excellent
depiction of Chicago in the 1890s. In short, such scenes—debuts, parties, women's teas—lack vitality, quite probably because the customs of
the young among the old rich and their emulators have generally been
seen by American writers as empty. Such stories and scenes tend to be
relegated today to certain kinds of women's magazines and novels.

As a group, the children of both the old and new wealthy, of successful businessmen, seem to follow self-destructive paths or else refuse to
follow their fathers into business. The children suffer and their families
disintegrate. New money or old money, the children are doomed, and
the authors do not suggest any reason other than money.

CHAPTER 7

"The Hog-Squeal of the Universe"

Plato had recommended it and the Pilgrims tried it, and when it failed, Bradford decided that communalism could not exist among depraved men. Private property and free enterprise were God's way for fallen man. Nevertheless, the communal urge resurfaced in the United States in the early nineteenth century, and most groups failed more quickly than the Pilgrims did. The New England literati established a communal settlement, Brook Farm, near Boston in 1841, which Hawthorne joined and quickly left. He later satirized the community in *The Blithedale Romance* (1852). Soon the Brook Farm Group, those "dreamy brethren" with their "impracticable schemes," as Hawthorne described them in *The Scarlet Letter* (1850),[1] read Fourier and designated themselves the Brook Farm Phalanx, although they never found the sixteen hundred souls necessary for a Fourier phalanx. The Brook Farm Phalanx dispersed in 1846, just two years before Marx and Engels issued *The Communist Manifesto*.

At first the Americans, whether proletariat, bourgeoisie or artists, paid little attention to Marx and Engels's *Manifesto*. In fact, the first mention of communism I can find in imaginative American literature is a poem published in 1874 in, of all places, a book of poetry for children, *A Voyage to the Fortunate Isles* by Mrs. S. M. B. Piatt. Mrs. Piatt was the author of a number of poetry books for children, and tucked between verses concerning elves and washing behind the ears are daring poems, which were perhaps intended to stimulate the mothers and fathers who had to read the other poems to their children. As can be seen in "The Palace-Burner. A Picture in a Newspaper," Mrs. Piatt's own response to communism is quite ambiguous, although she preaches otherwise to her child.

She has been burning palaces. "To see
    the sparks look pretty in the wind?" Well, yes—
And something more. But women brave as she
    Leave much to cowards, such as I, to guess.

But this is old, so old that everything
    Is ashes here—the woman and the rest,
Two years are—oh! so long. Now you may bring
    Some newer pictures. You like this one best?

You wish that you had lived in Paris then?—
    You would have loved to burn a palace, too?
But they had guns in France, and Christian men
    Shot wicked little Communists like you.

You would have burned the palace?—Just because
    You did not live in it yourself? Oh! Why
Have I not taught you to respect the laws?
    You would have burned the palace—would not *I*?

Would I? Go to your play. Would I, indeed?
    I? Does the boy not know my soul to be
Languid and worldly, with a dainty need
    For light and music? Yet he questions me.

Can he have seen my soul more near than I?
    Ah! in the dust and distance sweet she seems,
With lips to kiss away a baby's cry,
    Hands fit for flowers, and eyes for tears and dreams.

Can he have seen my soul? And could she wear
    Such utter life upon a dying face;
Such unappealing, beautiful despair:
    Such garments—soon to be a shroud—with grace?

Has she a charm so calm that it could breathe
    In damp, low places till some frightened hour;
Then start, like a fairy subtle snake, and wreathe
    A stinging poison with a shadowy power?

Would *I* burn palaces? The child has seen
    In this fierce creature of the Commune here,
So bright with bitterness and so serene,
    A finer being than my soul, I fear.[2]

Mrs. Piatt and her husband were friends of William Dean Howells, and so perhaps it is understandable that the first communist character in an American novel is Berthold Lindau of Howells's *A Hazard of New Fortunes* (1890), a "German Socialist," who becomes a naturalized American citizen and a veteran who lost an arm in the Civil War. Lindau is an old friend of Howells's literary spokesman in the novel, Basil March, who explains Lindau's background. " 'When I first knew him out in Indianapolis he was starving along with a sick wife and a sick newspaper. It was before the Germans had come over to the Republicans generally, but Lindau was fighting the anti-slavery battle just as naturally at Indianapolis in 1858 as he fought behind the barricades at Berlin in 1848' " (p. 77). March eventually manages to have Lindau hired as a translator at his magazine; however, when old Jacob Dryfoos, the magazine's financial "angel," finally discovers Lindau's sentiments, he demands that Lindau be fired. But when Lindau discovers that Dryfoos has made his money by speculation, not "by voark," he quits.

Capitalism and free enterprise are roundly condemned in *A Hazard of New Fortunes*. In the midst of union strikes in New York City, Lindau debates with Colonel Woodburn, a "Southern gentleman," who also dislikes free enterprise. Woodburn, as Lindau quite correctly perceives, preaches a kind of feudalism in which "the enlightened, the moneyed, the cultivated class shall be responsible to the central authority—emperor, duke, president . . .—for the national expense and the national defence" (p. 295). This enlightened class is also responsible to the working class "for homes and lands and implements, and the opportunity to labor at all times" (p. 295). This ideal community will come into being, Woodburn asserts, when "the last vestige of commercial society is gone" (p. 295).

In his vision of a future utopia, Lindau responds that the State will assume all responsibility for the working man. The State, which is "the whole beople," will own the land, the mills, the roads, and the mines (p. 295). In such a state, Lindau claims, "there shall be no rich and no boor; and there shall not be war any more" (p. 295).

The only spokesmen for free enterprise and private capitalism are old Dryfoos and his toady Fulkerson. Fulkerson's defense of capitalism generally revolves around an attack on Lindau, the "red-mouthed labor agitator"; people like Lindau, Fulkerson contends, should not be "allowed to come here. If they don't like the way we manage our affairs let 'em stay at home" (p. 297). Dryfoos, the farmer on whose land natural gas was discovered and who subsequently made a fortune on the market, is generally depicted as a heartless old man who cannot understand the striker's demands: "They lie, and you *know* they lie. . . . and what do you think the upshot of it all will be, after they've ruined business for another week, and made people hire hacks, and stolen the money of honest men? How is it going to end?" (p. 362).

Dryfoos's son Conrad is killed in the strike, and although March admits that he does not agree with Lindau and that there are "as many good, kind, and just people among the rich as there are among the poor" (p. 300), Lindau is nevertheless a sympathetic character and Conrad is a martyr. Moreover, while Lindau appears to be an atheist, Conrad associates Marxism with Christianity. "Didn't the Saviour Himself say, 'How hardly shall they that have riches enter into the kingdom of God'?" (p. 300). By the time Howells wrote *A Traveller to Altruria* (1894), he could describe what he saw as a deterioration of the free enterprise system in the forty years from 1850 to 1890. "If a man got out of work, he turned his hand to something else; if a man failed in business, he started in again from some other direction; as a last resort, in both cases, he went West, pre-empted a quarter section of public land, and grew up with the country. Now the country is grown up; the public land is gone; business is full on all sides, and the hand that turned itself to something else has lost its cunning. The struggle for life has changed from a free fight to an encounter of disciplined forces, and the free fighters that are left get ground to pieces between organized labor and organized capital."[3]

The late nineteenth century was an age of literary Utopias, perhaps the earliest being *Looking Backward 2000–1887* (1888) by Edward Bellamy. Although Bellamy advocated a kind of socialism, it is not a deterministic Marxist socialism because there is no proletariat-bourgeois clash. The development of Bellamy's socialism occurred as giant capitalistic trusts simply evolved into the government-owned and controlled National Trust. *Looking Backward* hardly qualifies as imaginative literature, because of its heavy dose of economic theorizing. However, Bellamy does provide a voice for capitalism, Julian West, a man more articulate and intelligent than old Jacob Dryfoos, Howells's capitalistic spokesman in *A Hazard of New Fortunes*. West understands that the greatest danger of the National Trust is the potential loss of personal freedom for individual citizens. " 'That is, . . . you [of the National Trust] have simply applied the principle of universal military service . . .

to the labor question.'"[4] As the socialist spokesman, Dr. Leete soon converts West, who finally admits that capitalism is "anti-Christian."[5]

Dryfoos and West are not effective spokesmen for capitalism, and of course the arguments are weighted against them. However, Bellamy and Howells at least supply spokesmen. In many of the radical novels to follow, part of that group that would soon be labeled "proletarian literature," the writer centers only upon the plight of the worker in a capitalistic society, with vicious factory owners only cardboard characters. In 1906 the first of America's proletarian novels was published, Upton Sinclair's *The Jungle*. The novel concerns a Lithuanian immigrant family who first settle in Chicago and find work in and around the stockyards. Sinclair emphasizes that the workers in a capitalistic society are no better than the cows and pigs that pass through the stockyard slaughterhouses.

> It was all so very businesslike that one watched it fascinated. It was pork-making by machinery, pork-making by applied mathematics. And yet somehow the most matter-of-fact person could not help thinking of the hogs; they were so innocent, they came so very trustingly; and they were so very human in their protests—and so perfectly within their rights! They had done nothing to deserve it, and it was adding insult to injury, as the thing was done here, swinging them up in the cold-blooded, impersonal way, without a pretence at apology, without the homage of a tear. . . .
>
> One could not stand and watch very long without becoming philosophical, without beginning to deal in symbols and similes, and to hear the hog-squeal of the universe.[6]

Capitalists do not really appear in *The Jungle*, although a family named Durham is used to symbolize all the capitalistic owners of industry. After recognizing the vicious spirit of competition built into the Durham company, from top management to lowest worker, the main character Jurgis can explain the essential corruption of capitalism. "So from top to bottom the place was simply a seething cauldron of jealousies and hatreds; there was no loyalty or decency anywhere about it, there was no place in it where a man counted for anything against a dollar. And worse than there being no decency, there was not even any honesty. The reason for that? Who could say? It must have been old Durham in the beginning; it was a heritage which the self-made merchant had left to his son, along with his millions" (p. 60).

For Jurgis and his family, things go predictably from bad to worse. Then, however, Jurgis hears a speech by Comrade Ostrinski, and he dedicates himself to the socialist cause. The comrade's long speech in Chapter 28 established both vocabulary ("Working men!" "oppressed," "disinherited," "the fierce wolves," "the ravening vultures") and sentiments ("The Voice of Labor" versus "The Masters of Slaves") for the proletarian literature that would finally reach its peak in America in the 1930s. Perhaps the only deviation from the party line in Ostrinski's speech is his association of Christianity and God with communism—a strangely recurring phenomenon among American socialist authors, at least until the 1930s.

As John Chamberlain has pointed out in "The Businessman in Fiction," the passage of the Pure Food and Drug Act (1906) was to some extent a result of the terrible slaughterhouse conditions depicted by Sinclair in *The Jungle*. Chamberlain wonders, however, why Sinclair continued to write as if businessmen "were impervious to suggestion." The answer to Chamberlain's consternation, of course, is that a legislative act to alter food processing practices would not be adequate for Sinclair, whose sympathies lie with Jurgis and Comrade Ostrinski's theories.

Native proletarian novels also condemned an economic system that relied heavily upon machinery and technology, a theme already evident in nineteenth-century American literature, as we have seen. In *The Jungle* the workers are depicted as slaves to the machine and thus as slaves to the economic system. "It was October, and the holiday rush had begun. It was necessary for the packing machines to grind till late at night to provide food that would be eaten at Christmas breakfasts; and Marija and Elizbieta and Ona, as part of the machine, began working fifteen or sixteen hours a day" (p. 142).

The proletarian novel thus condemned capitalism and its system of economic competition while extolling Marxist socialism or communism.[7] At the same time, in such American novels, plays, or poems, technology and machinery were seen as enslaving extensions of the capitalistic system. And, finally, at least until the 1930s, native American communists, as fictional characters, associated the ideals of Christianity with Marxist economics. There were, of course, variations on these themes.

One of the finest novels to come from this group is Abraham Cahan's

The Rise of David Levinsky (1916). Cahan depicts the upwardly mobile Levinsky from his youth in Russia to his subsequent success in the New York garment industry. It is the Ben Franklin story again, but with emptiness and loneliness the result of Levinsky's success. The novel is not a simple morality tale, however, nor, at least until the concluding pages, does the stark dichotomy of Capitalist Evil and Communist Good appear. Levinsky is by no means bad, and the reader is even allowed to understand that some benefits have come from capitalism and technology. As Levinsky views the garment district of New York's Fifth Avenue, he reflects,

> The new aspect of that section of the proud thoroughfare marked the advent of the Russian Jew as the head of one of the largest industries in the United States. Also, it meant that as master of that industry he had made good, for in his hands it had increased a hundredfold, garments that had formerly reached only the few having been placed within the reach of the masses. Foreigners ourselves, and mostly unable to speak English, we had Americanized the system of providing clothes for the American woman of moderate or humble means. The ingenuity and unyielding tenacity of our managers, foremen, and operatives had introduced a thousand and one devices for making by machine garments that used to be considered possible only as the product of handwork. . . . We had done away with prohibitive prices and greatly improved the popular taste. Indeed, the Russian Jew had made the average American girl a "tailor-made" girl.[8]

Levinsky falls in love with a girl whose family are Jewish intellectual socialists. By the family, he is called "Mr. Capitalist," and of course the socialists continually ask him for monetary contributions to their cause. At one point, Anna, the girl he loves, observes that "the methods of the Russian [Czarist] Government rendered [revolutionary] terrorism not only justifiable, but inevitable" (p. 479). The young people—Anna and her friends—are atheists, but their father, Tevkin, has become religious in his old age and even demands that the family celebrate Passover in the traditional fashion. During the ceremonies, Levinsky realizes that one cause of his spiritual emptiness is his neglect of his Jewish heritage when he came to America and became a business success.

However, he also believes that another cause of his spiritual emptiness and loneliness is his choice of business and his pursuit of financial success. Although he never becomes a communist, he gains sympathy for the cause. As an old man, he reflects,

> "There are cases when success is a tragedy."
> There are moments when I regret my whole career, when my very success seems to be a mistake.
> . . . The day when that accident turned my mind from college to business seems to be the most unfortunate day in my life. . . .
> The business world contains plenty of successful men who have no brains. Why, then, should I ascribe my triumph to special ability? I should probably have made a much better college professor than a cloak-manufacturer, and should probably be a happier man, too. I know people who have made much more money than I and whom I consider my inferiors in every respect.
> (p. 529)

Another variation within American proletarian literature is the concentration of a single work upon the evils of capitalistic technology and machines for the individual, without the prolonged pitch for socialism. In Elmer L. Rice's *The Adding Machine: A Play in Seven Scenes* (1923), Mr. Zero is replaced by a machine, after twenty-five years of faithful service. In Eugene O'Neill's *The Hairy Ape* (1922), Paddy's praise of the now past life of sailors on sailing ships as opposed to their entrapment on the modern steamship is accented by Long's socialist-Christian inclinations.

> Listen 'ere, Comrades! Yank 'ere is right. 'E says this 'ere stinkin' ship is our 'ome. And 'e says as 'ome is 'ell. And 'e's right! This is 'ell. We lives in 'ell, Comrades—and right enough we'll die in it. (*Raging.*) And who's ter blame, I arsks yer? We ain't. We wasn't born this rotten way. All men is born free and ekal. That's in the bleedin' Bible, maties. But what d'they care for the Bible—them lazy, bloated swine what travels first cabin? Them's the ones. They dragged us down 'til we're on'y wage slaves in the bowels of a bloody ship, sweatin', burnin' up, eatin' coal dust! Hit's them's ter blame—the damned Capitalist clarss!
> (pp. 191–92)

But Long is yelled down by his shipmates.

With the Great Depression, the production of proletarian literature intensified. The variety of poems, essays, short stories, and novels can best be seen in *Proletarian Literature in the United States: An Anthology*, published in 1935 and edited by Granville Hicks, Michael Gold, Isidor Schneider, Joseph North, Paul Peters, and Alan Calmer. Among the contributors are Theodore Dreiser, who switched to communism from his pessimistic naturalistic period during which he had written the Cowperwood trilogy and *An American Tragedy*, Jack London, Upton Sinclair, Erskine Caldwell, Nelson Algren, James T. Farrell, Kenneth Fearing, Langston Hughes, Muriel Rukeyser, Richard Wright, Archibald MacLeish, Clifford Odets, and John Dos Passos, who was soon to shift his economic preferences.

Perhaps the most representative literary expression of this 1930s group is Clifford Odets's play, *Waiting for Lefty* (1935). The characters who appear in a series of brief sketches are stereotypes, with the capitalists or their representatives presented as all evil, and the workers as downtrodden and exploited, sincere and desirous of only a decent wage. The conflicts are the result of the economic situation, and the only suggested solution is the overthrow of the capitalistic system.

As usual, in Odets's proletarian drama, the American capitalist is accused of heartlessness. "If big business were sentimental over human life there wouldn't be big business of any sort!" Businessmen are also immoral; they produce poison gas. They are racial bigots, and they have even infiltrated the unions with their own men, such as Fatt. By the 1930s, native communists had adopted atheism, and only the capitalist Grady bothers to cross himself. On the other hand, the United States Constitution is now understood to be a document for capitalists. "Spirit of '76! [My] Ancestors froze at Valley Forge! What's it all mean? Slops! The honest workers were sold out then, in '76. The Constitution's for rich men then and now. Slops!"[9]

As the depression became World War II, the communist movement among the literati lost momentum. Odets's play and other works by the proletarian writers of the 1930s represent, it now appears, nearly the end of the vicious, one-sided attacks on the American capitalist. Other American writers in the 1930s were attacking the stereotypes created by the proletarian writers, and Ernest Hemingway viciously characterized the proletarian writer himself in *To Have and Have Not* (1937), as I will discuss later.

CHAPTER 8

The Boobus Americanus
and the Artist

The uncultured nineteenth-century American capitalist, be he the small businessman like Hawthorne's Peter Hovenden or the wealthy speculator like James's Christopher Newman, who sought culture in Europe, presented new problems to the American artist as he entered the twentieth century. The American artist discovered that patronage from wealthy American capitalists was potentially a dangerous way of financial and moral survival. Even more dangerous, actually, were the children and grandchildren of old Peter Hovenden. The small or middle-class businessman began to appear in our literature not only as uncultured but even as apathetic to the artist and, alas, sometimes hostile. Such negatively conceived businessmen, the Rotarian and his Rotary Ann, whom H. L. Mencken included in his designation of Boobus Americanus, began to people a number of poems, plays, novels, and short stories. The American middle class, at least in the mind of the American artist, represented the general cultural taste (or lack of taste) of America.

Ezra Pound mounted the attack on the taste of the age in part II of "Hugh Selwyn Mauberley" (1920).

> The age demanded an image
> Of its accelerated grimace,
> Something for the modern stage,
> Not, at any rate, an Attic grace;
>
> Not, not certainly, the obscure reveries
> Of the inward gaze;

Better mendacities
Than the classics in paraphrase!

The "age demanded" chiefly a mould in plaster,
Made with no loss of time,
A prose kinema, not, not assuredly, alabaster
Or the "sculpture" of rhyme.[1]

And if American readers could not understand Pound, Ernest Hemingway bluntly echoed his sentiments five years later.

THE AGE DEMANDED

The age demanded that we sing
And cut away our tongue.

The age demanded that we flow
And hammered in the bung.

The age demanded that we dance
And jammed us into iron pants.

And in the end the age was handed
The sort of shit that it demanded.[2]

In plays and novels, the Boobus Americanus—the middle-class or
upper middle-class American businessman—was more specifically depicted as insensitive to art and even cruelly repressive of the artist. In
Willa Cather's "The Sculptor's Funeral" (1905), the body of sculptor
Harvey Merrick is brought home to the little Kansas town in which he
was born. Merrick's student, Steavens, accompanies the body and
serves as the outside observer of the narrow-minded townspeople. As
they come to pay their respects, the townspeople have nothing good to
say of Merrick, who had left his home to become a famous and respected artist in the East. Said a local cattleman, " 'Harve never could
handle stock none. . . . He hadn't it in him to be sharp.' " Said the coal
and lumber dealer, " 'Harve never was much account for anything practical, and he shore was never fond of work.' " Banker Phelps added,
" 'Where the old man [Harve's father] made his mistake was in sending
the boy East to school.' "[3]
Only the town lawyer, who had been a friend of Merrick's and had
once shared his ideals, has kind words for Merrick and in fact turns on

the townspeople who, he says, had " 'drummed nothing but money and knavery into their [own sons'] ears from the time they wore knickerbockers' " (p. 286).

> "Now that we've fought and lied and sweated and stolen, and hated as only the disappointed strugglers in a bitter, dead little Western town know how to do, what have we got to show for it? It's not for me to say why, in the inscrutable wisdom of God, a man like Harvey should ever have been called from this place of hatred and bitter waters; but I want this Boston man [Steavens] to know that the drivel he's been hearing here to-night is the only tribute any truly great man could have from such a lot of sick, side-tracked, burnt-dog, land-poor sharks as the here-present financiers of Sand City—upon which town God have mercy!" (pp. 286–89)

It was primarily citizens like those of Cather's Sand City, Kansas, or Sherwood Anderson's *Winesburg, Ohio* (1919) who were portrayed as being so very narrow and insensitive to the artist—the small-town financiers and businessmen. Such businessmen were labeled Philistines by the literati of the 1920s (a term borrowed from Matthew Arnold). Philistines denied freedom to any independent spirit, including and especially the artists. Opposed to the Philistines were the Bohemians or those who, by some quirk of individualism (usually artistic), appeared to be Bohemians to the business community and who felt themselves forced to flee to New York's Greenwich Village or to Europe. Those who fled to Europe after World War I were called by that other derogatory term, "expatriates." John Reed described the poverty and freedom of the Village Bohemians in "The Day in Bohemia, or Life Among the Artists."

> Inglorious Miltons by the score,
> And Rodins, one to every floor,
> In short, those unknown men of genius
> Who dwell in third-floor-rears gangreneous,
> Reft of their rightful heritage
> By a commercial, soulless age.
> Unwept, I might add—and unsung,
> Insolvent, but entirely young.[4]

Bill Gorton, Jake Barnes's friend in Ernest Hemingway's *The Sun Also Rises* (1926), described just what the American Boob believed the expatriate to be. " 'You're an expatriate. You've lost touch with the soil. You get precious. Fake European standards have ruined you. You drink yourself to death. You become obsessed by sex. You spend all your time talking, not working. You are an expatriate, see? You hang around cafes.' "[5] Replied Jake, who is an expatriate living in Paris, " 'It sounds like a swell life.' "

Thus a new skirmish was sounded in that old conflict between the artist and the American public. Not only could the American businessman be insensitive, even hostile, to the artist, but should he offer patronage, his aid might very well corrupt the purity of the artist. Whereas earlier generations of artists were apparently willing to accept the patronage of millionaires like Cowperwood, the twentieth-century American artist celebrated his own individuality, his own independence, even to the point of starvation, from the Boobus Americanus. For poets like Pound, such a separation was extreme. His disdain for and disregard of the American public was expressed as early as October 1914 in his essay "The Audience," published in *Poetry*. "It is true that the great artist has in the end, always, his audience, for the Lord of the universe sends into the world in each generation a few intelligent spirits, and these ultimately manage the rest."

Such an attitude among many of our poets and novelists, primarily in the post–World War I period, eventually and unfortunately alienated much of the American reading public in the first half of the twentieth century. It is still a rumbling argument, as Saul Bellow in his 1976 Nobel Prize acceptance speech has told the world. Bellow himself rejects such Poundian arrogance: "In the West a separation between great artists and the general public took place. . . . [As historian Erich Auerbach tells us,] 'Many of them took no trouble to facilitate the understanding of what they wrote—whether out of contempt for the public, the cult of their own inspiration, or a certain tragic weakness which prevented them from being at once simple and true.' . . . One can't tell writers what to do. The imagination must find its own path. But one can fervently wish that they—that we—would come back from the periphery. We do not, we writers, represent mankind adequately."[6]

Other artists in the early twentieth century, however, were not so extreme as Pound and sought to communicate with the Rotarian and his Rotary Ann. A writer like Ernest Hemingway, whom Gertrude Stein de-

scribed as 90 percent Rotarian,[7] depicted a number of fictional characters whose lionization by American patrons had destroyed their art.
Such is one problem of that complex character of *The Sun Also Rises*,
Robert Cohn, as Jake reflects. "That winter Robert Cohn went over to
America with his novel, and it was accepted by a fairly good publisher
. . . and when he came back he was quite changed. He was more enthu-
siastic about America than ever, and he was not so simple, and he was
not so nice. The publishers had praised his novel pretty highly and it
rather went to his head. Then several women had put themselves out to
be nice to him, and his horizons had all shifted."[8] Harry, in Hemingway's "The Snows of Kilimanjaro" (1936), allows his writing, his discipline, and his creativity to decay by his acceptance of an easy life
among the rich.[9]

It was primarily the commercialization of art that the artist seemed to
fear in the Boobus Americanus. In George S. Kaufman and Marc Connelly's *Beggar on Horseback* (1924), the young and impoverished com-
poser Neil McRae must choose between a poor but sympathetic girl,
Cynthia Mason, and the Philistine daughter of a wealthy industrialist,
Gladys Cady. The Cady family is a characterization of the newly rich
Boobus Americanus —a breed willing to "buy" an artist for the daughter's amusement just as they would be willing to buy their son an expen-
sive motor car. Much of the play is an enactment of Neil's dream, a
satiric exaggeration of what his life might be, should he marry Gladys
Cady. Businessmen are depicted as empty-headed conformists. Mr.
Cady's rise to wealth as a widget manufacturer was swift and easy. The
Cady children —Gladys and Homer—are worthless; Gladys's chief interest in life is dancing, and Homer, a spoiled young man, is aggres-
sively negative. During the course of the dream, Neil kills the Cady
family and is found guilty by a jury of dancing masters. The judge —
old Mr. Cady, whom Neil has killed—sentences Neil to the commercialization of his art.

> [JUDGE] CADY: This thing of using the imagination has got to
> stop. We're going to make you work in the right way. You see,
> your talents belong to us now, and we're going to use every bit of
> them. We're going to make you the most wonderful song writer
> that ever lived.
> NEIL: But I can't write that kind of music! You know I can't!
> CADY: You can do it by our system. You are sentenced to be at

the Cady Consolidated Art Factory at eight o'clock tomorrow
morning!
    NEIL: Art factory?

And there the next morning Neil is placed in a cage next to the cages of
the "world's greatest novelist," "the world's greatest magazine artist,"
and "the world's greatest poet." [10] Tourists observe these artists at work,
much as visitors observe animals at a zoo. Suffice it to say, when Neil
awakens from his dream, he quickly says good-bye to Gladys Cady and
runs off to the country with Cynthia Mason.

    The most typical work of this kind, however, the novel which con-
tributed a new word to the American language, is Sinclair Lewis's *Babbitt* (1922). Lewis had already explored small-town Boobism in *Main
Street* (1920), but in *Babbitt* he focused more carefully on the middle-
sized town's businessman, who lived in the midwestern city of "Zenith
the Zip City—Zeal, Zest, and Zowie," [11] a growing city with a popula-
tion of "between three and four hundred thousand inhabitants."

    Babbitt contains all the aspects and criticism of the American Boobs
that appeared in other novels or in poems, plays, and short stories of
this time. Moreover, Lewis's presentation—his story, his ironies, his
language, and his characters—are so obvious that his message could
not be missed by any Boob, such as Babbitt, who might venture into the
book. Lewis's novel can serve as a summary of many of the antibusiness
themes of previous books.

    For example, the businessman's antagonism to socialism and labor
agitators: " 'A good labor union is of value because it keeps out radical
unions, which would destroy property. No one ought to be forced to
belong to a union, however. All labor agitators who try to force men to
join a union should be hanged. In fact, just between ourselves, there
oughtn't to be any unions allowed at all; and as it's the best way of fighting the unions, every business man ought to belong to an employers' association and to the Chamber of Commerce. In union there is
strength. So any selfish hog who doesn't join the Chamber of Commerce ought to be forced to' " (p. 44).

    Lewis realized, even before the proletarian writers themselves, that
organized religion—a religion, that is, organized around business principles—would oppose socialism or radical unionism of any kind. The
Zenith businessmen bring the evangelist Mike Monday to speak at the
fairgrounds because they had heard "that in every city where he had

appeared, Mr. Monday had turned the minds of workmen from wages and hours to higher things, and thus averted strikes" (p. 99). Later, during a strike, the minister of Babbitt's church, the Chatham Road Presbyterian—a minister who writes Sunday messages entitled "The Dollars and Sense Value of Christianity"—preaches a sermon opposing the striking workers (p. 204).

Moreover, in *Babbitt*, the businessman is corrupt, but only slightly corrupt. Babbitt is involved in several shady business transactions. His children follow the now well-established pattern: daughter Verone, who has just graduated from Bryn Mawr, leans toward economic radicalism, but not militantly; son Ted rejects college and the business world for a life in the factories. Both husband and wife yearn for acceptance from their social betters—in *Babbitt*, the McKelveys. Parties and teas are described in detail. Furthermore, Babbitt himself represents the deterioration of vigorous pioneer stock. He reflects to himself, "Wish I'd been a pioneer, same as my grand-dad. But then, wouldn't have a house like this'" (p. 89).

Lewis is particularly careful to delineate the attitude of the Boobs toward art. The upwardly mobile Boob such as Babbitt does not, of course, openly resent "artists." Rather, he takes pride in knowing and being a fellow club member with "T. Cholmondeley Frink, who was not only the author of 'Poemulations,' which, syndicated daily in sixty-seven leading newspapers, gave him one of the largest audiences of any poet in the world, but also an optimistic lecturer and the creator of 'Ads that Add'" (p. 111). Frink has his poems set as prose because "it added a neat air of pleasantry to them" (p. 112). Frink is the poet of the Boob—a man who can enjoy bootleg whiskey during Prohibition and yet write this kind of poem:

> I sat alone and groused and thunk, and scratched my head and sighed and wunk, and groaned, "There still are boobs, alack, who'd like the old-time gin-mill back; that den that makes a sage a loon, the vile and smelly old saloon!" I'll never miss their poison booze, whilst I the bubbling spring can use, that leaves my head at merry morn as clear as any babe new-born! (p. 113).

In Babbitt's world, poetry and religion both seem to be the opiates of the people.

In their appreciation of art, however, Babbitt and his fellow businessmen have advanced to some extent beyond the citizens of the small town

Willa Cather had depicted or even those Lewis himself had created in *Main Street*. Babbitt welcomed the poet such as Chol Frink and, in fact, praised the American artist in an address before the Zenith Chamber of Commerce.

> "In other countries, art and literature are left to a lot of shaggy bums living in attics and feeding on booze and spaghetti, but in America the successful writer or picture-painter is indistinguishable from any other decent business man; and I, for one, am only too glad that the man who has the rare skill to season his message with interesting reading matter and who shows both purpose and pep in handling his literary wares has a chance to drag down his fifty thousand bucks a year, to mingle with the biggest executives on terms of perfect equality, and to show as big a house and as swell a car as any Captain of Industry! But, mind you, it's the appreciation of the Regular Guy who I have been depicting which has made this possible, and you got to hand as much credit to him as to the authors themselves." (p. 182)

That Regular Guy who supports the artists is, according to Babbitt, a man who reads in the evenings "a chapter or two of some good lively Western novel if he has a taste for literature" (p. 181). Thus, the influence and tastes of a Babbitt were particularly invidious to the serious American artist; while claiming to support "Art," Babbitt wanted to control and standardize art. A "poet" like Chol Frink only reinforced and reassured Babbitt in his tastes and beliefs.

Despite the fact that Lewis's Babbitt has become a noun of derogation with a limited definition (Webster's *New Collegiate Dictionary*: "a business or professional man who conforms unthinkingly to prevailing middle-class standards"), we have overlooked several important contributions this novel made to the Scrooge syndrome.

First, Lewis recognized that, as a rule, the era of the industrial giants, of aggressive capitalistic individualism was over. William Washington Eathorne is Zenith's surviving relic of this bygone era, a man who lives, symbolically, in a Victorian mansion. "But the house has an effect not at all humorous. It embodies the heavy dignity of those Victorian financiers who ruled the generation between the pioneers and the brisk 'sales-engineers' and created a somber oligarchy by gaining control of banks, mills, land, railroads, and mines" (p. 213). Babbitt and the other businessmen in the novel are "sales engineers," men who are trapped in their standardized world of business, but who attempt to see themselves as a new kind of hero. "To them, the Romantic Hero was no longer the knight, the wandering poet, the cowpuncher, the aviator, nor the brave young district attorney, but the great sales-manager, who had an Analysis of Merchandizing Problems on his glass-topped desk, whose title of nobility was 'Go-Getter,' and who devoted himself and all his young samurai to the cosmic purpose of Selling—not of selling anything in particular, for or to anybody in particular, but pure Selling" (p. 143). And so that no one will miss the underlying premise that private capitalism is the corrupting element, Lewis introduces a British nobleman and capitalist, Sir Gerald Doak, who is as much a Boob as Babbitt.

Nevertheless, Babbitt is a pathetic but sympathetic character. He is not the cold Peter Hovenden whom Hawthorne depicted, nor is he the somewhat admirable, but corrupt and amoral, Frank Cowperwood of Dreiser's trilogy. He is not the heartless cardboard capitalist of the proletarian novels, nor is he even the pathetic old millionaire Jacob Dryfoos of *A Hazard of New Fortunes* or the fallen Silas Lapham. Unlike the others, Babbitt is aware of the shallowness of his life. He attempts a variety of rebellions—from washing his face with the family guest towel to his adamant refusal to join the proto-fascist Good Citizens League. In each attempt, he is frustrated. The life of his best friend, Paul Riesling, who had always hoped to be a violinist but who had settled instead for Zenith and business, ends in tragedy. Babbitt is at least sensitive enough to understand that something is wrong with his world and that he himself is trapped.

Perhaps his most interesting attempts to escape Zenith, his business, and his family and to gain some perspective are his two trips to Maine, the first with Paul and the second by himself. The retreat to the woods has been, in American literature, the salvation of many a male character —from Natty Bumppo in Cooper's Leather-Stocking Tales, who sought the anarchy of the wilderness, through Henry David Thoreau, who lived at Walden Pond in order to escape a "life of desperation," even to Ernest Hemingway's Jake Barnes, who, with Bill Groton by his side, idyllically enjoys the Irati River and male companionship in *The Sun Also Rises*.

During the first trip, Paul and Babbitt succeed in finding a certain peace, and Babbitt returns from the fishing trip with new resolutions, which he quickly forgets. On the second trip, Babbitt, who has admired the close-mouthed and masculine Maine fishing guides, ventures into "the real wilds" with his favorite guide Joe. Happily settled in the woods, Babbitt "felt virile" and wants to learn more about this man whose life he had thought of imitating.

> "Joe, what would you do if you had a lot of money? Would you stick to guiding, or would you take a claim 'way back in the woods and be independent of people?"
> For the first time Joe brightened. He chewed his cud a second, and bubbled, "I've thought of that! If I had the money, I'd go down to Tinker's Falls and open a swell shoe store."
> (pp. 299–300)

Realizing that the woodsman too has been corrupted by business, a disappointed and lonely Babbitt retreats to Zenith.

Sinclair Lewis's *Babbitt* set the tone for much of the criticism of the new American middle-class businessman, the sales engineer, in the years following its publication. Babbitts are rampant in James T. Farrell's Studs Lonigan trilogy (1932, 1934, and 1935). Babbitt is transformed into Jason Compson in William Faulkner's *The Sound and the Fury* (1929). In popular literature, he finally escapes the business world in Sloan Wilson's *The Man in the Gray Flannel Suit* (1955). On stage, he is even more helplessly pathetic as Willy Loman in Arthur Miller's *Death of a Salesman* (1949). And yet, at the same time, many American writers were beginning to assert that the businessman, the private capitalist, had certain admirable qualities, that a Babbitt could at least recognize his deficiencies, and that perhaps, just perhaps, capitalism might have some benefits for the artist after all.

CHAPTER 9

"Is Money Money or Isn't Money Money?"

No one except Gertrude Stein could possibly have written such a statement, and so she did in 1936 in the first of her five articles on "Money," published that year in the *Saturday Evening Post*. By the 1930s, Gertrude Stein was undoubtedly one of our most respected writers. We tend to think of her influence as predominant in the 1920s, when groups of young American artists flocked for tea and advice to the familiar rooms on the rue de Fleurus in Paris. Her influence upon young writers, such as Ernest Hemingway, is well known. Yet, in the 1920s, Stein herself was little known in America. A decade later, however, Stein, accompanied by Alice B. Toklas, made a lecture tour of America, telling American crowds of her theories and reading her work. Moreover, her opera, *Four Saints in Three Acts*, with music by Virgil Thomson, had a startling success in Boston, New York, and Chicago in 1936. Because of her new fame, in the 1930s magazines like the *Saturday Evening Post* opened their pages to Stein, and she chose to tell America what she thought about money.

At that time America was not yet out of the Depression, although Franklin Delano Roosevelt's New Deal was well underway when Stein wrote her little essays on money, in which she stoutly defended private capitalism and attacked what she felt was the growing monetary control of the federal government. She was not alone among writers in defending capitalism in the 1930s, although it is only too clear that when we think of writers representative of the 1930s, of those whose works are taught in universities today, they are writers who followed an anti-capitalist line in their writings.

It was in the 1930s that the proletarian writers flourished, with their manifestoes, anthologies, and Marxist literary theories. Among their group: Granville Hicks, Theodore Dreiser, Floyd Dell, Jack London, Upton Sinclair, Nelson Algren, James T. Farrell, Erskine Caldwell, Josephine Herbst, the poets Kenneth Fearing, Kenneth Patchen, and Muriel Rukeyser, as well as Langston Hughes, Malcolm Cowley, Horace Gregory, Richard Wright, and Clifford Odets. For a time, John Dos Passos and E. E. Cummings joined the throng, but each, for his own reasons, soon turned from such radicalism. Other writers were not associated with the proletarian movement per se but nevertheless produced works harshly critical of capitalism, for example, Sinclair Lewis and John Steinbeck. The writers and intellectuals read *The Masses*, the *New Leader*, and the *Socialist Call* and joined John Reed clubs, which were the forerunners of the American Writers' Congresses of 1935, 1937, and 1939. Alone among America's major twentieth-century poets, T. S. Eliot declared himself a royalist and became an English citizen in 1927, and Ezra Pound was in Italy defending Mussolini and fascism in the 1920s.

Some writers in the 1930s, however, either refused to participate actively in any political or economic movement, such as William Faulkner, or refused to accept the radical line, such as Gertrude Stein, Ernest Hemingway, and Laura Riding; or, like Cummings, Dos Passos, and Edna St. Vincent Millay, they became aware before the mid-1930s that the radical Marxist dogma was dangerous for the American artist and for America. Indeed, a profound change was taking place in the American artist's attitude toward capitalism and the businessman—a change that would not be fully reflected in imaginative literature until after 1945. It was in the 1930s, however, that the shift began.

As Stein claimed in *Everybody's Autobiography* (1936), her essays on money were inspired by the fact that she was finally managing her own money.[1] Her reflections on money and her defense of capitalism in the *Saturday Evening Post* essays range from the abstractly philosophical to the eminently practical. Philosophically, Stein, a student of William James at Harvard and a well-educated woman who had studied medicine at Johns Hopkins, contended that money is that factor that separates man from animals.

> It is very funny about money. The thing that differentiates man from animals is money. All animals have the same emotions and the same ways as men. Anybody who has lots of animals around knows that. But the thing that no animal can do is count, and the thing no animal can know is money.

Men can count, and they do, and that is what makes them have money.

And so, as long as the earth turns around there will be men on it, and as long as there are men on it, they will count, and they will count money.[2]

Problems arise, Gertrude Stein contended, when governments decide that money is not money. In the United States, Congress and FDR did not understand that money is money.

Everybody who lives on it every day knows that money is money but the people who vote money, presidents and congress, do not think about money that way when they vote it. I remember when my nephew was a little boy he was out walking somewhere and he saw a lot of horses; he came home and he said, oh papa, I have just seen a million horses. A million, said his father, well anyway, said my nephew, I saw three. That came to be what we all used to say when anybody used numbers that they could not count well anyway a million or three. That is the whole point. When you earn money and spend money every day anybody can know the difference between a million and three. But when you vote money away there really is not any difference between a million and three. And so everybody has to make up their mind is money money for everybody or is it not.

In Stein's view, Russia is not so very different, although in 1936 she was a bit more optimistic about the Russians. "In Russia they tried to decide that money was not money, but now slowly and surely they are coming back to know that money is money."[3]

For Stein, the question of unemployment—a severe problem in 1936—is related to the government's definition and enunciation of unemployment.

One of the funny things is that when there is a great deal of unemployment you can never get any one to do any work. It was true in England it is true in America and it is now true in France. Once unemployment is recognized as unemployment and organized as unemployment nobody starts to work. If you are out of work and you find some work then you go to work. But if you are part of the unemployed then you are part of that, and if work comes you have to change your position from the unemployed to the employed, and then perhaps you will have to change back again, so perhaps you had better just stay where you are.[4]

Stein further contended that eliminating wealthy people or "the rich" is a disastrous error.

Getting rid of the rich does not end up very funnily. It is easy to get rid of the rich but it is not easy to get rid of the poor. Wherever they have tried it they have got rid of the rich all right and so then everybody is poor and also there are . . . more than ever . . . of ever so much poorer. And that is natural enough. When there are the rich you can always take from the rich to give to the poor but when everybody is poor then you cannot take from the poor to give to the ever so much poorer and there you are.[5]

At the heart of much of Stein's "economic theory" is her defense of the individual, her fear of organization, whether it be political or monetary. Organization, she believed, is a kind of slavery, encouraged primarily in her time by politicians such as FDR. The concept of individuality is intertwined with private capitalism, as Stein concluded her series of essays.

Organization is a failure and everywhere the world over everybody has to begin again.

What are they going to try next, what does the twenty-first century want to do about it? They certainly will not want to be organized, the twentieth century is seeing the end of that . . . perhaps they will begin looking for liberty again and individually amusing themselves again and old-fashioned or dirt farming.

One thing is sure until there are rich again everybody will be poor and there will be more than ever of everybody who is even poorer.

That is sure and certain.

Other writers were not so sure and certain that an economic system was intertwined with liberty. E. E. Cummings, a classmate of John Dos Passos at Harvard, contributed in the 1920s to *The Liberator* and in the August 1931 issue of *Literature of the World Revolution* published a translation of Louis Aragon's "Front Rouge," a poem that ends in an optimistic ecstasy for the Russian state.

It's the song of man and his laughter
It's the train of the red star
which burns the stations the signals the skies
SSSR October October it's the express
October across the universe SS
SR SSSR SSSR
SSSR SSSR[7]

With high hopes and a letter of introduction to Soviet writers from Dos Passos, Cummings visited Russia for five weeks in 1931. The result was *Eimi*, a diary of the journey published in 1933 and now a book most difficult to find. What Cummings discovered in Russia stunned him from his communist sympathies: hypocrisy, the subordination of art to the state, an antiquated technology, a "world of Was," a land of "peopleless people," "a new realm whose inhabitants are made of each other," "a joyless experiment in force and fear."[8] *Eimi*, which opens with Cummings on a train bound for Russia, begins in this way: "SHUT seems to be The Verb" (p. 3). As he emerges from Russia five weeks later, Cummings concludes his book:

Voice
(Who:
Loves;
Creates,
Imagines)
OPENS (p. 432)

Yet Cummings was still not entirely certain that the Marxist state did not hold possibilities. In *Eimi*, he had described it as a "streetsprinkler" run "amok"—with the implication that a "streetsprinkler" is potentially a beneficial machine (pp. 106–7).

In 1935, however, he published one certainly anti-Marxist poem in the volume *no thanks*; poem #30 begins "kumrads die because they're told)." Cummings cites "hate" as the dominant feature of "Kumrads."[9] By 1938, he began to associate economic liberty with artistic and personal liberty, as in poem #15 from *New Poems* (1938).

economic secu
rity" is a cu
rious excu

se
(in

use among pu
rposive pu
nks) for pu

tting the arse
before the torse[10]

By the end of World War II, Cummings's conversion is clear, as he
plainly spoke in poem #IV of *1x1* (1944).

of all the blessings which to man
kind progress doth impart
one stands supreme i mean the an
imal without a heart.

Huge this collective pseudobeast
(sans either pain or joy)
does nothing except preexist
it hoi in its polloi

and if sometimes he's prodded forth
to exercise her vote
(or made by threats of something worse
than death to change their coat

—which something as you'll never guess
in fifty thousand years
equals the quote and unquote loss
of liberty my dears—

or even is compelled to fight
itself from tame to team)
still doth our hero contemplate
in raptures of undream

that strictly (and how) scienti
fic land of supernod
where freedom is compulsory
and only man is god.

Without a heart the animal
is very very kind
so kind it wouldn't like a soul
and couldn't use a mind[11]

In 1951 Cummings proclaimed in *Jottings*, #6, "private property began the instant somebody had a mind of his own." [12]

In the meantime, a number of American critics and scholars had become disillusioned with Marxist literary theory and had begun a dialogue with the proletarian Marxist artists. The major philosophical statement of the anti-Hegelian and anti-Marxist group was by Max Eastman, whose life resembles an allegorical pilgrim's progress from Marxism to capitalism. In 1934, his *Artists in Uniform: A Study Of Literature and Bureaucratism* condemned artists who gave themselves to the Marxist cause. Responded Michael Gold in *The New Masses*, "Shameful! Disgusting! Horrible! Nauseating! Criminal!" [13] Among the literary critics, it was perhaps Edmund Wilson's "Marxism and Literature," published in *The Triple Thinker* in 1938, which most completely represented the then dominant position of the literati.

Probably more chilling and more damning to the position of the proletarian writers and critics was Ernest Hemingway's fictional depiction of a proletarian writer, Richard Gordon, in *To Have and Have Not* (1937). Gordon, full of high sentiment (" 'A writer has to know about everything,' Richard Gordon said. 'He can't restrict his experience to Bourgeois standards'")[14] uses his politics to go to bed with a wealthy socialite who "collects writers"; he judges people by appearances, as his view of Marie Morgan testifies. He even decides to work Marie into his new novel.

> He sat down at the big table in the front room. He was writing a novel about a strike in a textile factory. In today's chapter he was going to use this big woman [Marie] with the tear-reddened eyes he had just seen on the way home. Her husband when he came home at night hated her, hated the way she had coarsened and grown heavy, was repelled by her bleached hair, her too big breasts, her lack of sympathy with his work as organizer. He would compare her to the young firm-breasted, full-lipped little Jewess that had spoken at the meeting that evening. It was good. It was, it could be easily, terrific, and it was true. He had seen, in a flash of perception, the whole inner life of that type of woman. (pp. 176–77)

Richard Gordon had been fooled by appearances, by superficialities; Harry and Marie Morgan are a happily married, sexually dynamic and compatible couple. Harry is no labor organizer, but a free spirit, an anarchist by nature, had he ever tried to define his politics—a man who hated "revolutionaries." "What the hell do I care about his revolution. F——— his revolution. To help the working man he robs a bank and kills a fellow works with him and then kills that poor damned Albert that never did any harm. That's a working man he kills. He never thinks of that. With a family" (p. 168).

The proletarian writer, Richard Gordon, finds his only fan to be the insane and homosexual Herbert Spellman, who reads Gordon's novels as escape literature. The only true communist depicted in *To Have and Have Not* is Nelson Jacks, who comments concerning Gordon's novels, " 'I thought they were shit' " (p. 210). Ironically, Gordon loses his wife Helen to John MacWalsey, an economics professor. In their final scene together, Helen denounces Gordon for a number of reasons, one of which is his hypocrisy. " 'If you were just a good writer I could stand for all the rest of it maybe. But I've seen you bitter, jealous, changing your politics to suit the fashion, sucking up to people's faces and talking behind their backs' " (p. 186).

As if the creation of Richard Gordon weren't enough, Hemingway finally alienated the Writers' Congress members in 1940 with *For Whom the Bell Tolls*, a novel that condemned both fascism and communism but that did not necessarily support capitalism either. During the Spanish Civil War, Hemingway had gone to Spain, like many American writers, firmly convinced that fascism and Franco had to be defeated. Hemingway had been strongly antifascist from the time he had interviewed Mussolini for a newspaper article in 1923; his propaganda movie *The Spanish Earth* (1937) was a plea for funds for the Spanish Republic. However, when Hemingway came to write the novel, the Republican generals, journalists, and soldiers are discovered to be as cruel and vindictive as the fascists. In particular, Hemingway described the powerlessness of the individual in the Republican-Marxist camp, the slavery of "Liberation." " 'All of you should come in to the Republic and join the army,' the officer said. 'There is too much of this silly guerilla nonsense going on. All of you should come in and submit to our Libertarian discipline.' " [15] André Marty, an actual person who was the leader of the International Brigades, is a particularly unfavorable portrait.

It was, for writers like Hemingway and Dos Passos, the old American theme of anarchy, of individualism, which tended to turn them against communism, rather than any kind of positive support of capitalism, at least at this time. As Hemingway wrote Dos Passos on 30 May 1932, "I can't be a Communist because I hate tyranny and, I suppose, government. . . . I can't stand *any* bloody government I suppose." [16] Dos Passos had had a career similar to that of Cummings and Max Eastman—from left to right. In the 1930s Dos Passos published the three volumes of *USA*, a work condemning both industrialists and communists, capitalists and socialists. In the complex whirl of the America that Dos Passos depicted, there was no center, either moral or economic, that could order or give meaning to the lives of a Charley Anderson or a Mary French. Babbittry, greed, and corruption abound among the capitalists; hypocrisy, hate, and stifling discipline among the Marxists. Although Marxists in the 1930s hailed *USA* as a handbook in class hatred—a prelude, they hoped, to a later triumphant Marxist statement—it is not difficult to read *USA* as a statement of America's complexity, as an example of literary naturalism, and as a prelude of Dos Passos's soon-to-be-announced libertarianism.

Perhaps most interesting in the 1930s, however, is that there finally appeared literary depictions of capitalists, of businessmen who are not greedy, not destructive to workers and society, not narrow-minded and conformist Babbitts. Such capitalists are not pathetic, nor are their stories morality pieces, like "A Christmas Carol" or *The Rise of Silas Lapham*. On the other hand, those authors who chose to create these more favorable portraits of capitalists were unable to create round or realistic characters. In this very early stage of a more positive depiction of a capitalist, the writers could only sketch his character in a short piece or create a nearly allegorical figure. Thus, in *To Have and Have Not*, Hemingway's Jon Jacobson, the father of "a pleasant, dull and upright family," may have some qualities of a Babbit. However, Hemingway described him as a man "who opposed prohibition, is not bigoted and is generous, sympathetic, understanding and almost never irritable." His money comes from a patent medicine that is cheaply marketed and is effective. "There are," the narrator concludes, "no suicides when money's made that way" (pp. 238–40).

The most fully developed favorable depictions of capitalists in works by Americans in the 1930s appeared in the writings of two American women, Edna St. Vincent Millay and Ayn Rand. The original and then still unpublished manuscript of Millay's *Conversation at Midnight* was destroyed in a fire in 1936. Millay put the manuscript together again from already published sections, from notes, and from memory. In

1937, the poem, in the form of a closet drama, appeared, neither a critical nor a financial success, but not entirely ignored either.

The poem is a dialogue shared by seven men, among them Carl the
communist, the liberal Ricardo, and the businessman Merton. If, in
fact, Ricardo is given the best lines in this poem of political, economic,
and religious debate, Carl is given the worst lines and Merton is at least
treated with respect. Indeed, he represents the position of the capitalist
in several articulate speeches, as, for example, these selections.

[spoken to Carl the Communist]
            Do you think I don't know
That with *you* in power I wouldn't stand the chance of a rat
In a research laboratory?—Yet here you come and go
Unmolested, and shoot off your mouth, and publish the Daily Worker,
and insist
On your rights under a liberal Constitution! Tell me, would you care
To try publishing in Moscow today a paper called The Daily
Capitalist?
Or preach the blessings of the profit-system to a crowd in the Red
Square?

[spoken after Carl declares the imminent fall of capitalism]
The fittest to survive may well derive some satisfaction,
But should refrain from finding cause for pride, in that:
The value of a life is not determined by that life's protraction:
The fittest to survive in a sewer, is a sewer rat.

[on the status of workers]
The surplus value that today, unjustly or justly,
Is taken over by the individual factory-owner to re-invest
In implements and materials, or to speculate with, or to fritter away,
Will be seized by the State, less adroitly but more ruthlessly even,
To be dispensed as the State sees fit, for sound or injudicious
purchasing, . . .
The worker will be quite as helpless then as now: he will
earn a living of sorts, and the rest will go to his employer, that is, the
State, and he will have nothing to say.

[to Carl]
If you had your way, we'd live in a two-dimensional world,
All dutifully munching mulberry-leaves for the State.
Every man for the State, and the devil take the individual.[17]

Merton, however, is an "elitist" and Carl's accusation of Babbittry is not entirely unfounded. Yet Millay had found several admirable characteristics in Merton the businessman: some sense of an interrelationship between freedom and economics, an appreciation for and support of the arts, a respect for tradition and good manners, and, surprisingly, a love of and respect for nature (a most favorable quality in the context of the poem, because Carl the communist finds "sparrow-cuddling" only a bourgeois fad).

The Russian-born Ayn Rand's first major work was *Night of January 16th*, a play written in 1933 that had a successful Broadway run in 1935. The play is a courtroom drama, with the dead man, Bjorn Faulkner, a capitalist entrepreneur (based roughly on Ivan Kreuger, the Swedish "Match King") and with Faulkner's mistress, Karen Andre, on trial for his murder. As he is described by evidence given during the trial, Faulkner is a new kind of Frank Cowperwood, more admirable in his individuality, as anarchic as American heroes have tended to be, but a capitalist, one who clearly associated economic freedom with personal freedom. He is, however, not wholly admirable; he breaks laws, and he enjoys "a whip over the world." [18]

Nevertheless, Rand had created a new American hero, the entrepreneur, a kind of old-fashioned con man and Yankee Peddler, although not viewed as a destructive person. Perhaps the character owes something to Thorstein Veblen's distinction between the industrial innovator,[19] which Faulkner was, and the financial manipulator, but Rand herself tends to associate this new kind of hero with another tradition. In her introduction, Rand states that "The events [of the play] feature the confrontation of two extremes, two opposite ways of facing existence: passionate self-assertiveness, self-confidence, ambition, audacity, independence—versus conventionality, servility, envy, hatred, power-lust." [20] She has purposely chosen a somewhat shady entrepreneur like Faulkner to represent the first of her two extremes because "for the purpose of dramatizing the conflict of independence versus conformity, a criminal—a social outcast—can be an eloquent symbol." [21]

Rand has thus associated Faulkner with the long American tradition of outcast, lonely heroes—with the woodsman Natty Bumppo, who escapes from a jail in Templeton, New York, and flees to the woods in James Fenimore Cooper's *The Pioneers*; with the adulteress Hester Prynne, who lived on the edge of civilization in Hawthorne's *The Scarlet Letter*; even with Jay Gatsby, whose illicit fortune, however, marred his dream. Nevertheless, in this early work, Rand outlined a character who was to reappear in post–World War II fiction—the hero as private, capitalistic entrepreneur, for some authors the only kind of character strong enough to withstand the pressures of conformity and of organization in the second half of the twentieth century in America.

Such heroes, however, were not by any means the dominant protagonists in our fictional landscape of the 1930s. America's two major novelists, William Faulkner and Ernest Hemingway, created no such character, nor did such important writers as John Steinbeck and Theodore Dreiser. The proletarian writers were condemning the capitalist. On the other hand, the private, capitalistic entrepreneur had been introduced to the American literary scene in at least a sympathetic rendering before World War II began.

CHAPTER 10

The Businessman and the
Corporate Capitalist

As early as 1901, Frank Norris had identified the corporation as an octopus, a monster in the form of a railroad that destroyed the farmers
(even wealthy farmers), their homes, and their free lives. Norris's *The
Octopus* was the first part of an unfinished trilogy that was ultimately
intended to extol wheat as a life force. Within this framework, the corporation is seen as an evil.

> "They [the Railroad] own us, these task-masters of ours; they
> own our home, they own our legislatures. We cannot escape from
> them. There is no redress. We are told we can defeat them by the
> ballot-box. They own the ballot-box. We are told that we must
> look to the courts for redress; they own the courts. We know
> them for what they are—ruffians in politics, ruffians in finance,
> ruffians in law, ruffians in trade, bribers, swindlers, and trick-
> sters. No outrage too great to daunt them, no petty larceny too
> small to shame them; despoiling a government treasury of a mil-
> lion dollars, yet picking the pockets of a farm hand of the price of
> a loaf of bread.
> "They swindle a nation of a hundred million and call it Finan-
> ciering; they levy a blackmail and call it Commerce; they cor-
> rupt a legislature and call it Politics; they bribe a judge and
> call it Law; they hire blacklegs to carry out their plans and call it
> Organization; they prostitute the honour of a State and call it
> Competition." [1]

If Norris considers wheat a life force, the monopolistic corporation is
clearly a death force, something beyond the control even of its presi-

dent, Selgrim. In fact, Selgrim himself is depicted in somewhat sympathetic terms as a man who has some compassion for his workers but who is himself caught up in the force of the corporation. Moreover, the group of farmers who form a league and who, in a communist-inspired novel, would have been depicted as proletarian heroes are here depicted as inept, dishonest, and disorganized, but also as a potentially violent mob—a potential "Red Terror."[2] With such a dismal prospect for the future of humanity, it is probably no wonder that Norris turned to a mystical vision of wheat as a life force.

One remarkable quality of Norris's novel is its distinctions among different kinds of capitalists as businessmen. The farmers are both wealthy and poor and are generally depicted favorably, as are the small businessmen in the local community. The banker, however, is vicious and cutthroat—an agent of the railroad. The corporation and its officials are generally destructive and devious. What is perhaps more remarkable, given the 1901 publication date of *The Octopus*, is Norris's indictment of the unions as a cooperative and integral part of the corporate octopus. Striking brotherhood members are welcomed back to the company, but one nonmember of the brotherhood who worked during the strike is not only fired, but also blacklisted from work on other railroads. Norris was thus able to do what other American writers were generally unwilling (or unable) to do until much later in the century—to differentiate among capitalists, to distinguish between private capitalism and corporate capitalism, and finally to suggest that together the unions and the corporation might well be, despite their occasional conflicts, a powerful, destructive force against the individual's freedom.

In the 1920s, the middle-class businessman and the corporation president—Sinclair Lewis's Babbitt and Mr. Cady in Kaufman and Connelly's *Beggar on Horseback*—were depicted by the American artist as essentially identical, despite their different financial bases. In the 1930s, the entrepreneur—heroic because of his individuality and financial daring—appeared in Rand's *Night of January 16th*. Similar to Rand's Faulkner, but less a symbol and more a sympathetic character, is F. Scott Fitzgerald's Monroe Stahr, the protagonist of *The Last Tycoon*, a novel left unfinished at Fitzgerald's death in 1940, but published with outline and other material in 1941, with an introduction by Edmund Wilson. Far from being a negative and destructive character, the Hollywood producer Stahr is a strongminded but compassionate tycoon surrounded by corrupt colleagues. As a kind of feudal lord of his studio,

Stahr still has time to give personal help to a cameraman Pete Zavras and is willing to let the studio lose money on a quality picture, much to the disbelief and opposition of his colleagues. Reasons Stahr, "we have a certain duty to the public."[3] The novelist Boxley, whom Stahr has hired to write scripts (and who undoubtedly is a reflection of Fitzgerald himself) recognizes that "Stahr like [Abraham] Lincoln was a leader carrying on a long war on many fronts; almost single-handed he had moved pictures sharply forward through a decade, to the point where the content of 'A productions' was wider and richer than that of the stage. Stahr was an artist only, as Mr. Lincoln was a general, perforce and as a layman" (p. 137). Cecilia Brady, the daughter of one of Stahr's corrupt partners, sees Stahr "as a sort of technological virtuoso" (pp. 162–63).

This is not to say that Monroe Stahr does not embody several qualities already associated with businessmen by American authors. He is paternalistic in his approach to his corporation—a quality which indicates real weakness during his drunken discussion with the communist union organizer Brimmer. He is, moreover, relatively uneducated and, when he wants to learn about communism, he has "the script department get him up a two-page 'treatment' of the *Communist Manifesto*" (p. 154). Although his paternalism makes it difficult for him to understand the union movement, he was perhaps correct in his suspicions for, as Edmund Wilson interpreted the outline of the unfinished portion of *The Last Tycoon*, Fitzgerald obviously "intended to exploit the element of racketeering and gangsterism revealed in the [union] organization."[4]

Nevertheless, *The Last Tycoon* depicts Stahr as a kind of hero in Wilson's summary of the projected conclusion of the novel. "The split between the controllers of the movie industry, on the one hand, and the various groups of employees, on the other, is widening and leaving no place for real individualists of business like Stahr, whose successes are personal achievements and whose career has always been invested with a certain glamour. He has held himself directly responsible to everyone with whom he has worked; he has even wanted to beat up his enemies himself."[5]

In the post–World War II period, other writers began to distinguish more carefully between the private capitalist, often a small businessman, and the corporate capitalist, in contrast to the pre-1945 writers, who generally grouped all businessmen together. The corporation, that octopus Norris had described nearly half a century before, became more clearly identified as a destructive force. The small, private businessman and the "businessman-employee" of a corporation become sympathetic characters at about the same time the National Association of Manufacturers substituted the phrase "American Free Enterprise System" for "American Capitalism" in their pronouncements.

One representative and well-known play which strikingly demonstrated the difference between a businessman and a destructive capitalist is Arthur Miller's *Death of a Salesman* (1949). Willy Loman is a white-collar worker, a middle-class man with middle-class ambitions for his sons, a salesman—a businessman. His employer, Howard Wagner, is a capitalist, a man for whom profit is more important than loyalty to a long-employed salesman. In a sense, Miller has simply substituted the businessman for the laborer or cabdriver of Odets's *Waiting for Lefty*. In either case, the capitalist and his system are seen as corrupting even for a salesman, a latter-day Yankee Peddler, like Willy.

The "system" run by men like Howard Wagner and, in *The Last Tycoon*, Pat Brady soon was more fully identified by our writers with corporate capitalism or big business. Correspondingly, the small businessman began to emerge as a kind of sympathetic antihero. The earliest, most explicit example is Morris Bober in Bernard Malamud's *The Assistant* (1957). Bober has owned his little neighborhood grocery store for twenty-one years but is slowly being put out of business by his rival, Heinrich Schmitz. A compassionate man, Bober extends credit to the poor of the neighborhood. "He had labored long hours, was the soul of honesty— he could not escape his honesty, it was bedrock; to cheat would cause an explosion in him, yet he trusted cheaters—coveted nobody's nothing and always got poorer. . . . He was Morris Bober and could be nobody more fortunate." Moreover, as Bober recognizes, big business is destroying the small businessman. "The chain store kills the small man." [6]

Bober is the victim of a robbery, but because his cash register contains so little—$10, his entire day's take—he is hit and injured by the robbers. However, one of the robbers, Frank Alpine, feels so guilty that he returns to help Bober, and Bober, with great compassion, gives Frank a job. Frank takes over the store while Bober is recuperating and business improves, even though Frank pockets some of the money. In the end, Bober dies, and Frank rents the store and seems destined to repeat Bober's life as a marginal shopowner and a (converted) Jew. There are other small businessmen in *The Assistant*, such as the liquor store owner, Julius Karp, but Bober with his compassion and humanity represents "the persistence of [Jewish] values uncorrupted and the relevance of the Jewish tradition of idealism to life in present-day America," as observed by Josephine Zadovsky Knopp.[7] It is significant that Bober, this symbolic figure, is a small businessman, a private capitalist, although an unsuccessful one to be sure; in the late 1950s, the American writer was not yet ready to grant both goodness and success to the small businessman.

Perhaps the most striking example of the post–World War II indictment of the corporation and the union is John Dos Passos's *Midcentury: A Contemporary Chronicle* (1961). Many of Dos Passos's themes had already been introduced in his 1930s trilogy *USA*, but in *Midcentury* the destructive nature of union-business cooperation is brought into sharper focus. Such entanglements, further compounded by Mafia and racketeering interests, not only make it nearly impossible for a private capitalist like Will Jenks to begin his own business, but they also take advantage of honest union men such as Terry Bryant. Although *Midcentury* is generally viewed as a pessimistic book that attacks all aspects of capitalism, critics seem to have overlooked the fact that Will becomes successful for a number of reasons, not the least of which is his aggressive advertising campaign to the people of the community—a campaign that asserts the value of free enterprise and the classical economist's argument against monopoly.

> In his releases Will took high ground. His fight for competition was a fight to preserve the free enterprise way, the American way.
> . . . Will had typed out a five page story explaining how the Halloran interests were strangling the growth of Duquesne by their monopoly of transportation through Redtop Cabs. . . .
> *Corrupt Labor joins corrupt Management to strangle Competition.*[8]

Dos Passos depicts the early twentieth-century union movement favorably in the career of Blackie Bowman, an IWW and a self-proclaimed "atheist anarchist." At this early point of union development, Dos Passos implies, there was a need to fight the dominant business leaders, who employed violent tactics to break up the unions. However, the unions adopted these same tactics and allowed communists like Kate Levine to speak for them, as Dos Passos continues the story. In time, the union leader became only another kind of monopolistic, corporate capitalist investing union funds in private ventures and even, like the Worthingtons, assuming social pretensions which in earlier American novels were assigned to the newly rich industrialists. Lillian Worthington, wife of the president of the fictional International Rubber Workers Union, bought "a lot out near the Country Club. They built themselves a neat Cape Cod cottage on it, plain roomy and unassuming. They had to think of the girls growing up. Lillian was president of the PTA. She was in the League of Women Voters and was invited to join the Ladies' Garden Club. The girls were asked to the really nice dances" (p. 131).

Besides the union-business alliance, Dos Passos also condemns corporations for destroying free, entrepreneurial capitalism. As John P. Diggins has observed in *Up From Communism: Conservative Odysseys in American Intellectual History*, "Dos Passos was . . . convinced that those who controlled big business no longer represented capitalism." [9] Jaspar Milliron meets opposition from high and distant corporate management when he attempts to implement a new production process for his company; an example of Veblen's industrial innovator, he is, like Monroe Stahr, "a technical virtuoso" defeated by unimaginative financiers. One of the financiers depicted by Dos Passos is Judge Lewin, who lives in the world of "pure finance" (p. 458).

> I do not consider myself an evil man, yet my business, my hobby, my science is that special little section of arithmetic known as finance . . . insignificant from the point of view of great minds like Einstein's or Spinoza's, but still a sort of poor relation of mathematics. When I assume control of a corporation through the use of my own private skills, I have to consider it a problem in pure finance. I can't be bothered with what it takes or what it sells. I can't be distracted by worrying about administration, who gets fired from what job, all the grubby little lives involved.
> (p. 475)

Finally, Dos Passos also explores another danger for the entrepreneur—big government—a theme already introduced into American literature in Ayn Rand's *Atlas Shrugged* (1957). In one of the biographical sections of real people scattered among the sections of fiction, Dos Passos records the story of Robert R. Young, who gained control of the Allegheny Railroad with strong hopes of reforming and refinancing the failing line. He "talked public service and the interest of the small investor" (p. 290); he "pleaded the cause of honest management, streamlining, modernization, service" (p. 291). But in the end he failed.

> He died many times a millionaire. Money meant power, but not power enough. He was a skillful financial manipulator but not skillful enough
> to bring a successful reorganization of the railroads out from under the dead weight of the bankers' interests and the insurance companies' interests and the brotherhoods' interests
> and the seventy year old senile strangling head of the bureaucracy of the Interstate Commerce Commission.
> Restrictions, procedures, prerogatives hampered his every move. (p. 292)

In the fictional sketches, Dos Passos criticizes the NLRB as ineffective in controlling the racketeering and violent elements in the unions. With this theme—big government as dangerous to both free enterprise and the individual—Dos Passos suggested a thematic trend for novels in the 1970s.

The dangers of corporate capitalism also continue to be a major theme. Most recently, the corporation office appeared like this in Joseph Heller's *Something Happened* (1974).

> In the office in which I work there are five people of whom I am afraid. Each of these five people is afraid of four people (excluding overlaps), for a total of twenty, and each of these twenty people is afraid of six people, making a total of one hundred and twenty people who are feared by at least one other person. Each of these one hundred and twenty people is afraid of the other one hundred and nineteen, and all of these one hundred and forty-five people are afraid of the twelve men at the top who helped found and build the company and now own and direct it.[10]

In William Gaddis's *JR: A Novel* (1975), JR learns about the stock market in his sixth-grade class and, with a few telephone calls from a booth near the boys' room at his school, promptly builds a paper empire, a paper corporation. JR, the successful child capitalist, is a satiric portrait, a surrealistic spin-off of the corporate investor who, like Judge

Lewin in *Midcentury*, is involved in the game of pure finance with no thought of responsibilities or consequences.

The only fictional character in American literature who has been able to confront heroically and successfully big unionism and big business appeared to be the small, self-employed businessman. Will Jenks managed with some success in *Midcentury*, but he played only a minor role in a large and complex novel. However, Ken Kesey centered an entire novel, *Sometimes a Great Notion* (1964), around a heroic small businessman, Hank Stamper. Stamper is a character whose origins can be described in terms of the heroism of Daniel Boone and Natty Bumppo. Owner of a small, family lumbering company in Oregon, Stamper was also an all-state football player and a veteran of the Korean war.

Kesey has consciously surrounded his fictional hero with a myriad of nearly mythological associations. Hank's intellectual brother Lee associates Hank with Daniel Boone: *"Who played at Dan'l Boone in forest full of fallout?"* [11] Old Henry, Hank's father, is described as "a Norse hero . . . [an] old warrior" (p. 221). Although Hank realizes that "you can make the river stand for all *sorts* of other [sentimental, mystical] things" (p. 105), he himself is strong enough to confront the river and its force. "It was like me and that river had drawn ourselves a little contract, a little grudge match" (p. 104). Hank's personality becomes associated with tall tales. "Old Henry says Hank's so godawful stout because something odd happened to Hank's muscle tissue because of all the sulphur his first wife, Hank's real ma, ate while she was pregnant with him" (p. 312). The family motto is "NEVER GIVE AN INCH!" (p. 30), and at one point Hank announces, "I don't care much for cages" (p. 99).

Hank and his small lumbering firm are caught between the big lumber corporations, which seem to have captured the market and have been squeezing the small companies, and the union, whose members are striking Hank's small company. In order to fight the union, Hank hires only members of his family and even sends east for his half-brother Lee, who has failed his doctoral exams in literature and, at the time he receives Hank's letter, is popping pills and contemplating suicide. The union resorts to sabotage and violence, alternated with honeyed moralisms about teamwork and community spirit. On the other hand, Hank is able to deal with the large corporations at this time because they too are suffering from a strike and can meet their own contracts only by buying lumber from men like Hank.

Hank represents individualism—a self-sufficiency and strength traced to his nomadic, pioneering ancestors. Kesey quite properly does not put words like "free enterprise" and "capitalism" in Hank's mouth, but lets Hank speak out for an individuality that can be expressed through his business and through his ability to confront the unions, which to Hank represent only conformity and mediocrity. As Hank tells the union president, in response to his sweet sentiments about the common good and community spirit and the American way,

> "I'm just as concerned as the next guy, just as loyal. If we was to get into it with Russia I'd fight for us right down to the wire. And if Oregon was to get into it with California I'd fight for Oregon. But if somebody—Biggy Newton or the Woodsworker's Union or anybody— gets into it with *me*, then I'm for *me*! When the chips are down, I'm my own patriot. I don't give a goddam the other guy is my own *brother* wavin' the *American* flag and singing the friggin' 'Star Spangled Banner!'" (p. 346)

Hank's individual strength is ultimately and ironically a community strength, much as the king's strength was the community's strength in classical drama. When, at one point, Hank appears to have given in to union demands, the town is sad and the high school football team loses a game.

In an innovative and startling fashion, Kesey has thus adapted an ancient myth. The interrelationship of leader and community in a modern democracy can never be that of the ancient leader, such as Oedipus, and his people. However, Kesey implies that the heroic and free individual such as Hank Stamper does indeed have a positive and healthy effect on his community. Hank's struggle to meet his business and moral responsibilities and his refusal to buckle to the unreasonable union demands and the union leader's sweet sentiments concerning community spirit make explicit the strength and integrity of the small businessman.

In contrast to Hank's strength is this description of the union members on their way to a meeting:

> And there is nothing like feeling special for hustling a citizen out to round up every other comrade he can locate with a corresponding feeling; there is nothing like a sense of *difference* for getting a man lined up, shoulder to shoulder, with everybody as different as he is, in a dedicated campaign for the Common

> Good; which means a campaign either for the ramming of that
> difference down the throat of an ignorant and underprivileged and
> *unholy* world—this is only true, of course, in the case of a bona
> fide *holy* difference—or, at the other extreme, a campaign for the
> stamping-out of the thing that caused the damned difference in
> the first place. (p. 404)

Thus, according to the narrator, the union members are joining to im-
pose conformity to their own standards.

Hank's half-brother, Lee, is by contrast an academic, an intellectual,
a socialist, who returns home not to help Hank but to destroy him. Lee
hates Hank because Hank had slept with Lee's mother, Hank's step-
mother, and because Lee hates Hank's self-sufficiency and strength. Lee
reviles their father, Old Henry, because he is a capitalist. Lee attempts to
win by losing, while Hank attempts to win by winning. When Lee se-
duces Hank's wife, Viv, he feels that he has defeated his brother. Although Hank falters and admits that he has learned something from Lee,
it is finally Lee who stays with Hank and tells the reader what Hank's
integrity means.

> For there is always a sanctuary more, a door that can never be
> forced, whatever the force, a last inviolable stronghold that can
> never be taken, whatever the attack; your vote can be taken, your
> name, your innards, even your life, but that last stronghold can
> only be surrendered. And to surrender it for any reason other
> than love is to surrender love. Hank had always known this with-
> out knowing it, and by making him doubt it briefly I made it
> possible for both of us to discover it. I knew it now. (p. 594)

The contrast of Hank and Lee is perhaps a variation of the old American theme of the westerner and the dude. The two men, however, more
fully represent the independent individual of the free-enterprise system
and the group-oriented, academic, intellectual socialist. During the
1960s, American authors had regularly been attacking academic intellectuals for one reason or another:[12] Bernard Malamud's *A New Life* appeared in 1961; Saul Bellow's *Herzog*, 1964; and John Barth's *Giles
Goat-Boy; or, The Revised New Syllabus*, 1966. However, it is significant that the small businessman Hank has something to teach the academic Lee. Unlike Kesey's *One Flew Over the Cuckoo's Nest* (1962), in
which McMurphy is simply an individualistic rebel against a system,

the characters in *Sometimes a Great Notion* are more carefully specified and delineated. According to this novel, it is only the small businessman who is strong and self-sufficient enough to confront the union, big business, and academics and, at the same time, to bring strength to his community.

CHAPTER 11

"The Great American
Tradition of Tinkers"

Technology has always been a paradoxical problem for the American artist. On the one hand, Founding Fathers like Thomas Jefferson feared factories and a large urban populace but at the same time welcomed the small craftsman. Jefferson himself was, like Benjamin Franklin, a tinker, an inventor of a "polygraph" and a seven-day clock. Franklin, however, was the tinker par excellence, with his lightning rod, his bifocals, and Franklin stove. It is Franklin to whom Ralph Ellison's black, unnamed *Invisible Man* (1952) traces his background.

> Yet when you have lived invisible as long as I have you develop a certain ingenuity. I'll solve the problem. And maybe I'll invent a gadget to place my coffee pot on the fire while I lie in bed, and even invent a gadget to warm my bed—like the fellow I saw in one of the picture magazines who made himself a gadget to warm his shoes! Though invisible, I am in the great American tradition of tinkers. That makes me kin to Ford, Edison, and Franklin. Call me, since I have a theory and a concept, a "thinker-tinker." [1]

In the nineteenth century, as we have seen, artists like Melville and Thoreau feared the machine as destructive and enslaving for mankind. Melville's Maids of Tartarus were dominated and transmogrified into robots by the machine. Except for Walt Whitman's enthusiasm for world-spanning transportation, the nineteenth-century Industrial Revolution seemed to be the actualization of Jefferson's fears: urban centers festering with poor, machines replacing the small craftsman while clogging the sky with smoke and destroying the land.

The machine, within the capitalistic system, was generally viewed as a monster, as Frank Norris's farmers believed in *The Octopus* (1901).

> Then, faint and prolonged, across the levels of the ranch, he heard the engine whistling for Bonneville. Again and again, at rapid intervals in its flying course, it whistled for road crossings, for sharp curves, for trestles; ominous notes, hoarse, bellowing, ringing with accents of menace and defiance; and abruptly Presley saw again, in his imagination, the galloping monster, the terror of steel and steam, with its single eye, Cyclopean, red, shooting from horizon to horizon; but saw it now as the symbol of a vast power, huge, terrible, flinging the echo of its thunder over all the reaches of the valley, leaving blood and destruction in its path; the leviathan, with tentacles of steel clutching into the soil, the soulless Force, the iron-hearted Power, the Colossus, the Octopus.[2]

Just the year before *The Octopus* was published, Henry Adams had also realized the force and power of the Dynamo at the Paris Exposition of 1900. In "The Dynamo and the Virgin," Adams comes to understand that the Dynamo has taken the place of the medieval Virgin Mary in America, and the displacement is not a fortunate one. Although both the Virgin and the Dynamo represent a fecundity, the Dynamo is inhuman and devoid of art.

> [St. Gaudens and Matthew Arnold] felt a railway train as power; yet they, and all the other artists, constantly complained that the power embodied in a railway train could never be embodied in art. All the steam in the world could not, like the Virgin, build Chartres.
>   . . . Symbol or energy, the Virgin had acted as the greatest force the Western world ever felt, and had drawn man's activities to herself more strongly than any other power, natural or supernatural, had ever done.[3]

In *The Machine in The Garden: Technology and the Pastoral Ideal in America*, Leo Marx has summarized Adams's dichotomy between the Virgin and the Dynamo. "On the one side [the Virgin] he lines up heaven, beauty, religion, and reproduction; on the other side: hell, utility, science, and production."[4]

In *Dynamo* (1929), Eugene O'Neill extended Adams's implications and blended the images of the Great Mother and the Dynamo in the mind of a crazed Reuben Light, the son of a fundamentalist minister. Reuben hopes to establish a religion of the Dynamo.

> Did I tell you that our blood plasm is the same right now as the sea was when life came out of it? We've got the sea in our blood still! It's what makes our hearts live! And it's the sea rising up in clouds, falling on the earth in rain, made that river that drives the turbines that drive Dynamo! The sea makes her heart beat, too!—but the sea is only hydrogen and oxygen and minerals, and they're only atoms, and atoms are only protons and electrons—even our blood and the sea are only electricity in the end! And think of the stars! Driving through space, round and round, just like the electrons in the atom! But there must be a center around which all this moves, mustn't there? There is in everything else! And that center must be the Great Mother of Eternal Life, Electricity, and Dynamo is her Divine Image on earth! Her power houses are the new churches![5]

At much the same time, Carl Sandburg was worried about the exaltation of the machine in *Smoke and Steel* (1920); Mr. Zero in Elmer L. Rice's *The Adding Machine: A Play in Seven Scenes* (1923) was fired and replaced by a machine; and Charlie Chaplin was tangling with a factory assembly line in *Modern Times* (1936). The radical writers of the 1920s and 1930s were having their own soul-searching sessions about the machine, as Russia attempted to develop technology rapidly. Finally, the Twelve Southerners who authored *I'll Take My Stand: The South and the Agrarian Tradition* (1930) rehearsed Jefferson's arguments in hope of maintaining the South as an agrarian society. "If a community, or a section, or a race, or an age, is groaning under industrialism, and well aware that it is an evil dispensation, it must find the way to throw it off."[6] Attacking the "new so-called industrial 'slavery,'" John Crowe Ransom called for the South to reenter United States politics as part of the Democratic party, which would advocate "a principle [which] can now be defined as agrarian, conservative, anti-industrial."[7]

And yet, throughout the history of American literature, the inventor of all this technology, the man who was incorrectly called a tinker, remained a sympathetic character. Not quite a hero, and only occasionally a villain, the American Tinker is part of a "Great Tradition," as Ellison's Invisible Man affirmed. A unique character, created by American authors, the Tinker is probably a descendant of Ben Franklin and

Thomas Jefferson and, in literature, of that itinerant Yankee Peddler who had to mend the household utensils soon after he had sold them. "To tinker" properly means to repair or adjust in an amateurish manner, but the American Tinker was in actuality identified with Thomas Edison, Alexander Graham Bell, the Wright Brothers, even Henry Ford. In literature, an early American Tinker is Owen Warland, Hawthorne's Artist of the Beautiful, who became a tinker-artist when he turned his watchmaker's skills to the creation of the Beautiful, a mechanical butterfly.

Perhaps the most representative Tinker of nineteenth-century American literature is Hank Morgan of Mark Twain's *A Connecticut Yankee in King Arthur's Court* (1888). A versatile and clever mechanic, Morgan is transposed to sixth-century England to the court of King Arthur, Merlin, and Sir Launcelot. Morgan is described as a "practical Connecticut man," [8] a direct descendant of those Yankee Peddlers whose home state Irving identified as Connecticut. Morgan is not particularly well educated and is employed as a shop foreman before he enters the world of King Arthur, where he is appalled at the monarchy and the low status of the common people. He plans to destroy the monarchy and the Church, both of which he feels perpetuate the slavery of the people. Morgan opens schools and colleges to educate the people. Finally, he "reinvents" the technology of the nineteenth century, which he believes will help the people of Arthur's kingdom lead more healthy and comfortable lives and which, moreover, will prove superior to black magic and superstition. A master mechanic, Morgan is delighted with the prospect of technologically transforming sixth-century England into nineteenth-century America.

> There were no books, pens, paper, or ink, and no glass in the openings they believed to be windows. It is a little thing—glass is—until it is absent, then it becomes a big thing. But perhaps the worst of all was, that there wasn't any sugar, coffee, tea, or tobacco. I saw that I was just another Robinson Crusoe cast away on an uninhabited island, with no society but some more or less tame animals, and if I wanted to make life bearable I must do as he did—invent, contrive, create, reorganize things; set brain and hand to work, and keep them busy. Well, that was in my line. [9]

Hank Morgan is also an advocate of private property and free enterprise: each is ultimately necessary for a free democracy and for individual freedom. As a mechanic/tinker, he immediately establishes industries to manufacture products from telephones to soap to gun powder. Technology, private enterprise, and democracy are all intertwined in Morgan's explanations to King Arthur's subjects. As Henry Nash Smith pointed out, *A Connecticut Yankee in King Arthur's Court* "represents a bold attempt to evaluate the industrial revolution from the standpoint of the business community itself rather than from the standpoint of genteel literary and moral tradition." [10]

As close as Morgan comes, however, to reaching a kind of heroic stature, he ultimately fails, and his very failures indicate some of the problems to be examined by later American novelists. First, simply because of the governmental situation in sixth-century England, Morgan must become part of the feudal structure in order to effect any change. Thus he is "Sir Boss" and moves from tinker/mechanic/inventor/engineer to a managerial role, with more and more of his time devoted to managerial duties.

Second, Sir Boss's technology succeeds in improving life in sixth-century England only in minor ways. He does turn the knights from killing and dragon chasing to the stock market, and the English citizens do learn to use soap. In the end, however, in a dreadful scene of death and decaying bodies, Morgan's technology turns back upon him, and he and his men find themselves trapped within their own electronic barricade. It is Merlin's black magic that ultimately conquers and sends Morgan back to nineteenth-century Connecticut. Although the early part of Twain's fable is a celebration of the Tinker and his technology, the final pages outline the dangers inherent in a technology thoughtlessly used.

Finally, the people whom Morgan had hoped to help do not appreciate much of his technology and return to their old ways of primitive customs and superstition, under the influence of the Church and the monarchy. Indeed, it is ultimately the failure of the people that leads Morgan to the desperate measure of the electronic barricade. In short, although technology is seen as potentially dangerous, the people themselves are in essence more "evil"—selfish and ignorant— than technology, a misanthropic view also explored by Twain in other works. Finally, the ultimate leaders of Morgan's society, the Church and government "managers," fear Morgan's innovations and frustrate his plans.

Twain's book is an anti-Utopian novel of a rather grim kind, but it explores the Tinker in a sympathetic manner and tends to view issues in more depth and perspective than did the muckraking, radical, and Utopian novels written by other Americans at the turn of the century. Later writers who explored these same issues tended to give at least respect to the technological tinker; hence, even Ellison's Invisible Man can announce that he is part of the "great tradition" of the American Tinker.

The theme of the Tinker who becomes corrupt as he gradually assumes more of a managerial and capitalistic role was perhaps most completely explored in Sherwood Anderson's *Poor White* (1920). Hugh McVey, born a poor white in "a little hole of a town stuck on a mud bank"[11] on the Mississippi River in Missouri, is taken under the wing of Sarah Shephard, a woman of New England origins whose husband works for the railroad. Mrs. Shephard urges young Hugh out of his "stupor" and provides him with the spiritual thrust for his later career. Anderson reflects his own mixed emotions toward the New England tradition when he summarizes the character of Mrs. Shephard and others like her. "If they, with the frugal and sometimes niggardly New Englanders from whom they were sprung, have given modern American life a too material flavor, they have at least created a land in which a less determinedly materialistic people may in their turn live in comfort" (p. 10).

McVey leaves his hometown and, after a period of wandering and a variety of jobs, settles in Bidwell, Ohio. McVey is a shy and isolated man, unable to make friends with men or to court women. In order to alleviate his loneliness, he amuses himself by making mathematical calculations, then begins a period of self-education, and soon invents an agricultural machine which gives him money, prestige, and a large role in a company established by local promoters. The amateur tinker had succeeded, although he had "but little conception of the import in the lives of the people about him of the things he did." Drawn more and more into the managerial aspect of the plant, Hugh loses his ability to invent or to be a Tinker. At the same time, however, he advances beyond the level of Tinker to what is, according to Anderson anyway, a new, albeit undefined, level of consciousness. "The time of the comparatively simple struggle with definite things, with iron and steel, had passed. He fought to accept himself, to understand himself, to relate himself with the life about him" (p. 364). McVey is finally "saved" by the love of his wife Clara, who hates "the whole mechanical impulse of her generation" (p. 334), and by the birth of their son.

Anderson does not hesitate to tell the reader what he should learn from this tale.

A new force that was being born into American life and into life everywhere all over the world was feeding on the old dying individualistic life. The new force stirred and aroused the people. It met a need that was universal. It was meant to seal men together, to wipe out national lines, to walk under seas and fly through the air, to change the entire face of the world in which men lived. Already the giant that was to be king in place of old kings was calling his servants and his armies to serve him. He used the methods of old kings and promised his followers booty and gain. Everywhere he went unchallenged, surveying the land, raising a new class of men to positions of power. Railroads had already pushed out across the plains; great coal fields from which was to be taken food to warm up the blood in the body of the giant were being opened up; iron fields were being discovered; the roar and clatter of the breathing of the terrible new thing, half hideous, half beautiful in its possibilities, that was for so long to drown the voices and confuse the thinking of men, was heard not only in the towns but even in lonely farm houses, where its willing servants, the newspapers and magazines, had begun to circulate in ever increasing numbers. . . . The Morgans, Fricks, Goulds, Carnegies, Vanderbilts, servants of the new king, princes of the new faith, merchants all, a new kind of rulers of men, defied the world-old law of class that puts the merchant below the craftsman, and added to the confusion of men by taking on the air of creators. They were merchants glorified and dealt in giant things, in the lives of men and in mines, forests, oil and gas fields, factories, and railroads. (pp. 62–63)

In such a world, the true craftsman/tinker, the survivor of "the old dying individualistic life," has no chance, unless he chooses to join the merchant princes of the new faith. Undoubtedly, Anderson had been directly influenced by Thorstein Veblen's distinction between the technological innovator and the manager manipulator, and yet this theme had, as we have seen, already been developed in American literature before Veblen identified it in his treatises. Sponge, a character in Anderson's later *Dark Laughter* (1925), represents a Hugh McVey who has lost his own small shop, but is able to remain whole and healthy even though he must labor in a factory. Charley Anderson of Dos Passos's 1930s trilogy *USA* is an expert mechanic and aviator destroyed when he assumes a managerial role. However, his old friend and personal mechanic, Bill

Cermak, maintains a certain purity. In the post–World War II period, Ellison's Invisible Man can only retreat to his underground room in order to become a "thinker-tinker." Invisible Man had seen what had happened to the craftsman of the old individualistic school, Lucius Brockway, who, threatened by the unions and fearing replacement by "an *engineer*," [12] simply blows up the paint furnaces of the Liberty Paint Factory.

The failure of technology ultimately to improve man's condition is another nineteenth-century theme further developed in post–World War II literature. In such works, the Tinker's inventions have been taken over by the more educated and specialized engineers, and the Tinker himself has been excluded from the dominant technological system. The Tinker, therefore, is vested with a kind of innocence, and the evil is shifted to the engineers. At this point, the engineers become a kind of mad and inhuman scientist, an old type of character borrowed early by American writers from their English brethren. Nathaniel Hawthorne's Aylmer in "The Birthmark" (1846), Rappaccini in "Rappaccini's Daughter" (1844), even old Roger Chillingworth of *The Scarlet Letter* (1850) are early variations of the mad scientist.

In *Player Piano* (1952) by Kurt Vonnegut, Jr., an anti-Utopian vision of the future, the United States has become a society in which nearly all work has been taken over by machines that are run by a few engineers and managers. The mass of people are relegated to the terrible fate of "leisure," with housewives having little to do in their automated homes and their men having the limited choices of serving in the army, of joining a kind of WPA for road repairs, or of owning a small business like a barbership or a bar. In this novel the Tinker is many men but lives away from the machines and works in the road repair gang. When an engineer's car breaks down, he is unable to fix it, but the men in the road repair gang are touchingly eager and very adept at repair.

> "Well," said Paul [the engineer], "guess I'd better call somebody to come and get it. Probably take a week to order a new gasket."
>
> "Five minutes," said the tall man. He took off his hat and, with an expression of satisfaction, ripped out the sweatband. He took a penknife from his pocket, laid the cap of the fuel pump over the sweatband, and cut out a leather disk just the right size. Then he cut out the disk's center, dropped the new gasket in place, and put the pump back together. The others watched him

eagerly, handed him tools, or offered to hand him tools, and tried
to get into the operation wherever they could. One man scraped
the green and white crystals from a battery connection. Another
went around tightening the valve caps on the tires.

"Now try her!" said the tall man.

Paul stepped on the starter, the motor caught, roared fast and
slow without a miss as he pumped the accelerator. He looked up
to see the profound satisfaction, the uplift of creativity, in the
faces of [the road repair men].[13]

The Tinker is, in this novel, a man who is common among the American people, who delights in tinkering, who is handy with tools, and who
can express his creativity in this way. Paul, a member of the engineer-
manager contingent, admires the Tinker and, in fact, within the confines
of a modern factory, has managed to preserve fairly intact Building 58,
"the original machine shop set up by Edison in 1886" (p. 6).

It soothed him [Paul] to look up at the wooden rafters, uneven
with ancient adze marks beneath flaking calcimine, and at the
dull walls of brick soft enough for men—God knows how long
ago—to carve their initials in: "KTM," "DG," "GP," "BDH,"
"HB," "NNS." Paul imagined for a moment—as he often imagined on visits to Building 58—that he was Edison, standing on
the threshold of a solitary brick building on the banks of the Iro-
quois, with the upstate winter slashing through the broomcorn
outside. The rafters still bore the marks of what Edison had done
with the lonely brick barn: bolt holes show where overhead shafts
had once carried power to a forest of belts, and the wood-block
floor was black with the oil and scarred by the feet of the crude
machines the belts had spun. (p. 6–7)

Filled with nostalgia for the Heroic Age of Tinkering, Paul soon becomes a rebel and joins both fellow engineers and the people in an
unsuccessful rebellion.

Vonnegut's satire is directed against the managers, who represent a
kind of Babbitt boosterism; against the engineers, one of whom is a Tinker and creates a machine to replace himself and thus finds himself out
of a job; and even against the people, many of whom are incipient and
potential Tinkers, who have created the technological foundation which,
ironically, developed into the static, nightmare society America has be-

come. The Tinker, however, still invests his inventions with humanity and is able to take creative satisfaction in his work.

Vonnegut's *Player Piano* is also notable for the appearance of a nearly anthropomorphic computer as a kind of character —a forerunner of many other such human-computers in American literature. EPICAC XIV is a super computer situated in the Carlsbad Caverns. EPICAC I had been developed during World War II to help with military operations and, through its various versions, has become, as described by the president of the United States, Jonathan Lynn, "the greatest individual in history[:] . . . the wisest man that had ever lived was to EPICAC XIV as a worm was to that wisest man" (p. 104). Although the American engineers agree with the words of President Lynn, the Shah of Bratpuhr, a visitor from a "less civilized" country, quickly recognizes EPICAC XIV as a "false god" when the computer cannot answer the shah's riddle. In this relatively early anthropomorphic form, the computer proves no match for a "primitive" like the shah, although it can still confound the engineers. Since 1952, when Vonnegut's novel appeared, the utilitarian yet destructive aspects of the computer have continued to be explored in science fiction novels and in cinema. In fiction, it is John Barth's Giles of *Giles Goat-Boy* (1966) who could finally confound the computer WESCAC. The sophisticated computer is an example of technology that has escaped the control of the Tinker.

Ellison's Invisible Man, although "in the great American tradition of tinkers," is not finally an inventor of gadgets, although he creatively designs his underground room with 1,369 electric lights as a way of finding truth ("The truth is the light and light is the truth") and as a way of establishing visibility ("Light confirms my reality, gives birth to my form"[14]). Invisible Man is speaking symbolically when, early in the novel, he proclaims his allegiance to Edison and Franklin. Only at the conclusion of the book does the reader understand what the Tinker represents for Ellison's Invisible Man. Throughout the course of the story, Invisible Man has had to escape from corrupt corporate capitalism, from suffocating communism, from selfish unionism, from social and racist paternalism, from racial prejudice and militancy, from insanity, and from many other evils in order to proclaim and affirm the meaning of the Tinker.

> Now I know men are different and that all life is divided and that only in division is there true health. Hence again I have

stayed in my hole, because up above there's an increasing passion
to make all men conform to a pattern. . . .

Whence all this passion toward conformity anyway?—diversity
is the word. Let man keep his many parts and you'll have no
tyrant states.[15]

"I yam what I yam,"[16] the black man from the South has learned to say.
It is the creative individualism of the Tinker, an individualism allowed
by the diversity of an America that produced Edison and Franklin, both
of them businessmen and both of them in "the great tradition of American tinkers."

CHAPTER 12

"Hello, Babies. Welcome to Earth"

The children of rich American capitalists tended to suffer in pre–World War II novels, as we have seen. Many, such as Daisy and Tom Buchanan in *The Great Gatsby*, are corrupted by the wealth. Others, such as the children of Theodore Dreiser's Frank Cowperwood in *The Financier*, are simply ignored as their fathers pursue money. Children of the newly rich, such as the Marshall children of Henry Blake Fuller's *With the Procession*, must scramble to gain acceptance from the children of the older families of wealth. One type of rich man's child, for example, Conrad Dryfoos of William Dean Howells's *A Hazard of New Fortunes*, acquires a missionary conscience and dies a martyr attempting to help downtrodden workers.

In the post–World War II period, several of these stereotypes survive, but with crucial shifts in perspective. Saul Bellow's *Henderson the Rain King* (1959) not only inherited three million dollars after taxes but is even descended from an old, cultured, and public-spirited family among whom are a secretary of state, ambassadors to England and France, and a "famous scholar," Henderson's own father. A war veteran and a successful businessman in his own right, Henderson is nevertheless miserable: one marriage with five children ends in divorce; his second marriage, with twin sons, is also failing as the book opens, with Henderson threatening to commit suicide. By reversing the American's traditional westward course, Henderson travels east to darkest Africa to find man's primitive roots, to become a Rain King, to restore myth to his Waste Land. He returns—via New Found Land—with a lion cub and, we can only presume, a way to deal with his world of money and culture—not to mention his marriage. Although *Henderson the Rain*

King is perhaps Bellow's least satisfying novel because of its fairy-tale conclusion, Bellow has rather convincingly broken the pattern of the doomed children of the rich. Henderson has a chance to survive, and he will be able to return to his family's money and traditions with a new spiritual health.

Henderson's pilgrimage to Africa is, in a sense, a later version of Babbitt's eastward trip from the Middle West to the Maine woods. However, Babbitt found only a fishing guide who, if given enough capital, would open a shoe repair store. Henderson finds Romilayu, an African noble savage. Moreover, the rich boys who can find honor and perhaps health had already appeared as minor characters in a number of other post–World War II novels. In Ellison's *Invisible Man* (1952), for example, the son of a wealthy white manufacturer reveals the duplicity of a college educator to Invisible Man—a duplicity which is particularly painful and damaging to the young black from the South. Young Mr. Emerson breaks all the rules in revealing the duplicity of the supposed benefactor to Invisible Man because, as Emerson admits, "I'm incapable of such cynicism." As Invisible Man leaves the office, young Mr. Emerson "stammered guiltily,"

> "Please, I must ask you never to mention this conversation to anyone."
> "No," he [Invisible Man] said.
> "I wouldn't mind, but my father would consider my revelation the most extreme treason. . . . You're free of him now. I'm still his prisoner. You have been freed, don't you understand? I've still my battle." He seemed near tears.[1]

Young Mr. Emerson demonstrates a sense of honor and honesty, although he is not yet "healthy."

Popular post–World War II literature had also expressed this tendency. In John P. Marquand's *Point of No Return* (1949), neither the son of wealthy parents, Tony Burton, nor Charles Gray, the son of a cultured and once wealthy family, is depicted as a corrupting or corrupted stereotype or as a starry-eyed rebel. Burton is an honest and successful banker whose reading is limited to the novels of Richard Harding Davis, but he is described as "both typical and exceptional—a rich man's son with inherited ability and with ambition that had somehow not been dulled by his having always been presented with what he had wanted." He is a man who is beginning to understand that words have "shades of meaning." [2] Charles Gray is struggling to become vice president of Burton's bank but hates the "obsequiousness" and the conformity involved in gaining the position. A bit of a rebel, he does gain the position eventually. [3] The 1970s opened with Erich Segal's *Love Story*, an amazingly popular romance in which old-money Oliver Barrett IV gives up his family milling inheritance for a wage earner's daughter, Jennifer Cavilleri, an American of Italian descent who is smart and poor. The couple have to work to put Oliver through law school, but they are happy. Oliver wins a job in a prestigious New York law firm, and they call themselves *nouveau riche*. Such happiness cannot last, of course, and Jenny dies of leukemia.

Clearly, American writers were depicting the children of the rich in different ways, with perhaps a balanced and more generous view. In fact, these children are just children with problems like any other children, although money and family pride may be their particular concerns. The writers seemed to be affirming that children had problems no matter who their parents were. Children of academics, such as Saul Bellow's protagonist in *Herzog* (1964), have little peace at home as their parents fight and separate, sleep with students and colleagues' wives, and generally create chaos in their lives. In Bernard Malamud's *A New Life* (1961), Sy Levin and his colleague's wife Pauline Gilley commit adultery, while Pauline's small children are left alone at night or in the daytime. The infant daughter of a kitchen gadget demonstrator, ex-high school basketball star Rabbit Angstrom in John Updike's *Rabbit, Run* (1960), drowns while being given a bath by her drunken mother. In *Midcentury* (1961), John Dos Passos depicted the children of union leaders joining a country club and aspiring to the best groups. And in 1969 Philip Roth made clear in *Portnoy's Complaint* that there were far worse kinds of parents to have than parents whose only qualifications were old or new money.

When John F. Kennedy became president in 1961, many old stereotypes were destroyed. The son of a "self-made" millionaire, Kennedy might have wasted his life in booze and polo, had he been a character in a pre-1945 novel. However, in a post-1945 novel, John O'Hara's *Ten North Frederick* (1955), which won the National Book Award in 1956, the aristocratic Joseph B. Chapin is a respected and honored man. Although he cannot be the lieutenant governor of Pennsylvania, as he had hoped, Chapin is nevertheless important enough that the governor attends his funeral. In his biography of John O'Hara, Matthew Bruccoli contends that O'Hara based Chapin's character upon that of Franklin Delano Roosevelt.[4] Despite Chapin's grace and legitimate financial success and the fact that "he had spent his life in a manner that did harm to the fewest possible people," he dies a slow alcoholic suicide; his son is an alcoholic; his wife Edith is emotionally estranged (both Joe and Edith had had brief affairs); and his daughter is divorced from her second husband after a hasty first marriage with a lower-class man and a subsequent abortion. O'Hara treats his characters with sympathy; Edith, for example, is admired by other people for her restraint at her husband's funeral. The rich have "class," as the local political boss comments.[5] Indeed, the futility of the Chapin family is not necessarily the result of their wealth and social class, but rather the result of the terrible world that O'Hara has chosen to depict. The "common" people suffer too.

In short, the attitude of the American writer toward the children of the rich capitalist in large part altered; the fate of the children was not so inextricably and predictably involved with their parents' money or social attitudes. As Eliot Rosewater, the fictional son and heir of the wealthy Rosewater family in Kurt Vonnegut's novel *God Bless You, Mr. Rosewater or Pearls Before Swine* (1965), muses on a proper baptism for infants, he says,

> Hello, babies. Welcome to Earth. It's hot in the summer and cold in the winter. It's round and wet and crowded. At the outside, babies, you've got about a hundred years here. There's only one rule that I know of, babies—:
> "God damn it, you've got to be kind."[6]

Eliot Rosewater is the antihero of a novel that can be read simultaneously as a parody of all preceding antibusiness novels and as a critical commentary about the misguided ambitions of capitalists. The title and its subtitle *God Bless You, Mr. Rosewater or Pearls Before Swine* indicate the paradoxical nature of Vonnegut's book. Eliot Rosewater, whose name suggests both Eliot Roosevelt and T. S. Eliot, is by right of primogeniture the president of Rosewater Foundation, a philanthropic foundation established by Eliot's old-wealth family. Eliot chooses to distribute funds among the poor of Rosewater County, Indiana—a charitable act which, in the context of most anticapitalist novels, would be a laudable choice for the son of a wealthy man. However, the poor people are quite probably the "swine" of the subtitle (some critics suggest that the rich might also be the "swine"), and most are ignorant, greedy, and pitiful. As a parody of anticapitalist novels, Vonnegut's *God Bless You, Mr. Rosewater* is filled with exaggerated caricatures of the stereotypes American novelists had been creating for years. The book begins in this way: "A sum of money is a leading character in this tale about people, just as a sum of honey might properly be a leading character in a tale about bees" (p. 1). The novel ends with Eliot, tennis racket raised in a kind of benediction, urging the children in Rosewater County "to be fruitful and multiply" (p. 217).

Eliot traces the wasteland that has become post-1945 America to the politicians and the free-enterprise system. The Rosewater fortune was created during the Civil War by Noah Rosewater, Eliot's great grandfather.

> When the United States of America, which was meant to be a Utopia for all, was less than a century old, Noah Rosewater and a few men like him demonstrated the folly of the Founding Fathers in one respect: those sadly recent ancestors had not made it the law of the Utopia that the wealth of each citizen should be limited. This oversight was engendered by a weak-kneed sympathy for those who loved expensive things, and by the feeling that the continent was so vast and valuable, and the population so thin and enterprising, that no thief, no matter how fast he stole, could more than mildly inconvenience anyone.
>
> Noah and a few like him perceived that the continent was in fact finite, and that venal office-holders, legislators in particular, could be persuaded to toss up great hunks of it for grabs, and to toss them in such a way as to have them land where Noah and his kind were standing. (pp. 20–21)

Eliot's explanation, of course, contains several contradictions, not the least of which is that, although free enterprise can be traced to the foolishness of the Founding Fathers, legislative corruption is necessary for the system to become foul, for Noah to grab his piece of the continent. In fact, *God Bless You, Mr. Rosewater* has been termed an antigovernment novel rather than an antibusiness novel by Raymond M. Olderman.[7] Moreover, the vision of a Utopia must not be taken literally in any novel by Vonnegut. Like his *Player Piano*, *God Bless You, Mr. Rosewater* argues that there never can be a Utopia. In other passages of the novel, not only businessmen and legislators but also religious leaders and journalists are corruptible and corrupted. Greed is a universal quality except, of course, for Eliot Rosewater, who is trying to give the foundation's money away.

Eliot's own motives in this apparently unselfish and altruistic project are not entirely clear. To some extent, he feels guilty for his inherited wealth, but he is also dissatisfied with giving money to artists and museums. "You can safely ignore the arts and sciences. They never helped anybody" (p. 23). Moreover, Eliot has his own illusions about the poor he is trying to help. "He would argue that the people he was trying to help were the same sorts of people who, in generations past, had cleared the forests, drained the swamps, built the bridges, people whose sons formed the backbone of the infantry in time of war—and so on" (p. 69). However, as depicted in the novel and as described by Eliot's father, "The people who leaned on Eliot regularly were a lot weaker than that—and dumber, too. When it came time for their sons to go into the Armed Forces, for instance, the sons were generally rejected as being mentally, morally, and physically undesirable" (p. 69–70).

Finally, there is some doubt as to whether Eliot, who preaches love and kindness, is himself actually motivated by love. Eliot is cruel to his father and to his wife, Sylvia. In fact, he "had ruined the life and health of a woman [Sylvia] whose only fault had been to love him" (p. 183). Eliot is a neurotic and alcoholic who wallows in dirty clothes and dirty rooms. His sexual drive has been "short circuited" (p. 87) as he seeks Utopia, according to his psychiatrist. Clearly, however, Eliot is a more sympathetic character than his father, Senator Lister Rosewater, who is undoubtedly meant to suggest Senator Barry Goldwater. (*The Conscience of a Conservative* is mentioned in Chapter 10.) And yet, Lister Rosewater does love his son Eliot and Sylvia and represents what one critic, Peter J. Reed, in *Writers for the Seventies: Kurt Vonnegut*, describes as a "capitalist ethic." "The capitalistic father sees the free distribution of money and love as indiscriminate, devaluing and contrary to the ethic that both things should be deserved. The egalitarian son feels all men inherently merit their share of both, and regards the hoarding of wealth and the withholding of love from one's fellows as mutually supporting vices."[8] Throughout the novel, Senator Rosewater advocates "the Free Enterprise System, as conceived by the Founding Fathers" and holds in contempt "the do-gooders, who thought people shouldn't ever have to struggle for anything" (p. 36).

Thus, the novel is complex. At one point, Eliot calls himself Hamlet, and the reader understands that Eliot will break rules in order to avenge what he feels is an injustice. However, at the same time, the reader is reminded of the tragic conclusion of *Hamlet*, with its many dead, including Hamlet himself. In short, the child of the capitalist in Vonnegut's novel resembles young Conrad Dryfoos of William Dean Howells's *A Hazard of New Fortunes*, but the purity of his motives is clouded and the capitalist father is not wholly evil.

Eliot's kind of philanthropy is a personal and individual act. As a single human being, he attempts to love all people equally, simply because they are human. He leaves his money to the children of Rosewater County by claiming that he is their father. Other children in post-1945 works become involved in larger social movements, but these children do not necessarily have capitalistic parents.

In Charles Gordone's *No Place to Be Somebody: A Black-Black Comedy* (1969), Mary Bolton, whose father has been the lawyer for a white Italian Mafia-like mob leader, is active in the civil rights movement. Johnny Williams, a young black, convinces her that the mob is racially discriminating against him by attempting to force him out of his legitimate business as the owner of a small bar. Actually, Johnny hopes to take over mob leadership in the territory, to create a "black Mafia." Mary, who believes Johnny's lie and thinks that he loves her, steals her father's files, which contain evidence enough to convict the white Mafia leader of murder. For her efforts, Mary is called a "stupid, naive little bitch." As a friend of Johnny explains to Mary, "What did you do it for, Mary? For love? Sheee! He hates you, you bitch. Hates everything you stand for. Nice little suffering white girl."[9] Like the earlier Mildred Douglas of Eugene O'Neill's *The Hairy Ape* (1922), Mary Bolton is a misguided and naive reformer, even though she does not come from an identifiably capitalistic background.

The most complex reformer daughter of a capitalist created by an American writer since 1945 is Linda Snopes, who is conceived and born in *The Hamlet* (1940), but who reaches middle age in the final two novels of William Faulkner's trilogy, *The Town* (1957) and *The Mansion* (1959). Linda bears the name Snopes, a label which in itself has become, through Faulkner's novels, representative of all the cumulative evils of selfish and acquisitive capitalism: Snopesism. Linda's stepfather is Flem Snopes, the leader of a large clan of Southern white trash, who outmaneuvers members of the old Southern aristocracy to become a bank president and the most prominent citizen of Jefferson in Faulkner's fictional Yoknapatawpha County, Mississippi.

Flem is generally recognized as a symbol of "finance-capitalism"—a man who is interested in manipulating money (and, hence, manipulating and destroying people). As the narrator notes during Flem's funeral, which occurs in the final pages of *The Mansion*, Flem "had no auspices either: fraternal, civic, nor military: only finance; not an economy—cotton or cattle or anything else which Yoknapatawpha County and Mississippi were established on and kept running by, but belonging simply to Money." [10] Like John Dos Passos's Judge Lewin of *Midcentury* but on a smaller, local scale, Flem inhabits the world of "pure finance." With no sense of honor or tradition, with no pretense even to culture, Flem destroys not just the families of old Southern aristocracy, but also "old folk society," as Cleanth Brooks noted. [11]

Linda's mother is Eula Varner Snopes, a sort of twentieth-century Earth Goddess from the small town of Frenchmen's Bend, near Jefferson. Eula is the daughter of Will Varner, the relatively wealthy owner of most of the land around Frenchmen's Bend. However, Varner never moves to town and has no social pretensions, although he is depicted in *The Mansion* as a political power in the area. As a girl and woman, Eula has an amazing and unconscious sexual appeal for all men; in the course of the trilogy, she is referred to as Helen of Troy, Venus, Semiramis, Judith, Lilith, Francesca, and Isolde. When, in *The Hamlet*, she leaves the community for a time, the land suffers a drought. Courted by many, Eula eventually becomes pregnant by Hoake McCarron, a "unique big buck," a "wild stag," who is Linda's father and an appropriate mate for Eula/Helen of Troy. [12] Hoake is not one of the country boys, however, but the well-educated son of a wealthy widow. After impregnating Eula in *The Hamlet*, he runs off and appears only briefly again at Linda's wedding in *The Mansion*.

Will Varner marries his pregnant daughter to his store assistant, the sexually impotent Flem Snopes. Having married the boss's daughter, Flem begins his ascent to the financial heights of Jefferson, Mississippi. In order to hide the fact that Eula is already pregnant, Flem and Eula take an extended honeymoon in Texas, where Linda is born. With an Earth Goddess for a mother and a sexually impotent and emotionally frigid capitalist for a stepfather, Linda grows to maturity.

When Linda is nineteen, Eula commits suicide, in part because Flem threatens to expose her adultery with the then president of the bank, old-family Manfred de Spain, and in part because she hoped to free Linda from Flem's control. With her mother's death, Linda is free enough from Flem's control to travel to Greenwich Village. The time is the 1930s, and Linda soon marries a communist, Jewish sculptor Barton Kohl. After Linda joins the communists, the Kohls fight in the Spanish Civil War, where Kohl loses his life and Linda, her hearing. Linda returns home to Jefferson—now a widow and a wounded war veteran—but with energy to burn for social reforming. However, the only two communists she can find in Jefferson are two immigrant Finns who are puzzled because the Jefferson proletariat has not joined them and does not even realize that it is a proletariat. Unable to establish a cell with the Finns, Linda tries to help the Negroes by initiating a project in their schools—a project which the Negroes themselves do not want. Her reforming ambitions are deflected when World War II breaks out, and she becomes a riveter in the Pascagoula shipyards. After the war, she returns to Jefferson, where she finds that even the two Finnish communists have become capitalists. By an elaborate plan, Linda precipitates Flem's murder, at the hands of Cousin Mink Snopes—she even helps Mink escape from the mansion after the murder—and after the funeral drives north in her new British Jaguar, as the trilogy ends.

Linda was bred of at least moderately wealthy parents, the natural daughter of Hoake McCarron and the granddaughter of Will Varner, a landowner of the Southern yeoman class. Varner's daughter is the wife of Flem Snopes, a finance capitalist. That Linda becomes a communist under such circumstances is not unusual in the course of American literature. However, she is not a naive reformer like Mildred Douglas or Mary Bolton. Faulkner does not simply end the story when her ideology is rendered ineffective, nor does he force her to die, as Howells did Conrad Dryfoos in *A Hazard of New Fortunes*. Faulkner allows her to reach middle age and lets the reader watch her plan and manipulate Flem's murder, probably to avenge her mother's suicide. Linda the communist then escapes in her new Jaguar. She is really not far up the ladder from Flem.

The most admirable or sympathetic characters who continue throughout the trilogy are Linda's mother, Eula, and V. K. Ratliff, the sewing machine salesman and the only person who gets the better of Flem in a financial transaction. (Flem later wins back his money and then some, however.) Eula would be an allegorical character—a fertility goddess—had she not had the integrity to commit suicide in order to free Linda from Flem's control. This admirable Eula is the daughter of the relatively wealthy landowner, Will Varner.

Ratliff, a kind of Yankee Peddler, is a traveling salesman who makes a modest living and who, by investing in other businesses, has become a small, private capitalist. The descendant of a Russian immigrant— V. K. stands for Vladimir Kyriltch—he is a contrast to Linda, the card-carrying American communist. Ratliff is shrewd and intelligent, as Cleanth Brooks has noted, "a spokesman for the traditional society," [13] the "most nearly trustworthy observer" and narrator of the novels. "Ratliff is a great man, a great student of humanity," Linda Welshimer Wagner observed. [14] Born in Frenchmen's Bend but traveling throughout the area, he is wise to the ways of both city and country folk. It is Ratliff who realizes what Linda is up to as she plans Flem's murder and who warns Lawyer Gavin Stevens, a gullible romantic who unwittingly aids Linda.

Ultimately, in this complex trilogy, the children of the rich are not necessarily doomed to corruption or communism. Flem, the finance capitalist, is the most corrupt of the characters, and he comes from white trash. Eula and V. K. are admirable and come from yeoman stock. Jason Compson, who represents the last remnant of an old aristocratic family, approaches the level of Flem in his financial manipulations but finally cannot outsmart Flem. In short, although family is important, especially in the Southern society Faulkner depicts, the child of wealthy parents is not doomed simply because of his parents' financial status. He or she must finally find his own way.

Although Joyce Carol Oates's 1969 novel *them* is primarily concerned with the Wendall family, who are urban poor whites, it depicts a wealthy young woman, Nadine Greene, who becomes the mistress of Jules Wendall. It would have been only too easy for Oates to rely on the traditional stereotype to create Nadine's character. However, Nadine's parents are "good" and she loves them. Nadine and Jules run off together and plan for Jules to make a million dollars in the Southwest; Nadine has confidence in Jules "because there are so many stupid people I know who are rich." [15] Their journey west ends abruptly as Jules becomes sick and Nadine deserts him. Nadine and Jules are drawn together "violently"; they share a "wildness," which, five years later, Nadine's husband—a corporate tax lawyer—cannot satisfy. Nadine is, in fact, verging on insanity, and when their affair resumes, she eventually tries to kill Jules. Yet Jules, who is certainly a sympathetic character in the context of the novel, always hopes to be reunited with Nadine. In the world of *them*, a novel that won the National Book

Award in 1970, children and adults suffer and go mad, no matter what their economic status.

The post-1945 novelists have generally depicted a world in which children have little chance for happiness, whether their mothers are Eula Varner Snopes, Mrs. Portnoy, or Loretta Wendall, or their fathers, Senator Lister Rosewater, Lawyer Bolton, Moses Herzog, or Rabbit Angstrom. Sylvia Plath proclaimed in "Daddy" (1962) to her academic father:

> You do not do, you do not do
> Any more, black shoe
> In which I have lived like a foot
> For thirty years, poor and white,
> Barely daring to breathe or Achoo.[16]

And Vonnegut's fictional Eliot Rosewater welcomed Babies to Earth with the encomium, " 'God damn it, you've got to be kind.' "

CHAPTER 13

The Businessman as Hero

Not many heroes of any kind have appeared in post–World War II American literature, heroes, that is, of the traditional sort. "Antihero," "novel of the absurd," "black comedy" are all terms used to describe serious novels written since 1945. No person, fictional or real, has been able to escape the novelist's or biographer's denigrating pen. Americans have learned that Camelot's Jack Kennedy kept track of his sexual encounters and that the apparently wise and gentle poet Robert Frost was a vicious critic and a jealous man; Americans have read in their fiction that all leaders are weak and vain—not just men and women from business, but also those from government, the unions, the ministry, academia, yes, even the novelists and poets themselves, such as Charles Citrine and Von Humboldt Fleisher in Saul Bellow's *Humboldt's Gift* (1975).[1]

The debunking of heroes had been occurring for some time, and, although E. E. Cummings declared in 1923 that "Buffalo Bill's / defunct," the writers of the post-1945 period extended and intensified the despair. In recent years, academics have organized interdisciplinary symposia to examine whether or not there are any heroes left and, if not, whatever happened to them. In the fall of 1976, during a two-and-a-half-day symposium at the University of Illinois at Urbana-Champaign, faculty and students heard Florence Howe, a professor and also president of the Feminist Press, describe the communist proletarian feminist as hero; they watched Joshua Taylor of the Smithsonian Institution delineate the traditional and historical depiction of the American hero but with no recent reference; and they listened to Thomas Murphy, chairman of the board of General Motors, acknowledge with relief that the bad old days of business "heroes" such as Vanderbilt are over and then plead for a new cooperation of business and academia because of their common problems, such as government control, and because of the need for sharing talent.

And yet no one mentioned that Ken Kesey had celebrated the small businessman in *Sometimes a Great Notion* in 1964. The novel itself has generally been viewed as too "romantic," with Hank Stamper too close to the nineteenth-century American hero of rugged individualism like Natty Bumppo of James Fenimore Cooper's Leather-Stocking Tales. Moreover, Stamper was a rural hero at a time when most people lived in the cities. Besides all that, Kesey's novel alienated both the academics, because of the depiction of Lee, and the liberal critics, because of his depiction of union leaders and members.

Kesey had, however, asserted that, in the face of unionism, academia, and big business, perhaps it was only the small, private businessman who could display courage and endurance. Kesey's 1964 novel was followed in the next thirteen years by three novels, written by recognizably important contemporary authors, all of which feature small businessmen or an entrepreneur as the central and most sympathetic character: Stanley Elkin's *A Bad Man* (1967) and *The Franchiser* (1976) and James Dickey's *Deliverance* (1970). Each novel treats the small businessman or entrepreneur in a different way. In fact, so different are these novels and their businessmen/heroes that I will divide this chapter into two sections.

"A Man of Franchise, a True Democrat"

Elkin's *A Bad Man* and *The Franchiser* share two themes. The first is that the salesman (in *A Bad Man*, the capitalist/salesman who owns a department store) and the franchiser of such businesses as a Howard Johnson's or a Fred Astaire Dance Studio are "democrats."[2] Both Leo Feldman of *A Bad Man* and Ben Flesh of *The Franchiser* attempt to help people buy what they want; they make available to people whatever they might need, from a green hat to Hallmark greeting cards. As Ben Flesh reflects, he wants to satisfy "convenience necessity and the universalized appetite" (p. 262). Isidore Feldman, Leo's father and a Jewish Yankee Peddler who is "eccentric," taught Leo as a boy that " 'It's no joke, it costs to live. Consumers, we're consumers. Hence our mortality. I consume, therefore I am.' " [3] The implications of Isidore's statements lie beyond the commercial metaphor. Man is a consumer, not just of McDonald's hamburgers, but also of air and water; the process of living is necessarily one of consuming. The expense is not just in terms of money, but in terms of man's very existence; man consumes so that he may live. When man consumes no more, he dies. "I consume, therefore I am." The expense and price are not only the potential deprivation of others, but also one's necessary "selfishness" (for want of a better word). The salesman and the franchiser offer their services to customers equally and democratically, just as Henry Ford had hoped to make his Model T available to all Americans.

The results of the efforts of both Feldman and Flesh are not always beneficial. In democratizing goods, in supporting franchises, Flesh is well aware that he risks making "Bar Harbor, Maine, look like Chicago, . . . quell[ing] distinction, obliterat[ing] differences, . . . would common-denominate until Americans recognize that it was America everywhere" (p. 164). Moreover, Flesh believes that people are "dumb"—and so are "businessmen." Describing American culture, Flesh observes,

> "We read shapes. The culture is preliterate. . . ."
> "It's tactile, a blind man's culture. . . . It's never been taken for granted that anyone can *read*! . . .
> "Why bulbs look like pears and how the world got its curly tail. Nobody. Nobody ever. Nobody with money invested ever took it for granted that a single mother's son of us could read. They think we're so *dumb*. We *are* so dumb. And they are, too. So we get these *symbols*. The mustard jar a symbol and the candy bar a symbol, too. We live with molds, castings, with paradigms and modalities. With recognizable shapes. With—*oh, God*—trademarks like the polestar. I could go it alone in an Estonian supermarket. We live in Plato's sky!" (pp. 195–96)

In *A Bad Man*, Leo Feldman also discovers that his attempts to fill customers' orders has led to strange dealings; he arranges for abortions, for prostitutes and pimps, for drugs, and for gay companions, even for a gun. It is for these illegal dealings that he lands in jail for a year—a "bad man," or, as his name suggests, a "felled man." Feldman, the wealthy owner of a department store, justifies himself in this way: " 'All right. I filled needs. Like a pharmacist doing prescriptions. Did you ever know anyone like me? A woman needed an abortion, I found a doctor. A couple needed a kid, I found a bastard. A punk a fix, I found a pusher. I was in research'" (pp. 16–17). And yet, as the novel continues, the reader discovers that there are men far worse than the "bad man" Feldman.

The "democrat"—salesman and franchiser—is a "realist," and reality is for him each person and his never-ending and always various needs. When Flesh remarks that "We live in Plato's sky," he is affirming that our "preliterate" culture based on shape and form is reality. Plato had adapted a word that literally meant "form" or "shape" (the Greek word $\iota\delta\acute{\epsilon}\alpha$) to describe the Essences which eternally exist in the sky or heaven and of which our present world is only a shadow. The Greek root $\iota\delta$ means "to see." Plato placed these ultimate Essences, literally "forms," far away from earth and man, who can view reality only as if he were chained in a cave and can see only shadows of others moving past. However, Elkin's Flesh affirms that reality is here and now. Flesh would agree with Plato that man is symbol-dominated and shape-oriented, but Flesh cannot believe that reality exists in Essences far away from man.

Elkin's depiction of reality is not very attractive, and in fact the doom of sex-driven men and pill-popping women, consumers all, might remind the reader of that dark vision of the world held by the early Puritans, who viewed man as eternally sinful, as granted only a partial atonement through Christ's sacrifice. For the Puritans, capitalism was God's way for fallen man. However, for Ben Flesh and for Leo Feldman, there is no Christ and not even partial atonement in this reality of Plato's sky. Elkin does offer, however, some partial resolutions for those of us who must live in Plato's sky. Certainly, the role of the franchiser and salesman— the "democrat"—is depicted in both novels as sympathetic and, in *A Bad Man*, even heroic. The quality of his heroism is the second theme these two novels share.

Leo Feldman is both a "bad man" and a "felled man." Before he goes to prison, he has been cruel to his wife and occasionally intimidating to his son. He has lied and cheated, but he has not stolen. He admits that he has "contributed to the world's gloom" (p. 13). The son of a Yankee Peddler, who also embodies the traditional image of the Wandering Jew, Feldman is a financially successful self-made man, a community leader, whose family lives in comfortable suburbia. When he enters prison, however, he is labeled a "bad man" not by society outside the prison, but by the warden and the prisoners themselves. As the novel progresses, it becomes clear that the warden and the system he creates represent a greater evil than does the "democratic" and somewhat anarchic "bad man" Feldman.

Warden Fisher, "a fisher of bad men," is the dictator of a system that attempts to reduce men to conformity and total state control. The jail is a system of confusing rules and regulations, "a place of vicious, plodding *sequiturs*, though not even the oldest lifers understood it, not even the warden" (p. 58). A system of imposed order, the jail teaches the men to acquiesce to rules that are said to represent order and civilization. Feldman is immediately marked as a "bad man" because of his different, individually tailored prison uniform. He and the other "bad men" are persecuted and spied upon, as the warden encourages the men to spy on each other.

Feldman is sent to solitary confinement and then, symbolically, spends a night sleeping in the electric chair. During these periods, he examines his past life and acknowledges his own weaknesses, yet he does not lose his indomitable individuality and energy. He never fully complies with the system and thus, to the warden and the prisoners, he remains a "bad man."

Feldman has embedded near his heart a homunculus, the now rock-hard remains of what was once his twin brother. This bit of otherness inside of him, so close to his heart, is dangerous: a blow to Feldman's chest could kill him. On the other hand, the homunculus also symbolizes both a "fossilized potential" in Feldman, as well as the sense of otherness in Feldman—an otherness which springs from his own sense of individuality and his willingness to value individuality in others. In this novel, evil comes not from individuality, not even from greed—the traditional sin of salesmen and consumers. "Nothing could last forever, not even greed," says Feldman (p. 132). In *A Bad Man*, evil comes from controlling others, from a system like Warden Fisher's with its rules, its conformity, its guilt, its spying, and its viciousness. Warden Fisher's jail, an agency of the government, is most obviously representative of a totalitarian state, with Feldman a kind of gulag bad man. At one point in the novel, however, the prison is also associated with big corporations.

In the end, just before Feldman is to be released from jail, the prisoners and the warden try him in a kangaroo court, through most of which Feldman sleeps. Warden Fisher and the men have been unable to break Feldman, to make him pliable; thus, he must be purged. The facts of Feldman's life are revealed, and he admits that he has made errors.

However, as the novel ends, he is found guilty of being a "bad man" and the prisoners begin to beat him—undoubtedly to beat him to death because of the homunculus. In a startling conclusion, however, Feldman the salesman is given the final words of the novel.

> "Why, I'm innocent," he thought. All along, the more they had talked, the more they had made their case, pushing him closer and closer to this last closed corner of their justice, the less guilt he had felt. He wasn't guilty. He was not. He was no bad man. How I love my life, he thought. How I cherish it. It is the single holiness. My icicle winter snots like the relics of saints. How pious I am, how blessed. I accept wars, history, the deaths of the past, other people's poverties and losses. Their casualties and bad dreams I write off. . . .
>
> Why, I *am* innocent, he thought, even as they beat him. And indeed, he felt so. (p. 336)

Feldman does not just happen to be a businessman/salesman. His character, as well as his crime, is interrelated with his profession as a businessman. As in *Sometimes a Great Notion*, only a small businessman could have the character and strength to maintain his sense of individuality against a totalitarian system such as Warden Fisher's. In *A Bad Man*, the salesman-businessman, despite his faults, is dynamic ("setting other things in motion"—p. 143), democratic, and life-affirming.

In his later novel *The Franchiser*, Elkin emphasizes the vitality of Ben Flesh—the dynamic aspect suggested, but not developed, in *A Bad Man*. Flesh has been allowed the use of his wealthy godfather's money for his various franchises, and the world of business offers him a veritable garden of variety and marvels: "inheritance and self-creation were not the only alternatives in the busy world of finance, . . . there were all sorts of success stories, qualititative distinctions, . . . the world was a fairyland still" (p. 19). Admitting that he doesn't understand money, Flesh crisscrosses the United States in his pale-blue Cadillac practicing his "shuttle finance" in the middle of a recession. Flesh is not involved in "high finance," which he describes as a kind of abstract capitalism, "some avatar of asset and credit and reserve and parity, all the complicated solvency of diversification and portfolio" (pp. 259–60). Flesh is thus the entrepreneur/franchiser on a limited scale, a Yankee Peddler of the 1970s who has found a means of pursuing individual business interests within the world of large corporations. On the periphery of the corporate Howard Johnson's or McDonald's, he is nevertheless able to remain a comparatively small businessman, far from corporate demands and the problems of high finance.

For Flesh, the world is a wonderful place, a land of infinite possibilities, and, of all the many kinds of people depicted in the novel, it is the franchiser who is able to cooperate with this miracle —the world. His response to the energy crisis is this. " 'There isn't enough [energy] in the world to run the world. There *never* was. How could there be? The world is a miracle, history's and the universe's long shot. It runs uphill. It's a miracle. Drive up and down in it as I do. Look close at it. See its moving parts, its cranes and car parks and theater districts. It can't be. It could never have happened. It's a miracle. I see it but I don't believe it' " (p. 257). Overwhelmed and fascinated by the myriad variety of the world, Flesh wants to contribute to this miracle. With the country in a recession, he wonders where the money will come from for new churches and schools, and he concludes, " 'Though it may be a franchiser, I think, who'll save us. Kiss off the neighborhood grocers and corner druggists and little shoemakers. A franchiser. Yes. Speaking some Esperanto of simple need, answering appetite with convenience food. Some Howard Johnson yet to be' " (p. 258).

Suffering from multiple sclerosis, Flesh continues to establish his franchises even as he knows that within weeks he will be confined to a wheelchair. Like Feldman, Flesh too affirms life. He too wants to "set other things in motion." He faces the end of his life with ecstasy.

> And ah, he thought, euphorically, ecstatically, this privileged man who could have been a vegetable or mineral instead of an animal, and a lower animal instead of a higher, who could have been a pencil or a dot on a die, who could have been a stitch in a glove or change in someone's pocket, or a lost dollar nobody found, who could have been stillborn or less sentient than sand, or the chemical flash of somebody else's fear, ahh. Ahh! (p. 342)

Of all our authors, Elkin has perhaps wrestled most directly with the problems of capitalism and the businessman. In his creation of the salesman and the entrepreneur, he recognizes that they are fallible people: they are both Flesh and Feldman. Moreover, free enterprise, as depicted in these novels, can have dangerous side effects: the self-gluttony of consumers, for example, and a tendency to standardize and homogenize. On the other hand, the businessmen—Flesh and Feldman—are strong individuals who can resist totalitarian control. However, they are not such isolated individuals that they have no concern for community;

they are democrats who attempt to make the world's miracle available to all people. Moreover, they are dynamic; it is they who "set things in motion," who thus can destroy any tendency toward a static state. Finally, in a society filled with guilt and fear, the franchiser and the salesman can see the miracle of life and can value themselves and others as human beings.

"What I Had Undervalued"

Elkin juxtaposed his entrepreneur against the world of totalitarianism, but James Dickey sent his businessman in another direction—to the woods. Dickey's *Deliverance* (1970) is the only novel by a man who is widely respected for his poetry. At the presidential inauguration of Jimmy Carter, his fellow Georgian, Dickey recited a poem written for the occasion and thus assumed a kind of informal poet laureateship. *Deliverance* is set in Georgia; the hero is Ed Gentry, the owner and partner in a small advertising agency, who, bored with his business and home life, is attracted by the romance of adventure of a canoe trip down a river through largely unsettled woods. The core of the book concerns the canoe trip, the episode around which the popular movie version centered. Overlooked by the filmwriters, unfortunately, were the scenes which surround the trip down the river.

Deliverance is a novel with a frame; opening and closing scenes take place in civilization, with the central section the canoe trip. Ed has joined this pilgrimage to the woods at the urging of his friend Lewis, a survival and fitness buff, who has learned wilderness skills in case civilization should destroy itself in a nuclear holocaust. Along with Ed and Lewis are Drew, a sales supervisor for a soft-drink company, and Bobby, a mutual fund salesman. In the opening scenes, it is clear that Ed decides to go to the woods because he seeks "deliverance" from his modestly successful small advertising agency and from the boring "normalcy" of his happy home life. As Ed reflects before he leaves on the trip, "The feeling of inconsequence of whatever I would do, of anything I would pick up or think about or turn to see was at that moment being set in the very bone marrow. How does one get through this? I asked myself. By doing something that is at hand to be done was the best answer I could give; that and not saying anything about the feeling to anyone. It was the old, mortal, helpless, time terrified human feeling, just the same." [4]

What Ed seeks—deliverance in the form of some sort of nineteenth-century heroic and pioneering self-sufficiency in the wilderness—is also involved in the softly sexual model his agency is using in a panty ad for the Kitt'n Britches company. The Kitt'n Britches model has gray eyes (the color of the eyes of beautiful women in medieval poetry), but in her left eye is "a peculiar spot, a kind of tan slice," a "gold-glowing mote" (pp. 21, 22). It is this lovely aberration which comes to symbolize Ed's quest and escape from "the old mortal, helpless, time terrified human feeling" into the woods.

Henry David Thoreau had gone to the woods from 1845 to 1847 because he wished to live "deliberately." He wanted to participate in the communion of squirrels and to examine Walden Pond, which was, as he said, "earth's eye." Moreover, Thoreau hoped to reaffirm the "animal" side of his nature, to let the instinctive element of his personality emerge from under the shadow of his intellect which, he believed, had dominated his pre-Walden life. It wasn't "wilderness," but rather "wildness" that Thoreau sought in the woods.

> As I came home through the woods with my string of fish, trailing my pole, it being now quite dark, I caught a glimpse of a woodchuck stealing across my path, and felt a strange thrill of savage delight, and was strongly tempted to seize and devour him raw; not that I was hungry then, except for that wildness he represented. Once or twice, however, while I lived at the pond, I found myself ranging the woods, like a half-starved hound, with a strange abandonment, seeking some kind of venison which I might devour, and no morsel could have been too savage for me. The wildest scenes had become unaccountably familiar. I found in myself, and still find, an instinct toward a higher, or, as it is named, spiritual life, as do most men, and another toward a primitive rank and savage one, and I reverence them both. I love the wild not less than the good. The wildness and adventure that are in fishing still recommend it to me. I like to take rank hold on life and spend my day more as the animals do.[5]

It was this same kind of wildness—the wildness of fishing—that George Babbitt had sought in 1920 in the Maine woods. Thoreau did not devour the woodchuck raw, but he did find some sort of balance and left the woods having experienced his communion with the squirrels and a sympathetic intercourse with the pine needles. A discouraged Babbitt returned to Zenith, however, when his woodsman guide suggested that what he really wanted to do was open a shoe repair store in the nearest town.

Dickey's four canoeists manage to discover "a primitive rank and savage" society in the woods, but it is not one of woodchucks and squirrels. When Ed and Bobby are briefly separated from Lewis and Drew, they meet two woodsmen, one of whom rapes Bobby and the other prepares to force Ed to a deviate sexual act. Lewis, who has returned with Drew to check on Ed and Bobby, shoots and kills one hillbilly from ambush, and the other hillbilly runs away. The two perverted hillbillys represent the degradation of these uncivilized woodspeople in the "hook-wormy" Country of Nine-Fingered People (p. 52). Their savagery and sickness are further emphasized by the blind and retarded albino boy with whom Drew plays a banjo and guitar duet, by the chicken heads floating in the river, and by the night attack of an owl on Ed's tent.

After Lewis has killed the hillbilly, the four businessmen must decide what to do with the body. Drew, the most civilized of the men, wants to take the body to Aintry and report the crime to the police. Lewis, however, views the situation in another way.

> "We ought to do some hard decision-making before we let ourselves in for standing trial up in these hills. We don't know who this man is, but we know that he lived up here. He may be an escaped convict, or he may have a still, or he may be everybody in the country's father, or brother or cousin. I can almost guarantee you that he's got relatives all over the place. . . . And I'm goddamned if I want to come back up here for shooting this guy in the back, with a jury made up of his cousins and brothers, maybe his mother and father too, for all I know." (pp. 123–24)

Bobby does not want the sodomy exposed in a public trial, and Ed is willing to go along with Lewis. So the hillbilly's body is buried, and the men set out again down the river.

In the course of their journey, Drew is killed, quite probably by a bullet from the second hillbilly's gun; Lewis's leg is shattered when the canoe crashes in the rapids; and, although Ed proves himself a "man," it is the kind of "primitive rank and savage" manhood of which he wants no part ever again. Drew's death is explained as an accident to the Aintry police, Lewis recovers, and the three men return to their lives in the city, but with a change. Their deliverance was indeed from boredom, but it was not a deliverance into a primitive, natural heroism; rather, their deliverance was release from such a romantic quest in "the land of impossibility" (p. 277) and into a new appreciation for their positions of moderately successful businessmen and family men. When Ed returns, he is happy to be with his wife who is "what I had undervalued" and he discovers renewed interest and creativity in his work.

That James Dickey would choose as his protagonist that most infamous of business villains, the advertising executive, indicates his conscious opposition to previous and contemporary denigrations of such a character. Moreover, Ed's discovery of his own primitive and savage instincts (animal/man analogies abound in the novel) suggests that civilized values and customs may be easily and quickly destroyed, but that such values are the most human, sane, and ultimately satisfying. When Ed returns from the trip down the river, he rehires an employee he had previously fired for indolence; George Holley, who considered himself a "real artist," had worked for Ed only to be able to support himself for serious painting. When Ed returns from the river and rehires Holley, he himself attempts to form collages that are "full of sinuous [river] forms threading among the headlines of war and student strikes" (p. 276), as a way, the reader can suppose, of suggesting the primitive and savage side of man that emerges even in "civilization." In short, the businessman can be moral, conscientious, generous, and creative.

The river, which runs through Ed's collages, is destroyed by a dam soon after the weekend adventure. Although the hillbillys who lived along the river were primitive and "nine-fingered," the river itself represents a kind of "primal energy." When Ed leaves Aintry to return home, he stops briefly by the river and "stood next to the water for the last time. I stooped and drank from the river" (p. 267). Later, Ed realizes, "The river and everything I remembered about it became a possession to me, a personal, private possession, as nothing else in my life ever had. Now it ran nowhere but in my head, but it ran as though immortally. I could feel it—I can feel it—on different places on my body. It pleases me in some curious way that the river does not exist, and that I have it. In me it still is, and will be until I die, green, rocky, deep, fast, slow, and beautiful beyond reality" (p. 275). It is an archetypal, animal world in which Ed has participated, the same world reflected in a number of Dickey's poems, such as "The Heaven of Animals."

> Here they are. The soft eyes open.
> If they have lived in a wood

It is a wood.
If they have lived on plains
It is grass rolling
Under their feet forever.

Having no souls, they have come,
Anyway, beyond their knowing.
Their instincts wholly bloom
And they rise.
The soft eyes open.

To match them, the landscape flowers,
Outdoing, desperately
Outdoing what is required:
The richest wood,
The deepest field.

For some of these,
It could not be the place
It is, without blood.
These hunt, as they have done,
But with claws and teeth grown perfect,

More deadly than they can believe.
They stalk more silently,
And crouch on the limbs of trees,
And their descent
Upon the bright backs of their prey

May take years
In a sovereign floating of joy.
And those that are hunted
Know this as their life,
Their reward: to walk

Under such trees in full knowledge
Of what is in glory above them,
And to feel no fear,
But acceptance, compliance.
Fulfilling themselves without pain

At the cycle's center,
They tremble, they walk

Under the tree,
They face, they are torn,
They rise, they walk again.[6]

The instinctive animal drive remains in men like Ed, who, in the course of the novel, does in fact "stalk" and "crouch on the limbs of trees" and who must be "More deadly than [he] can believe." He has gained "full knowledge" of what there is "in glory"; on the other hand, unlike the animals in the poem, he has a "soul" and he understands that he does not need to follow the "cycle" of the animals.

Further emphasizing Dickey's sense of man's soul-being are the many mentions of eyes in *Deliverance*. The "gold-glowing mote" of the left eye of the Kitt'n Britches model is associated with the wildness of the river and reappears in Ed's imagination at several points: just before he leaves on the canoe trip as he makes love to his wife, again as he struggles up the steep river bank to kill the second hillbilly, and again after he returns home as he realizes that "her gold-halved eye has lost its fascination. Its place was in the night river, in the land of impossibility" (p. 277). The most "decent" and caring people in the novel, Drew and Ed's wife Martha, wear glasses. Even in death, without his glasses, Drew's eyes are "blue and all-seeing and clear" (p. 216). The albino boy at Oree has one "rational" eye and one wandering eye (p. 54). A chicken head in the river has a "glazed eye half open" (p. 77). In short, in order to "see," man needs glasses, man-made aids for his vision and understanding.

When Ed returns to Martha and civilization, he has been delivered to a new appreciation of his middle-class roles of father, husband, and businessman. Such a situation is positive and even heroic, in the context of Dickey's novel; "indifference" and "mindlessness" (pp. 180, 178) exist for Ed in the wildness of the river and the savagery of the perverted hillbillys—an indifference to which Ed himself must succumb before he can kill the second hillbilly. From such mindlessness and indifference, Ed at first fears a return to civilization and "to men and their questions and systems" (p. 228): "the Drive-ins and Motels and Homes of the Whopper" (p. 267) are still there, of course, when Ed returns, but he is finally able to understand "what I had undervalued" and to find new meaning even in his advertising agency.

Certainly Dickey has challenged traditional American notions about the romance of the wilderness, the nature of manhood, and the sterility of middle-class life and business. With Kesey and Elkin, Dickey affirms the values of the middle-class businessman in the variety and richness of American life. In Dickey's *Deliverance*, Ed Gentry represents, as his name suggests, a gentleman, a person of gentle birth. In Kesey's *Sometimes A Great Notion*, Hank Stamper's name indicates the strength and individuality of a common man, a strength needed in the second half of the twentieth century to combat those forces that attempt to destroy the individual—unions, government, big business, even academia. As Elkin certifies, these small businessmen are not perfect; they are Flesh and Feldman. They are, however, producers and doers with creative energy. They are not the stagnant Scrooge whose capital only accumulates. They are participants in a society which that "thinker-tinker" Invisible Man recognizes as a healthy diversity; "diversity is the word. Let man keep his many parts and you'll have no tyrant state."[7]

To be sure, four sympathetic protagonists who are small, private businessmen created by three important post-1945 novelists do not compose a dominant trend, but they do at least suggest a shift in perspective at the same time that the more traditionally American heroic types are being debunked. Indeed, *Sometimes a Great Notion*, *A Bad Man*, *The Franchiser*, and *Deliverance* are strikingly affirmative novels in juxtaposition to other novels of the post-1945 period by those writers we generally regard as important. Kesey, Elkin, and Dickey have confronted the paradoxes of capitalism in the post-Modern period in an intellectually and artistically creative fashion.

CHAPTER 14

The Values of Capitalism

Most businessmen depicted in post-1945 television and serious literature are still characterized as greedy, unethical, and immoral (or amoral),
whether they are JR of William Gaddis's *JR: A Novel* or J.R. of "Dal-
las." Moreover, most serious novelists who depict a businessman as a
central character still condemn him for many of the same reasons evident in earlier novels. Thus, for example, Bruce Gold's father and
brother Sid in Joseph Heller's *Good as Gold* (1979) are stereotypical
greedy materialists and hedonists. The characterization of the young
speculator of Gaddis's *JR: A Novel* suggests that businessmen are child-
ish and irresponsible and that making money in the stock market is easy.
In *God Bless You, Mr. Rosewater* by Kurt Vonnegut, Jr., Eliot Rosewater contends that capitalism is destructive to the poor and stupid. Morris
Bober of Bernard Malamud's *The Assistant* claims that supermarket
corporations are destroying his small neighborhood grocery store.

A more subtle charge was recently made by poetry critic Valerie
Trueblood. By comparing "soft poetry" to capitalism, Trueblood condemns such poetry nearly beyond redemption.

> G. K. Chesterton wrote in an essay that capitalism had pro-
> duced "a peculiar thing, which may be called oppression by
> oblivion." When language helps a reader not to know, rather than
> to know, it is doing the same peculiar thing. At first capitalism
> may seem to be no kin of a kind of poetry, but both rely on
> stalwart credulousness as the state most receptive to their effects.
> Both seek with a sort of overmastering geniality to shake the
> hands of those they least serve. In addition to a sedative insis-

tence on the individual and his "needs," they share a highly
managed and strategic language, and a continual raising of
thresholds, persuading us we are missing something—not peace
and fairness, not revelation and delight, but a certain grade of
experience.[1]

In Trueblood's description, capitalism is a kind of opiate of the people,
seductive and subverting to a state not of knowledge, but of desire for a
useless "experience." Both the writer of soft poetry and the capitalist
become here a particularly destructive sort of con man.

So far as I can tell, few serious contemporary writers have explored
in fiction the areas in which businessmen today might be particularly
vulnerable. For example, no writer has attacked the businessman primarily for his pollution of the environment; in Richard Brautigan's
Trout Fishing in America (1967), pollution of America's trout streams
is caused as much by too many people and careless fishermen as by
industry. Nor has any writer explored the dangers of multinational corporations; perhaps the often secret intricacies of such corporate ar-
rangements are beyond the knowledge of the realistic writer. When
Milo Minderbinder forms a multinational cartel in Joseph Heller's
Catch-22 (1961), the details are vague and the situation unbelievable.
Finally, no writer has attacked capitalism for its emphasis upon and celebration of the individual. In fact, one of the most striking attacks on
egalitarianism written in the 1970s is an episode in Vonnegut's *Between
Time and Timbuktu; or, Prometheus-5, A Space Fantasy* (1972). The poet
Stony Stevenson is blasted into a time-warp and discovers that under the
243rd, 244th, and 245th amendments to the Constitution, everyone is
equal: bright people, like Stony, are required to wear radios to scramble
their brains, and talented ballerinas must wear springs attached to their
arms and legs to hinder their movement.[2]

The general attitude toward businessmen since 1945 is still negative,
yet certain other writers have created sympathetic, even heroic businessmen and have, in the process, suggested positive values of capitalism. Perhaps the most striking quality of recent American literature that
deals with capitalism in a sympathetic manner is the sensitivity of the
authors to the problems which capitalism as a system offers to all of us.
Except for Gertrude Stein's 1930s essays, the writers do not deal directly with economic theory, and none offers statistics, curves, charts,
or graphs, but rather each confronts the problems in an imaginative

mode with plots, characters, symbols, metaphors, and language. It is perhaps for this reason they can offer resolutions that are generally different from those of our economists, political scientists, and sociologists.

However, before the mid-twentieth-century writer could deal with capitalism in a creative and constructive manner, he had to accept the death of some old myths, or at least had to admit that these old myths were inappropriate for our time. The first myth is that of the possibility of Utopia, with its corollary, the perfectibility of mankind. This myth is the basis of our various attempts at communal living, of the willingness of certain Americans to accept the proletarian Utopia of Marx and Engels. As John Chamberlain pointed out, a perfect system exists only in the brain of the person imagining it. Even by the midthirties, intelligent American writers had accepted that such a Utopia was not to be. Thus, they set about dealing with a nonperfect (and even nonperfectible) man in a nonperfect world. With this assumption, a contemporary writer like Stanley Elkin is more easily able to admit that his businessmen are both Flesh and Feldman and can then seek real values and resolutions. Despite the fact that both Flesh and Feldman exist largely in an unreal, fictional landscape, they are complex characters, with both faults and virtues, unlike the cardboard capitalists of proletarian literature.

Another myth which writers had to dispel is that, with the frontier gone, rugged individualism could no longer exist in largely urban America. As early as 1894, in *A Traveller in Altruria*, William Dean Howells declared that the disappearance of public lands caused the "free fighter" to be destroyed by the combined forces of organized business and organized labor. A nostalgic yearning for the pioneer days floats throughout our literature, even in the musings of Sinclair Lewis's George Babbitt and of Eugene O'Neill's Mildred Douglas of *The Hairy Ape*. Until recently, it was assumed that such a rugged frontier individualism was not possible, except in John Wayne movies. However, in *Sometimes a Great Notion*, Ken Kesey depicted a man like Hank Stamper, who discovered that only by his rugged individualism could he escape the conformity and mediocrity of the unions. Furthermore, Ed Gentry of James Dickey's *Deliverance* no longer mourns the loss of the frontier per se; his trip down the river taught him that a "primitive rank and savage" life might be appealing to Henry David Thoreau at Walden Pond in the nineteenth century, but that civilized man does not need to follow the cycle of the animals, and that, in fact, the wilderness leads ultimately to nine-fingered people and the sexual perversions of the two hillbillys. By rejecting the wilderness, Gentry is "delivered." For Dickey, the wilderness is a kind of Conradian "Heart of Darkness" (1902), and civilization is a thin but highly valuable veneer.

A third myth which the American artist had to reject is that making money is easy and that businessmen are stupid. Certain contemporary writers, such as William Gaddis, whose *JR: A Novel* features a boy capitalist, continue to insist on the old myth. Other writers have rejected it. One way to destroy the myth is to assume that businessmen are not any more stupid than anyone else, as did Ben Flesh in *The Franchiser*. Another way, however, is to show that the businessman, such as Monroe Stahr in *The Last Tycoon*, has to work very hard indeed, or that a businessman, such as Ed Gentry in *Deliverance* or Merton in Edna St. Vincent Millay's *Conversation at Midnight*, can be both successful and intelligent.

A fourth myth which writers had to ignore is that capitalism developed directly from Puritanism. Not surprisingly, the creative writers understood the fallacy of Weber's position before our intellectual historians, critics, and scholars did. The Protestant ethic of having a calling and of self-help, in terms of Max Weber's definitions, is now simply not a consideration in a number of recent novels, as contrasted, for example, to Lewis's *Babbitt*, in which Weber's theories are rampant. On the other hand, even as recently as 1976, a cultural historian like Daniel Bell was still reciting Weber's theories in *The Cultural Contradictions of Capitalism*. In a curious fashion, Bell has inverted Weber's thesis. Following Weber, Bell asserts that Protestantism and capitalism were historically intertwined, but Bell understands this historical interrelationship as beneficial to capitalism. Protestant virtues, he believes, controlled the self-destructive and hedonistic aspects of capitalism; the Golden Age of capitalism came in the first half of the eighteenth century, the days of Benjamin Franklin and Jonathan Edwards. When Protestantism was submerged in "Modernism," according to Bell, the dangerous tendencies of capitalism became dominant.

However, for such writers as Gertrude Stein, Edna St. Vincent Millay, E. E. Cummings, Stanley Elkin, Ken Kesey, and James Dickey, capitalism is clearly separate from Puritanism and is not historically linked with a failed religion of asceticism. One interesting result of this perception on the part of our writers is that not one of their heroic small businessmen is religious. Any commitment to traditional religion is lacking in their characters. In fact, for Ben Flesh of Elkin's *The Franchiser*, we are now living in .Plato's sky; there is nothing else. Whether the atheist-businessman has been created as a way of avoiding the old myth of capitalism-Puritanism or whether atheism is a necessary part of the contemporary fictive landscape is as yet an unanswered question. It is possible that the artistic problems involved in creating this new character, the businessman as hero or even as a sympathetic character, have been so great for the writer that, like Pablo Picasso's and George Braque's early attempts at Cubism, he can at this point use only grays and tans.

This is not to say, however, that in the godless worlds these novelists evoke there are no transcendent values. Kesey, Elkin, and Dickey are not proponents of a despairing existentialism or of a secular naturalism in which man is a creature dominated by environmental factors. In Kesey's *Sometimes a Great Notion*, the mythological implications of Hank Stamper and his family at least suggest a larger and more universal frame for the action. Elkin's *A Bad Man* abounds with near-allegorical figures, beginning with Feldman's Wandering Jew/Yankee Peddler father and ending with Warden Fisher, the totalitarian tyrant in a system of static statism. The unreal landscape of *The Franchiser*, the multiple twins of the benefactor's family, and Flesh himself, who can describe his world in terms of Plato's Essences, all provide an intellectual context extending beyond any naturalistic interpretation. Finally, in *Deliverance*, the American myth of the frontier is inverted, while at the same time the protagonist reaffirms other values through metaphor, such as the varieties of sight or vision, and through the symbolic nature of the trip itself.

Under any circumstances, it has been our creative artists who first separated Puritanism and capitalism and thus have been able to concentrate imaginatively on the problems apparent in capitalism. With the old myths out of the way, these writers then seemed determined to examine the businessman while creating—perhaps in the very act of creating— their novels, poems, and plays. Although Henry Blake Fuller could with some confidence assert in *With the Procession* (1895) that there did exist a "mercantile morality," he did not define this morality any further, and antibusiness writers have not recognized any such morality. As Henry Nash Smith stated in "The Search for a Capitalist Hero," no positive moral values have sprung from capitalism. More recently, Daniel Bell asserted that "What [the] abandonment of Puritanism and the Protestant ethic does . . . is to leave capitalism with no moral or transcendent ethic" and, further, "American capitalism . . . has lost its traditional legitimacy, whch was based on a moral system of reward rooted in the Protestant sanctification of work."[3] A critic like Richard Hofstadter in *Anti-Intellectualism in American Life* would agree with Bell, but for different, Weberian reasons.

What the argument finally comes to is the relationship between the individual and society. Capitalism is understood as a system in which economic self-interest is allowed to motivate actions of the private individual. In *Wealth of Nations* (1776), Adam Smith asserted that the free economic expression of the individual's self-interest, coupled with man's "moral sentiments," would ultimately lead to freedom and community good. Those who oppose capitalism, such as the socialists, argue that the free expression of the individual is secondary to a planned society in which community good is valued beyond individual self-interest. Some writers, like Bell, argue that capitalism's free expression of individual self-interest has led to a new hedonism, in which the sense of the common community or culture or *civitas*, as Bell labels it, has disappeared. According to Bell, *civitas* is "the spontaneous willingness to make sacrifices for some public good."[4]

In very broad terms, the relationship of the individual and society is an old problem in American literature, with our major writers generally coming down on the side of the individual. As we all know, Henry David Thoreau's "Civil Disobedience" (1849) begins, "I heartily accept the motto, 'That government is best which governs least,'" and later in the essay Thoreau mourns that "the American has dwindled into an Odd Fellow,—one who may be known by the development of his organ of gregariousness, and a manifest lack of intellect and cheerful self-reliance."[5] Breaking the rules of the *civitas* by hunting deer out of season, Natty Bumppo escapes jail and flees to the woods in James Fenimore Cooper's *The Pioneers*. And in 1884, Mark Twain's Huck Finn rejected the *civitas* and "light[s] out for the territory," because, as Huck reasoned, "Aunt Sally she's going to adopt me and sivilize me, and I can't stand it. I been there before."[6] These works do not concern themselves with capitalism as such, but are representative of the elevation of the individual, at times bordering on anarchy, in the works of major American writers.

When certain American writers perceived that private capitalism seemed to be an economic system in which individual freedom and self-expression were theoretically not only allowed, but encouraged, the emphasis upon the individual already apparent in our previous literature found a new fictional background. In a new imaginative texture, writers like Kesey and Dickey enhanced the old theme of individual worth, as opposed to "organizations," as Gertrude Stein terms them, such as totalitarian government, corporate capitalism, monopolistic unionism, even academia. This is not to say that these writers depicted such characters as Hank Stamper and Leo Feldman as perfect beings; rather, given a choice between individual values and community domination (in whatever form), these writers opt for individual values.

What is striking about these writers and their imaginative creations is that the problems of the individual and the *civitas* are approached in several new ways, several perspectives different from any found in the theories of sociologists, economists, and cultural historians. Perhaps the first attempt to solve some of the problems is Ken Kesey's suggestion that the individual of strength and integrity has a beneficial effect on the community. Especially in *Sometimes a Great Notion*, Kesey has perhaps borrowed from the ancient Greek concept of leader and community. When King Oedipus sins, the community suffers a drought. However, Stamper is not Oedipus Rex; he is a private businessman whose problems are not with the gods and fate, but with unions and socialists like Lee. Nor can Stamper really be viewed as a nineteenth-century American Adam, a Natty Bumppo, who, as R. W. B. Lewis defined him, is "the innocent solitary" who springs "from nowhere, outside time, at home only in the presence of nature and God, who is thrust by circumstances into an actual world and an actual age."[7] The difference between the classical hero like Oedipus and the American Adam like Natty Bumppo is, according to Lewis, the relationship of hero/individual and society. "For the traditional [Classical] hero is at the center of [his] world, the glass of its fashion, the symbol of its power, the legatee of its history. But the American hero as Adam takes his start outside the world, remote or on the verges; its power, its fashions, and its history are precisely the forces he must learn, must master or be mastered by."[8]

It is with the American Adam that the academic Lee associates his half-brother Hank and finds Hank to be an anachronism (*"Dan'l Boone in a forest of fallout"*).[9] However, Lee learns that Hank is not finally a Daniel Boone or a Natty Bumppo, those asocial men who could not stand to be surrounded by close neighbors and who continually moved further west. Hank Stamper is quite capable of getting along in society, and he has a broad sense of family, of kinship. It is in association with his family that he is able to withstand the conformist pressures of the union.[10] In a sense, Hank Stamper represents a kind of middle ground between the two kinds of mythical heroes: the classical hero and the American Adam. In a democratic society, an Oedipus the King cannot exist; on the other hand, the self-centered and innocent American Adam is too isolated from others and too anarchic to find a place in society. Perhaps Hank represents a new kind of character, the strong individual of integrity who can ultimately bring a certain knowledge and health to his community. In this novel, private capitalism is not credited with any kind of moral or transcendent value, but it is apparent that private capitalism provides the only setting within which such a hero can act.

Kesey thus suggests that the paradox of individual and community is just that, a paradox, because, through Hank's free expression of self-interest, the community will, in some near-mythical manner, be more healthy. Kesey does not need to resort to Adam Smith's suggestion of man's "moral sentiments" to account for Hank's value to the community. Moreover, Kesey further suggests that it is not capitalism that has produced hedonism, but rather unionism with its sugary pleas for the "Common Good."

A second suggested resolution of the problem of the individual and society can be found in Elkin's *A Bad Man* and *The Franchiser*. In these novels, the individual, private businessman provides for all people luxuries which formerly would have been available only to the rich. The private businessman is therefore "a man of franchise, a true democrat."[11] A democratic economy is not a new defense of either capitalism or socialism, but Elkin carefully associates it with private capitalism. Elkin does point out that democratized consumerism can lead to both cultural homogenization and hedonism; the alternative, however, seems to be worse: the totalitarian state, where men like Warden Fisher reduce men to pliability. Fisher is the supreme rationalist, a man whose rules are sequiturs. However, Elkin goes beyond a simple assertion of the values of democratic economics to suggest several ways that such an economic system and the individual are interrelated. First, the private capitalist, the businessman, is a catalyst to society; he is the one who "set[s] . . . things in motion."[12] He is the doer, the producer, juxtaposed to the static statism of Warden Fisher's prison. Elkin here assumes that the act of becoming is preferable to a state of being, that the dynamic self-starter is not a danger to society, as Daniel Bell has suggested, but is the one alternative to static statism. One benefit of such motion and such dynamism is the contribution of the capitalist to new schools and churches, as Ben Flesh suggests in *The Franchiser*. (The reader can be reminded here of Gertrude Stein's theory as to why there should always be wealthy people in any society.)

Furthermore, Elkin suggests still another justification for the validity of the private capitalist's free expression of self-interest and the resulting dynamic democratic economy. By identifying and respecting himself as an individual, the private businessman learns to value other people as individuals, to allow them to be individuals. In short, capitalism, at least in Elkin's novels, contains paradoxes that work to the ultimate good of the community; the private businessman creates a dynamic, democratic economy in which individual self-interest can result in an otherness, a respect for another individual.

A third possible resolution to the problem of the individual and the *civitas* within a capitalistic system has been suggested in Dickey's *Deliverance*. In this novel, the value of the capitalistic system is affirmed in contrast with primitivism. The wilderness is shown to be a place of degradation, a land of nine-fingered people and of sexually perverted hillbillys. The isolated individual in the woods will succumb to "mindlessness" and "indifference" (pp. 180, 78), just as Ed Gentry was forced to succumb as he killed the second hillbilly. In many ways, *Deliverance* is an affirmation of middle-class values in a large urban area—values that Daniel Bell, for one, claims have disappeared as the modern world saw "an agrarian, small-town, mercantile, and artisan way of life" disappear.[13] For the Weberians, such middle-class values, or the Protestant Ethic, in combination with capitalism, are damaging anyway. Dickey's novel is a variation of Joseph Conrad's "Heart of Darkness," in which civilization is only a thin veneer and reversion to savage primitivism is only too easy. However, Conrad's ultimate negativism is contradicted by Dickey, who suggests that private capitalism provides a proper background for the free expression of man's most generous and creative instincts. After all, the hedonists in Dickey's book are the perverted hillbillys, not the businessmen. The paradox here is that within a *civitas* based on capitalism, free expression of economic self-interest is directly related to a valuation of family and community, or, as Ed Gentry terms it, "what I had undervalued" (p. 270).

Despite these three different approaches to the paradoxes of the individual and community within a capitalistic system, Kesey, Elkin, and Dickey suggest that it is the private businessman who values himself, others, and the "miracle" that is the world, as Ben Flesh affirmed.[14] Stamper, Flesh, and Gentry are not, to be sure, egalitarians like Kurt Vonnegut's Eliot Rosewater, nor are they elitists like Senator Lister Rosewater. Unlike Eliot, they do not pity; unlike Senator Rosewater, they do not extol only the strong. Rather, Ed Gentry, Hank Stamper, and Leo Feldman tend to respect the differences among men. It is the unionists, the preachers of community good, the totalitarian leaders, and the uncivilized hillbillys who denigrate and destroy, who violate and reduce.

These three approaches to the problems of capitalism—the relationship of individual and community—are not simple solutions, nor are they complete. They are not simple in that each author has grappled in a creative and imaginative way with the problems and has decided that they are in fact paradoxes. Paradoxes are more complex than conflicts or even contradictions and can be only partially resolved. In the neat intellectual world of treatises and theories, final answers and resolutions are sought. However, these authors seem to be suggesting that the values of capitalism lie in its very paradoxical nature—an essence which Ken Kesey, for example, can describe at this point only in a semi-mythological context.

Furthermore, these authors have refused to rely on old and obvious defenses of capitalism. For example, the wealthy businessman who endows a charity or museum or university is following a historical pattern established by Benjamin Franklin. Although Elkin's Leo Feldman does give generously to charities, this is only one factor of his complex capitalistic character. Moreover, it is clear that this kind of community consciousness and generosity is especially manifest now. Bennett Schiff pointed out in a recent issue of *Smithsonian* magazine that the Babbitts and Dodsworths of the 1970s are active just this way and in other ways as well.

> Today, you will find them sitting on the boards of their local art commissions, steady visitors to the museums and galleries of the world, regular clients of subscription series to the theater, concert hall, opera and dance. And, not alone that, they are themselves (we will come to their children in a moment) acting in the community theater, painting, sculpting, potting, weaving, dancing, taking pictures that are more than snapshots. For it is here, in

these intimate areas of the collective inner environment of the
country, that our national character has been transformed. Do
not, please, think of it as a "culture boom." We are not speaking
of merchandising, but of one of the basic pattern-breaking
changes in the history of a society—a restructuring of
sensibility.[15]

Brave words and correct ones, perhaps, but also words which suggest
that businessmen must change their sensibility in order to support and/
or participate in the arts, that merchandising is somehow different from
these other activities. This differing sensibility is not the case in such
characters as Ed Gentry or his employee George Holley. The point here
is that, for writers like Dickey and Elkin, the expression of economic self-interest in a pluralistic society will ultimately lead to these
other activities—that business and artistic sensibilities might well be
interrelated.

These writers thus suggest that private capitalism provides the framework for a pluralistic society in which the individual and the *civitas* are
suspended in a paradoxical but healthy relationship. Monopolistic
unionism, corporate capitalism, state capitalism, totalitarianism, and
other kinds of government control can and do destroy the balance. Thus
far, it has been only this private capitalist who has been depicted in a
heroic manner. Such heroism is not the result of repentance and refor-
mation after unethical business dealings, as in the cases of Silas Lapham
and Ebenezer Scrooge. Although the heroic businessman might not always follow wholly ethical business practices, the alternatives to private
capitalism presented by the authors are far less satisfactory. The businessman's role is affirmed as potentially heroic in itself, especially in
terms of his beneficial effect on society. He is celebrated for his sense of
individuality and for his social dynamism. However, the corporate capitalist is still viewed with suspicion by these fictional characters, except,
seemingly, for Ben Flesh, who ironically claims that he does not understand corporate finance even though he himself is a corporate franchiser. One must finally wonder about the future of the businessman as
hero. As a relatively recent arrival on the American literary scene, he
has already assumed several interesting forms. However, his survival is
probably precarious both in fiction and in life. While our writers tell us
that his heroism depends on a balance of paradoxes, our government
tells us that the number of private businessmen declines each year.

NOTES

Introduction: The Scrooge Syndrome

1. John Chamberlain, "The Businessman in Fiction," p. 146. All subsequent references to this article are from pp. 146 and 148.

2. Two studies that center upon the antibusiness novelist and the radical and economic novel of the twentieth century are Taylor's *The Economic Novel in America* and Rideout's *The Radical Novel in the United States, 1900–1954*. In a brief overview of the businessman in "economic novels," Taylor finds the image negative because speculative businessmen violate the "middle class code" of thrift and industry, because large corporations are dangerous to the individual, and because businessmen and politicians form corrupt alliances. Like Chamberlain, Taylor tends to place the origins of business hostility in the post–Civil War period. Rideout's work centers upon the radical novelists, primarily leftist novelists, and traces their rise and decline. By the very nature of such works, businessmen receive little attention, except for the accusation of a general "moral viciousness" and a perverted sex life.

With reference to the cinema, Jonas Spatz contends that Hollywood filmmakers since 1950 have been attempting to project the image of a tycoon who is both businessman and artist. In *Hollywood in Fiction*, Spatz observes that "in an age when the efficiency, as well as the ethics, of capitalism is being questioned, the [film] tycoon has felt the need for the first time to justify his way of life" (p. 80).

With a wide-ranging approach, but one largely hostile to businessmen, Charles Burden, Elke Burden, Sterling Eisiminger, and Lynn Ganim anthologized a number of poems, essays, and short fiction pieces in *Business in Literature*.

3. John Gardner, "Moral Fiction," p. 32.

4. Richard Hofstadter, *Anti-Intellectualism in American Life*, pp. 42, 238, 239.

5. Henry Nash Smith, "The Search for a Capitalist Hero," pp. 78 and 79 (hereinafter cited parenthetically in text). In their emphasis upon the post–Civil War period as the spawning ground for antibusiness hostility, both Chamberlain and Smith agree with the historical view of businessmen asserted by Sigmund Diamond in *The Reputation of the American Businessman*.

Chapter 1: Capitalism is God's Way for Fallen Man

1. Certainly the most complete explanation of the financial structures of the English colonies is Sir Percival Joseph Griffith's *A License to Trade*.

2. John Smith, *The Generall Historie of Virginia, New-England, and the Summer Isles*, pp. 210, 219.

3. For the economic situation of the Massachusetts Bay Colony, a particularly reliable study is Thomas Jefferson Wertenbaker's *The Puritan Oligarchy*. Also helpful, but reflecting the theories of Max Weber, is Larzer Ziff's *Puritanism in America*.

4. William Bradford, *Bradford's History of Plymouth Plantation 1606–1646*, pp. 146–47.

5. Ibid., p. 146.

6. John Winthrop, *Winthrop's Journal "History of New England" 1630–1649*, p. 112.

7. Ziff, *Puritanism in America*, p. 149.

8. Michael Wigglesworth, "The Day of Doom," pp. 260, 259, 264.

9. As quoted in Wertenbaker, *The Puritan Oligarchy*, p. 204.

10. Vernon L. Parrington, *Main Currents in American Thought*, p. 97.

11. Henry Nash Smith, "The Search for a Capitalist Hero," p. 86.

12. Max Weber, *The Protestant Ethic and the Spirit of Capitalism*, p. 111. Hereinafter cited parenthetically in text.

13. *The Twenties*, p. 357.

14. D. H. Lawrence, *Studies in Classic American Literature*, p. 15.

15. It is ironic that the refusal to read historical evidence is a charge directed successfully against Weber and his followers. Hofstadter indicts the businessman for the same reason. "Contempt for the past" is an attitudinal basis for the businessman's anti-intellectualism, according to Hofstadter, *Anti-Intellectualism*, p. 238.

16. Michael Walzer, "Puritanism as a Revolutionary Ideology," pp. 31, 34–35. John Chamberlain is another scholar who has refuted Weber's thesis of the Puritan origin of capitalism. In *The Roots of Capitalism*, Chamberlain terms Weber's and Tawney's argument a "whopping *non-sequitur*" (p. 47) and then traces the roots of capitalism to much earlier historical periods.

17. Samuel Sewall, *The Diary of Samuel Sewall*, p. 172.

18. *Anti-Intellectualism*, p. 238.

19. Bercovitch is here quoting from William Haller's *The Rise of Puritanism*, pp. 4–5.

20. *The Puritan Origins of the American Self*, pp. 17–18. In a later work, *The American Jeremiad*, Bercovitch contends that the correspondence of Puritan contradictions "yielded the secular basis of . . . the sacral view of free enterprise economics" (p. 94). For example, Bercovitch points out ironically that even Jonathan Edwards "sanctified a worldliness he would have despised" (p. 109). Edwards and others, according to Bercovitch, "played important roles in harnessing the Puritan vision to the conditions of eighteenth-century life . . . some to redefine the city on the hill as a model of middle-class economy, others to translate the wonders of the chiliad into the virtues of democratic capitalism (legal equality, open opportunity, self help)" (p. 110).

21. *Anti-Intellectualism*, p. 399.

22. Ralph Waldo Emerson, "Napoleon; or, The Man of the World," *Complete Works*, IV, 253–55, 258.

Chapter 2: The Problems of Liberty

1. *The Autobiography of Benjamin Franklin*, pp. 125–26.

2. "The Way to Wealth," *Papers of Benjamin Franklin*, VII, 347–49.

3. "On the Price of Corn, and the Management of the Poor," ibid., XIII, 514.

4. "Information for Those Who Would Remove to America," *Benjamin Franklin: Autobiography and Selected Writings*, p. 262.

5. Charles Wilson, "The Other Face of Mercantilism," p. 120.

6. Michael Kammen, *Empire and Interest*, p. 117.

7. Franklin, "The Education of Youth," *Papers of Benjamin Franklin*, III, 417–18, 419.

8. *The Autobiography of Benjamin Franklin*, pp. 149–50.

9. Ibid., p. 146.

10. Ibid., p. 155.

11. Everett Emerson, "The Cultural Context of the American Revolution," *American Literature 1764–1789*, p. 16.

12. Alexis de Tocqueville, *Democracy in America*, I, 64.

13. Nathaniel Hawthorne, *Hawthorne and His Publisher*, p. 141.

14. As quoted by Everett Emerson, "The Cultural Context of the American Revolution," p. 14.

15. *Works*, I, 495–96.

16. As quoted by Everett Emerson, "The Cultural Context of the American Revolution," p. 15.

17. Benjamin T. Spencer, *The Quest for Nationality*, p. 68.

18. Barlow, *Works*, II, 382.

19. Ibid., 324.

20. Philip Freneau, "To the Americans of the United States," in *Poems of Freneau*, pp. 149–50.

21. In ibid.; all quotations are from p. 353.

22. *Complete Works*, IX, 120.

23. *Collected Poems*, p. 40.

24. Freneau, "Advice to Authors by the Late Mr. Robert Slender," *The Prose of Philip Freneau*, pp. 91, 93.

25. *Works*, I, 496.

26. Timothy Dwight, *Greenfield Hill*, in *The Major Poems of Timothy Dwight*, p. 511.

27. Thomas Jefferson, *Notes on the State of Virginia*, pp. 164–65. Hereinafter cited parenthetically in text.

28. As quoted by A. Whitney Griswold, "Jefferson's Agrarian Democracy," Harry C. Dethloff, ed., *Thomas Jefferson and American Democracy*, pp. 49–50.

29. Dwight, *Greenfield Hill*, p. 481.

Chapter 3: The Yankee Peddler and the Con Man

1. *Poems of William Cullen Bryant*, p. 14.

2. *Complete Works*, IX, 35.

3. Washington Irving, *Knickerbocker's History of New York*, p. 118. Hereinafter cited parenthetically in text.

4. Constance Rourke, *American Humor*, p. 35.

5. In *Form and Fable in American Literature*, Daniel G. Hoffman examines both the Yankee Peddler and the Confidence Man. Two other valuable discussions of the Confidence Man are "The Confidence Man in American Literature," a dissertation by Victor Hoar, Jr., and, more recently, Warwick Wadlington's *The Confidence Game in American Literature*. Wendy Martin has pointed out a very early appearance of the Confidence Man in Hugh Henry Brackenridge's *Modern Chivalry*, which was written in parts from 1792 to 1805, with final editions in 1815, in her valuable article, "The Rogue and the Rational Man," pp. 179–92.

6. Thomas Chandler Haliburton, *The Clockmaker*, p. 9.

7. Johnson J. Hooper, *Adventures of Captain Simon Suggs, late of the Tallapoosa Volunteers*, all references to page 8.

8. In *The Works of Herman Melville*, VII, 93.

9. Ibid., VI, 472.

10. Ibid., XIII, 239–40, 244.

11. Henry David Thoreau, *Walden and Other Writings*, pp. 6, 7.

12. Melville, "The Lightning Rod Man," *Works*, X, 171.

13. *Herman Melville*, p. 251.

14. A full discussion of the possible influence of Barnum's *Autobiography* upon *The Confidence-Man* can be found in John Seelye's introduction to *The Confidence-Man*, pp. xxiv–xxxiii.

15. Melville, *The Confidence-Man*, in *Works*, XII, 115.

16. Ibid., p. 103.

17. Ibid., p. 209.

18. Ibid., p. 42.

19. Ibid., pp. 262, 264, 266.

20. Ibid., pp. 270–71.

21. *Form and Fable*, p. 307.

22. *The Confidence-Man*, in *Works*, XII, 253, 250.

23. Hofstadter, *Anti-Intellectualism*, p. 399.

Chapter 4: "The American" and the Artist

1. *Democracy in America*, I, 64.

2. Hawthorne, *Hawthorne and His Publisher*, p. 141.

3. Nathaniel Hawthorne, "The Artist of the Beautiful," *Complete Works*, II, 506. Hereinafter cited parenthetically in text.

4. Herman Melville, "Bartleby the Scrivener: A Story of Wall Street," *Works*, X, 20. Hereinafter cited parenthetically in text.

5. *Herman Melville*, p. 242. In *The Businessman in Literature: Dante to Melville*, Michael J. McTague argues that "Bartleby the Scrivener" develops the "negative qualities of business" (p. 64).

6. Walt Whitman, "Song of Myself," *Walt Whitman, Representative Selections*, pp. 51–52.

7. Whitman, *Democratic Vistas*, ibid., p. 427. Hereinafter cited parenthetically in text.

8. Whitman, "Passage to India," ibid., pp. 256, 259.

9. Ernest Hemingway, *Across the River and into the Trees*, p. 16.

10. Henry James, *The American*, p. 32. Hereinafter cited parenthetically in text.

Chapter 5: Crooked Money and Easy Money

1. William Dean Howells, *The Rise of Silas Lapham*, pp. 2, 4. Hereinafter cited parenthetically in text.

2. Edwin Arlington Robinson, "Richard Cory," *Collected Poems*, p. 82.

3. Ernest Hemingway, *To Have and Have Not*, pp. 235, 236.

4. *William Faulkner*, pp. 185, 222.

5. H. L. Mencken, Introduction to Theodore Dreiser, *An American Tragedy*, p. 12.

6. F. Scott Fitzgerald, *The Great Gatsby*, p. 74. Hereinafter cited parenthetically in text.

7. William Dean Howells, *A Hazard of New Fortunes*, p. 72. Hereinafter cited parenthetically in text.

Chapter 6: The Generation Trap

1. John P. Marquand, *The Late George Apley*, p. 116.

2. Eugene O'Neill, *The Hairy Ape*, in *Three Plays of Eugene O'Neill*, p. 203. Hereinafter cited parenthetically in text.

3. Philip Barry, *Holiday*, p. 128. Hereinafter cited parenthetically in text.

4. John Dos Passos, *The Big Money*, in *USA*, p. 300. Hereinafter cited parenthetically in text.

5. William Faulkner, *Absalom, Absalom!*, p. 14. Hereinafter cited parenthetically in text.

6. Henry Blake Fuller, *With the Procession*, pp. 42, 275, 32. Hereinafter cited parenthetically in text.

Chapter 7: "The Hog-Squeal of the Universe"

1. Nathaniel Hawthorne, *The Scarlet Letter*, in *Complete Works*, V, 43.

2. Mrs. S. M. B. Piatt, "The Palace-Burner. A Picture in a Newspaper," *A Voyage to the Fortunate Isles*, pp. 119–22.

3. Howells, *A Traveller to Altruria*, p. 212.

4. Edward Bellamy, *Looking Backward 2000–1887* , p. 46. *Utopias and Utopian Thought* contains articles by editor Frank Manuel and other scholars who explore such topics as "Varieties of Literary Utopias" and "Utopia and Democracy." See also Robert L. Shurter's *The Utopian Novel in America, 1865–1900.*

5. Bellamy, *Looking Backward*, p. 230.

6. Upton Sinclair, *The Jungle*, pp. 35–36. Hereinafter cited parenthetically in text.

7. Any number of studies deal with writers of the American left. Besides those of Walter Fuller Taylor and Walter B. Rideout, cited in n. 2 of the Introduction, of particular interest are Daniel Aaron's *Writers on the Left*; James Burkhart Gilbert's *Writers and Partisans*; and Fay M. Blake's *The Strike in the American Novel*. The emphasis of editor Jack Salzman's *Years of Protest* is to demonstrate that not all creative literature written in the 1930s was radical.

8. Abraham Cahan, *The Rise of David Levinsky*, p. 443. Hereinafter cited parenthetically in text.

9. Clifford Odets, *Waiting for Lefty*, in *Six Plays of Clifford Odets*, pp. 15, 28.

Chapter 8: The Boobus Americanus and the Artist

1. In *Personae*, p. 188.

2. In *Ernest Hemingway: 88 Poems*, p. 53.

3. Willa Cather, "The Sculptor's Funeral," *The Novels and Stories of Willa Cather*, VI, 282, 283. Hereinafter cited parenthetically in text.

4. As quoted in Frederick J. Hoffman, *The Twenties*, p. 35.

5. Ernest Hemingway, *The Sun Also Rises*, p. 115.

6. Saul Bellow, "Nobel Prize Speech," *Newsweek*, 27 December 1976, p. 62.

7. Gertrude Stein, *The Autobiography of Alice B. Toklas*, in *Selected Writings of Gertrude Stein*, p. 207.

8. Hemingway, *The Sun Also Rises*, p. 8.

9. Ernest Hemingway, "The Snows of Kilimanjaro," *Short Stories*, p. 158.

10. George S. Kaufman and Marc Connelly, *Beggar on Horseback*, pp. 210, 212.

11. Sinclair Lewis, *Babbitt*, p. 160. Hereinafter cited parenthetically in text.

Chapter 9: "Is Money Money or Isn't Money Money?"

1. Gertrude Stein, *Everybody's Autobiography*, p. 307.

2. Gertrude Stein, "All About Money," in *Gertrude Stein*, p. 333.

3. Stein, "Money," ibid., pp. 332, 333.

4. Stein, "Still More About Money," ibid., p. 335.

5. Stein, "My Last About Money," ibid., p. 335.

6. Ibid., p. 337.

7. In *E. E. Cummings: A Miscellany Revised*, ed. George J. Firmage, p. 273.

8. E. E. Cummings, *Eimi*, pp. 8, 21, 49. Hereinafter cited parenthetically in text.

9. Cummings, poem #30 of *no thanks*, in *Poems: 1923–1954*, p. 296.

10. Cummings, poem #15 of *New Poems*, ibid., p. 341.

11. Cummings, poem #IV of *IxI*, ibid., pp. 390–91.

12. Cummings, poem #6 of *Jottings*, in *E. E. Cummings*, p. 330.

13. As quoted in John P. Diggins, *Up from Communism*, pp. 28–29.

14. Hemingway, *To Have and Have Not*, p. 140. Hereinafter cited parenthetically in text.

15. Ernest Hemingway, *For Whom the Bell Tolls*, p. 376.

16. *Selected Letters 1917–1961*, ed. Carlos Baker, p. 360.

17. Edna St. Vincent Millay, *Conversation at Midnight*, pp. 105, 109, 107–8, 115.

18. Ayn Rand, *Night of January 16th*, p. 43.

19. For me, Thorstein Veblen's most clear explanation of the differences between the industrial innovator and the financial manipulator is *Engineers and the Price System*.

20. Rand, Introduction to *Night of January 16th*, p. 2.

21. Ibid.

Chapter 10: The Businessman and the Corporate Capitalist

1. Frank Norris, *The Octopus*, p. 261.

2. Ibid., p. 260.

3. F. Scott Fitzgerald, *The Last Tycoon*, p. 62. Hereinafter cited parenthetically in text.

4. Edmund Wilson, ibid., p. 169.

5. Ibid., pp. 170–71.

6. Bernard Malamud, *The Assistant*, pp. 16–17, 33.

7. *The Trial of Judaism in Contemporary Jewish Writing*, p. 109.

8. John Dos Passos, *Midcentury*, pp. 448, 449. Hereinafter cited parenthetically in text.

9. Diggins, *Up from Communism*, p. 250.

10. Joseph Heller, *Something Happened*, p. 13.

11. Ken Kesey, *Sometimes A Great Notion*, p. 116. Hereinafter cited parenthetically in text.

12. See John O. Lyons, *The College Novel in America*.

Chapter 11: "The Great American Tradition of Tinkers"

1. Ralph Ellison, *Invisible Man*, p. 7.

2. Norris, *The Octopus*, p. 48.

3. Henry Adams, *The Education of Henry Adams*, pp. 388–89.

4. Leo Marx, *The Machine in the Garden*, p. 347.

5. Eugene O'Neill, *Dynamo*, pp. 133–34.

6. Twelve Southerners, *I'll Take My Stand*, p. xx.

7. Ibid., p. 27.

8. Mark Twain, *A Connecticut Yankee in King Arthur's Court*, p. 36.

9. Ibid., p. 85.

10. "The Search for a Capitalist Hero," p. 89.

11. Sherwood Anderson, *Poor White*, p. 3. Hereinafter cited parenthetically in text.

12. Ellison, *Invisible Man*, p. 204.

13. Kurt Vonnegut, Jr., *Player Piano*, p. 61. Hereinafter cited parenthetically in text.

14. Ellison, *Invisible Man*, pp. 7, 6.

15. Ibid., p. 563.

16. Ibid., p. 260.

Chapter 12: "Hello Babies. Welcome to Earth"

1. Ellison, *Invisible Man*, pp. 186, 188–89.

2. John P. Marquand, *Point of No Return*, pp. 542, 552.

3. In *The Denatured Novel*, Albert Van Nostrand points out that *Point of No Return* spawned a number of popular novels in the 1950s that celebrate the "system" and the corresponding loss of individuality for men like Grey. He is, it seems to me, too hard on this book and has not considered the way Grey finally gets the job on his own terms.

4. Bruccoli, *The O'Hara Concern*, p. 238.

5. John O'Hara, *Ten North Frederick*, pp. 399, 359.

6. Kurt Vonnegut, Jr., *God Bless You, Mr. Rosewater; or, Pearls before Swine*, p. 110. Hereinafter cited parenthetically in text.

7. *Beyond the Waste Land*, pp. 217–18.

8. Peter J. Reed, *Writers for the Seventies*, p. 162. In view of Vonnegut's criticism of capitalism, I should note that in 1970 he urged the graduating class at Bennington College to "work for a socialist form of government. Free Enterprise is much too hard on the old and the sick and the shy and the poor and the stupid, and on people nobody likes. . . . Dwight David Eisenhower once pointed out that Sweden, with its many Utopian programs, had a great rate of alcoholism and suicide and youthful unrest. Even so, I would like to see America try socialism. If we start drinking heavily and killing ourselves, and if our children start drinking heavily and killing themselves, and if our children start acting crazy, we can go back to good old Free Enterprise again." "Address to Graduating Class at Bennington College, 1970," *Wampeters Foma & Granfalloons (Opinions)*, p. 168.

9. Charles Gordone, *No Place to Be Somebody*, p. 98.

10. William Faulkner, *The Mansion*, p. 419.

11. *William Faulkner*, p. 222.

12. Faulkner, *The Mansion*, pp. 121–22.

13. Brooks, *William Faulkner*, p. 217.

14. *Hemingway and Faulkner*, p. 220.

15. Joyce Carol Oates, *them*, pp. 288, 297.

16. In *Ariel*, p. 49.

Chapter 13: The Businessman as Hero

1. One of the more recent interesting characterizations of the American writer is Tom Wolfe's depiction of "the well-known American writer" who spends his money for ca-

terers and a summer home in the best middle-class tradition while writing a new book with the working title: *Recession and Repression: Police State America and the Spirit of '76.* Tom Wolfe, *Mauve Gloves & Madmen, Clutter & Vine*, pp. 2, 11.

2. Stanley Elkin, *The Franchiser*, p. 164. Hereinafter cited parenthetically in text.

3. Stanley Elkin, *A Bad Man*, p. 42. Hereinafter cited parenthetically in text.

4. James Dickey, *Deliverance*, p. 18. Hereinafter cited parenthetically in text.

5. Thoreau, *Walden*, pp. 81, 168, 189.

6. James Dickey, "The Heaven of Animals," *Poems 1957–67*, pp. 59–60.

7. Ellison, *Invisible Man*, p. 563.

Chapter 14: The Values of Capitalism

1. Valerie Trueblood, "Soft Poetry," p. 22.

2. Kurt Vonnegut, Jr., *Between Time and Timbuktu; or, Prometheus-5, A Space Fantasy*, p. 165.

3. Daniel Bell, *The Cultural Contradictions of Capitalism*, pp. 71, 84.

4. Ibid., p. 25.

5. Thoreau, "Civil Disobedience," *Walden*, pp. 635, 642.

6. Mark Twain, *Adventures of Huckleberry Finn*, p. 405.

7. *The American Adam*, pp. 92, 89.

8. Ibid., p. 128.

9. Kesey, *Sometimes a Great Notion*, p. 116.

10. Robert A. Nisbet in *Tradition and Revolt* has argued that one way to protect the individual from the state is through a pluralistic society containing many units, chief among them the family.

11. *The Franchiser*, p. 164.

12. *A Bad Man*, p. 143.

13. Bell, *The Cultural Contradictions of Capitalism*, p. 55.

14. Elkin, *The Franchiser*, p. 257.

15. Bennett Schiff, "Phenomena, Comments, and Notes," p. 20.

BIBLIOGRAPHY

Aaron, Daniel. *Writers of the Left: Episodes in American Literary Criticism*. New York: Harcourt, Brace and World, 1961.

Adams, Henry. *The Education of Henry Adams: An Autobiography*. Boston: Houghton Mifflin, 1918.

Anderson, Sherwood. *Poor White*. New York: B. W. Huebsch, 1920.

————. *Winesburg, Ohio: A Group of Tales of Ohio Small Town Life*. New York: Modern Library, [1941?].

Arvin, Newton. *Herman Melville: A Critical Biography*. New York: Viking Press, 1957.

Barlow, Joel. *Works*. 2 vols. Gainesville, Fla.: Scholars' Facsimiles and Reprints, 1970.

Barnum, Phineas Taylor. *The Life of P. T. Barnum, Written by Himself*. London: S. Low, 1855.

Barry, Philip. *Holiday: A Comedy in Three Acts*. New York: Samuel French, 1929.

Barth, John. *Giles Goat-Boy; or, The Revised New Syllabus*. Garden City, N.Y.: Doubleday, 1966.

————. *The Sot-Weed Factor*. New York: Grosset and Dunlap, 1960.

Bell, Daniel. *The Cultural Contradictions of Capitalism*. New York: Basic Books, 1976.

Bellamy, Edward. *Looking Backward 2000–1887*. New York: Modern Library, 1951.

Bellow, Saul. *Henderson the Rain King: A Novel*. New York: Viking Press, 1959.

————. *Herzog*. New York: Viking Press, 1964.

————. *Humboldt's Gift*. New York: Viking Press, 1975.

————. "Nobel Prize Speech" (copyright 1976 by the Nobel Foundation), as reprinted in *Newsweek*, 27 December 1976, p. 62.

Bercovitch, Sacvan. *The American Jeremiad*. Madison: University of Wisconsin Press, 1978.

————. *The Puritan Origins of the American Self*. New Haven, Conn.: Yale University Press, 1975.

Blake, Fay M. *The Strike in the American Novel*. Metuchen, N.J.: Scarecrow Press, 1972.

Bradford, William. *Bradford's History of Plymouth Plantation 1606–1646*. Edited by William T. Davis. 1908. Reprint. New York: Barnes & Noble, 1964.

Brautigan, Richard. *Trout Fishing in America*. New York: Dell, 1967.

Brooks, Cleanth. *William Faulkner: The Yoknapatawpha Country*. New Haven, Conn.: Yale University Press, 1963.

Brown, Wallace. *The Good Americans: The Loyalists in the American Revolution*. New York: William Morrow, 1969.

Bruccoli, Matthew J. *The O'Hara Concern: A Biography of John O'Hara*. New York: Random House, 1975.

Bryant, William Cullen. *Poems of William Cullen Bryant*. Oxford: Oxford University Press, 1914.

Burden, Charles; Burden, Elke; Eisiminger, Sterling; and Ganim, Lynn, eds. *Business in Literature*. New York: David McKay, 1977.

Cahan, Abraham. *The Rise of David Levinsky*. New York: Harper and Brothers Torchbooks, 1960.

Cather, Willa. "The Sculptor's Funeral." *The Novels and Stories of Willa Cather*. Library Edition. Vol VI. Boston: Houghton Mifflin, 1937.

Chamberlain, John. "The Businessman in Fiction." *Fortune*, November 1948, pp. 134–48.

———. *The Roots of Capitalism*. Rev. ed. Princeton, N.J.: D. Van Nostrand, 1965.

Cheever, John. *Bullet Park*. New York: Alfred A. Knopf, 1969.

Clemens, Samuel Langhorne. *See* Mark Twain.

Coleman, D. C., ed. *Revisions in Mercantilism*. London: Methuen, 1969.

Conrad, Joseph. "Heart of Darkness." *Complete Works*. Vol. 16. Garden City, N.Y.: Doubleday, Page, 1924.

Cooper, James Fenimore. *Notions of the Americans: Picked up by a Traveling Bachelor*. New York: Ungar, 1963.

———. *The Pioneers; or, The Sources of the Susquehanna*. New York: Rinehart, 1961.

Cummings, E. E. *E. E. Cummings: A Miscellany Revised*. Edited by George J. Firmage. New York: October House, 1967.

———. *Eimi*. New York: Covici, Friede, 1933.

———. *Poems: 1923–1954*. New York: Harcourt, Brace & World, 1954.

Dethloff, Henry C., ed. *Thomas Jefferson and American Democracy*. Lexington, Mass.: D. C. Heath, 1971.

Diamond, Sigmund. *The Reputation of the American Businessman*. New York: Harper & Row, 1965 (originally Harvard University Press, 1955).

Dickens, Charles. "A Christmas Carol." *Christmas Books*. New York: Harper and Brothers, 1854.

———. *The Life and Adventures of Martin Chuzzlewit*. London: MacMillan, 1927 (reprint of 1st ed.).

Dickey, James. *Deliverance*. Boston: Houghton Mifflin, 1970.

———. *Poems 1957–67*. Middletown, Conn.: Wesleyan University Press, 1967.

Diggins, John P. *Up From Communism: Conservative Odysseys in American Intellectual History*. New York: Harper and Row, 1975.

Dos Passos, John. *Midcentury: A Contemporary Chronicle*. Cambridge, Mass.: Riverside Press, 1961.

———. *USA*. New York: Modern Library, [1949].

Dreiser, Theodore. *An American Tragedy*. Cleveland: World, 1948.

———. *The Financier*. Cleveland: World, 1940.

————. *The Stoic*. Garden City, N.Y.: Doubleday, 1947.

————. *The Titan*. Garden City, N.Y.: Garden City Publishing, 1925.

Dwight, Timothy. *The Major Poems of Timothy Dwight (1752–1817)*. Gainesville, Fla.: Scholars' Facsimiles and Reprints, 1970.

Eastman, Max. *Artists in Uniform: A Study of Literature and Bureaucratism*. New York: Alfred A. Knopf, 1934.

Edwards, Jonathan. "Personal Narrative." *Jonathan Edwards: Representative Selections*. Edited by Clarence H. Faust and Thomas H. Johnson. Rev. ed. New York: Hill and Wang, 1962.

Elkin, Stanley. *A Bad Man*. New York: Random House, 1967.

————. *The Franchiser*. New York: Farrar, Straus, Giroux, 1976.

Ellison, Ralph. *Invisible Man*. New York: Vintage Books, 1972.

Emerson, Everett, ed. *American Literature, 1764–1789: The Revolutionary Years*. Madison, Wis.: University of Wisconsin Press, 1977.

Emerson, Ralph Waldo. *The Complete Works of Ralph Waldo Emerson*. Centenary Edition. 12 vols. Cambridge, Mass.: Riverside Press, 1904.

Farrell, James T. *Studs Lonigan: A Trilogy*. New York: Modern Library, 1938.

Faulkner, William. *Absalom, Absalom!* New York: Modern Library, 1951.

————. *The Hamlet*. New York: Vintage Books, 1964.

————. *The Mansion*. New York: Random House, 1957.

————. *The Sound and the Fury*. New York: Random House, 1956. Photographic reproduction of 1st ed.

————. *The Town*. New York: Vintage Books, 1961.

Fitzgerald, F. Scott. *The Great Gatsby*. New York: Charles Scribner's Sons, 1953.

————. *The Last Tycoon*. New York: Bantam Books, 1976.

————. "Winter Dreams." *The Stories of F. Scott Fitzgerald*. Selected by Malcolm Cowley. New York: Charles Scribner's Sons, 1954. Pp. 127–45.

Franklin, Benjamin. *The Autobiography of Benjamin Franklin*. Edited by Leonard W. Labaree and others. New Haven, Conn.: Yale University Press, 1964.

————. *Benjamin Franklin: Autobiography and Selected Writings*. Edited by Dixon Wecter and Larzer Ziff. Rev. ed. New York: Holt, Rinehart and Winston, 1969.

————. *The Papers of Benjamin Franklin*. Edited by Leonard W. Labaree and others. 21 vols. New Haven, Conn.: Yale University Press, 1959–78.

Freneau, Philip. *Poems of Freneau*. Edited by Harry Hayden Clark. New York: Harcourt, Brace, 1929.

————. *The Prose of Philip Freneau*. Selected and edited by Philip M. Marsh. New Brunswick, N.J.: Scarecrow Press, 1955.

Fuller, Henry Blake. *With the Procession: A Novel*. New York: Harper and Brothers, 1895.

Gaddis, William. *JR: A Novel*. New York: Alfred A. Knopf, 1975.

Gardner, John. "Moral Fiction." *Saturday Review*, April 1978, pp. 29–33.

Gilbert, James Burkhart. *Writers and Partisans: A History of Literary Radicalism in America*. New York: John Wiley and Sons, 1964.

Gordone, Charles. *No Place to Be Somebody: A Black-Black Comedy*. Indianapolis: Bobbs-Merrill, 1969.

Gould, Jean. *The Poet and Her Book: A Biography of Edna St. Vincent Millay*. New York: Dodd, Mead, 1969.

Griffiths, Sir Percival Joseph. *A License to Trade: The History of the English Chartered Companies*. London: E. Benn, 1974.

Haliburton, Thomas Chandler. *The Clockmaker; or, The Sayings and Doings of Samuel Slick of Slickville*. 1st ser. London: R. Bentley, 1838.

Haller, William. *The Rise of Puritanism; or, The Way to New Jerusalem As Set Forth in Pulpit and Press from Thomas Cartwright to John Lilburne and John Milton, 1570–1643*. New York: Columbia University Press, 1957.

Hawthorne, Nathaniel. *The Complete Works of Nathaniel Hawthorne*. University Edition. 13 vols. New York: Sully and Kleinteich, 1882–83.

———. *Hawthorne and His Publisher*. Edited by Caroline Ticknor. Boston: Houghton Mifflin, 1913.

Heller, Joseph. *Catch-22*. New York: Simon and Schuster, 1961.

———. *Good As Gold*. New York: Pocket Books, 1979.

———. *Something Happened*. New York: Alfred A. Knopf, 1974.

Hemingway, Ernest. *Across the River and into the Trees*. New York: Charles Scribner's Sons, 1950.

———. *Ernest Hemingway: 88 Poems*. Edited by Nicholas Georogionnis. New York: Harcourt Brace Jovanovich/Bruccoli Clark, 1979.

———. *Ernest Hemingway Selected Letters, 1917–1961*. Edited by Carlos Baker. New York: Charles Scribner's Sons, 1981.

———. *For Whom the Bell Tolls*. New York: Charles Scribner's Sons, 1940.

———. *The Short Stories of Ernest Hemingway*. New York: Charles Scribner's Sons, n.d.

———. *The Sun Also Rises*. New York: Charles Scribner's Sons, 1970.

———. *To Have and Have Not*. New York: Charles Scribner's Sons, 1970.

Herrick, Robert. *The Memoirs of an American Citizen*. New York: Grosset and Dunlap, 1908.

Hicks, Granville; Gold, Michael, and others. *Proletarian Literature in the United States: An Anthology*. New York: International Publishers, 1935.

Hoar, Victor, Jr. "The Confidence Man in American Literature." Ph.D. dissertation, University of Illinois at Urbana-Champaign, 1965.

Hoffman, Daniel G. *Form and Fable in American Fiction*. New York: Oxford University Press, 1961.

Hoffman, Frederick J. *The Twenties: American Writing in the Postwar Decade*. Rev. ed. New York: Free Press, 1962.

Hofstadter, Richard. *Anti-Intellectualism in American Life*. New York: Vintage Books, n.d.

Hooper, Johnson J. *Adventures of Captain Simon Suggs, late of the Tallapoosa Volunteers*. Southern Literary Classic Series. Chapel Hill: University of North Carolina Press, 1969.

Howells, William Dean. *A Hazard of New Fortunes*. New York: Bantam Books, 1960.

———. *The Rise of Silas Lapham*. Cambridge, Mass.: Riverside Press, 1912.

———. *A Traveller from Altruria*. New York: Harper and Brothers, 1894.

Irving, Washington. *Knickerbocker's History of New York*. New York: A. L. Burt, 1893.

James, Henry. *The American*. Edited by Matthew J. Bruccoli. Boston: Houghton Mifflin, 1962.

Jefferson, Thomas. *Notes on the State of Virginia*. Edited by William Peden. Chapel Hill: University of North Carolina Press, 1955.

Kammen, Michael. *Empire and Interest: The American Colonies and the Politics of Mercantilism*. Pilotbooks, Lippincott History Series. Philadelphia: J. B. Lippincott, 1970.

Kaufman, George S., and Connelly, Marc. *Beggar on Horseback*. New York: Boni and Liveright Publishers, 1924.

Kenner, Hugh. *A Homemade World. American Modernist Writers*. New York: William Morrow, 1975.

Kesey, Ken. *One Flew Over the Cuckoo's Nest*. New York: Viking Press, 1969.

————. *Sometimes a Great Notion*. New York: Bantam Books, 1965.

Knopp, Josephine Zadovsky. *The Trial of Judaism in Contemporary Jewish Writing*. Urbana: University of Illinois Press, 1975.

Lawrence, D. H. *Studies in Classic American Literature*. New York: Albert and Charles Boni, 1930.

Lewis, R. W. B. *The American Adam: Innocence, Tragedy, and Tradition in the Nineteenth Century*. Chicago: University of Chicago Press, 1955.

Lewis, Sinclair. *Babbitt*. New York: Harcourt, Brace, 1922.

————. *Dodsworth*. New York: Harcourt, Brace, 1929.

————. *Main Street*. New York: Harcourt, Brace and World, 1948.

Longstreet, Augustus B. "The Horse Swap." *Georgia Scenes; characters, incidents, etc. in the first half century of the Republic*. American Century Series. New York: Sagamore Press, 1957.

Lyons, John O. *The College Novel in America*. Carbondale: Southern Illinois University Press, 1962.

McTague, Michael J. *The Businessman in Literature: Dante to Melville*. New York: Philosophical Society, 1979.

Malamud, Bernard. *The Assistant*. New York: Farrar, Straus and Cudahy, 1957.

————. *A New Life*. New York: Farrar, Straus and Cudahy, 1961.

Manuel, Frank E., ed. *Utopias and Utopian Thought*. Boston: Houghton Mifflin, and Cambridge, Mass.: Riverside Press, 1966.

Marquand, John P. *The Late George Apley: A Novel in the Form of a Memoir*. Boston: Little, Brown, 1937.

————. *Point of No Return*. Boston: Little, Brown, 1949.

Martin, Wendy. "The Rogue and the Rational Man: Hugh Henry Brackenridge's Study of a Con Man in *Modern Chivalry*." *Early American Literature*, vol. 8, no. 2 (1973), 179–92.

Marx, Leo. *The Machine in the Garden: Technology and the Pastoral Ideal in America*. London: Oxford University Press, 1964.

Melville, Herman. *The Confidence Man: His Masquerade*. San Francisco: Chandler Publishing, 1968 (facsimile of the 1st ed.).

————. *The Works of Herman Melville*. Standard Edition. 12 vols. London: Constable, 1922.

Mencken, H. L. Introduction to *An American Tragedy*, by Theodore Dreiser. Cleveland: World, 1948.

Millay, Edna St. Vincent. *Conversation at Midnight*. New York: Harper and Brothers, 1937.

Miller, Arthur. *Death of a Salesman*. In *Collected Plays of Arthur Miller*. New York: Viking Press, 1957.

Moore, Marianne. "Poetry." *Collected Poems*. New York: Macmillan, 1952.

Nisbet, Robert A. *Tradition and Revolt: Historical and Sociological Essays*. New York: Random House, 1968.

Norris, Frank. *The Octopus: A Story of California*. Garden City, N.Y.: Doubleday, 1952.

——. *The Pit: A Story of Chicago*. New York: Doubleday, Page, 1903.

Oates, Joyce Carol. *them*. New York: Vanguard Press, 1969.

Odets, Clifford. *Six Plays of Clifford Odets*. New York: Modern Library, 1939.

O'Hara, John. *Ten North Frederick*. New York: Random House, 1955.

Olderman, Raymond M. *Beyond the Waste Land: The American Novel in the Nineteen Sixties*. New Haven, Conn.: Yale University Press, 1972.

O'Neill, Eugene. *Dynamo*. New York: Horace Liveright, 1929.

——. *The Hairy Ape*. In *Three Plays of Eugene O'Neill*. New York: Modern Library, 1937.

Parrington, Vernon Louis. *Main Currents in American Thought: An Interpretation of American Literature from the Beginnings to 1920*. New York: Harcourt, Brace, 1927, 1930.

Pearce, Roy Harvey. *The Continuity of American Poetry*. Princeton, N.J.: Princeton University Press, 1961.

Piatt, Sarah Morgan Bryan. *A Voyage to the Fortunate Isles*. Boston: J. R. Osgood, 1874.

Plath, Sylvia. *Ariel*. New York: Harper and Row, 1966.

Pound, Ezra. *Personae: The Collected Poems of Ezra Pound*. New York: New Directions Books, 1926.

Rand, Ayn. *Atlas Shrugged*. New York: Random House, 1957.

——. *Night of January 16th*. New York: New American Library, 1971.

Reed, Peter J. *Writers of the Seventies: Kurt Vonnegut*. New York: Warren Paperback Library, 1972.

Rice, Elmer L. *The Adding Machine: A Play in Seven Scenes*. New York: S. French, 1929.

Rideout, Walter B. *The Radical Novel in the United States, 1900–1954: Some Interrelations of Literature and Society*. Cambridge, Mass.: Harvard University Press, 1956.

Robinson, Edwin Arlington. *Collected Poems of Edwin Arlington Robinson*. New York: Macmillan, 1937.

Roth, Philip. *Portnoy's Complaint*. New York: Random House, 1969.

Rourke, Constance. *American Humor: A Study of the National Character*. Garden City, N.Y.: Doubleday-Anchor, 1953.

Salzman, Jack, ed. with Barry Wallenstein. *Years of Protest: A Collection of American Writings of the 1930s*. New York: Pegasus, 1967.

Sandburg, Carl. *Smoke and Steel*. New York: Harcourt, Brace and Howe, 1920.

Schiff, Bennett. "Phenomena, Comments, and Note." *Smithsonian*, May 1978, pp. 20–26.

Seelye, John. Introduction to *The Confidence-Man: His Masquerade*, by Herman Melville. San Francisco: Chandler Publishing, 1968 (facsimile of the 1st ed.).

Segal, Erich. *Love Story*. New York: New American Library, 1970.

Sewall, Samuel. *The Diary of Samuel Sewall*. Edited by Harvey Wish. New York: Capricorn Books, 1967.

Shurter, Robert L. *The Utopian Novel in America, 1865–1900*. New York: AMS Press, 1973.

Sinclair, Upton. *The Jungle*. New York: Viking Press, 1970.

Smith, Adam. *An Inquiry into the Nature and Causes of the Wealth of Nations*. Chicago: Henry Regnery, 1953.

Smith, Henry Nash. "The Search for a Capitalist Hero: Businessmen in American Fiction." In *The Business Establishment*, edited by Earl F. Cheit. New York: John Wiley and Sons, 1964. Pp. 77–112.

Smith, John. *The Generall Historie of Virginia, New-England, and the Summer Isles*. 1624. March of America Series, no. 18. Ann Arbor, Mich.: University Microfilms, 1966.

Smith, Seba. *The Life and Writings of Major Jack Downing of Downingville, away down East in the state of Maine. Written by himself* . . . . Boston: Lilly, Wait, Colman, and Holden, 1833.

Spatz, Jonas. *Hollywood in Fiction: Some Versions of the American Myth*. The Hague: Mouton, 1969.

Spencer, Benjamin T. *The Quest for Nationality: An American Literary Campaign*. Syracuse, N.Y.: Syracuse University Press, 1957.

Stein, Gertrude. *Everybody's Autobiography*. New York: Vintage Books, 1972.

———. *Gertrude Stein: Writings and Lectures 1909–1945*. Edited by Patricia Meyerowitz. Baltimore: Penguin Books, 1974.

———. *Selected Writings of Gertrude Stein*. Edited by Carl Van Vechten. New York: Modern Library, 1962.

Taylor, Walter Fuller. *The Economic Novel in America*. Chapel Hill: University of North Carolina Press, 1942.

Thoreau, Henry David. *Walden and Other Writings*. Edited by Brooks Atkinson. New York: Modern Library, 1937.

Tocqueville, Alexis de. *Democracy in America*. Translated by Henry Reeve. Rev. ed. 2 vols. New York: Colonial Press, 1899.

Trueblood, Valerie. "Soft Poetry." *American Poetry Review* 9, no. 2 (March/April 1980), 22.

Twain, Mark. *Adventures of Huckleberry Finn*. New York: Harper and Brothers, 1918.

———. *A Connecticut Yankee in King Arthur's Court*. San Francisco: Chandler Publishing, 1963 (facsimile of the 1st ed.).

———. *The Mysterious Stranger and Other Stories*. New York: Harper and Brothers, 1922.

———, and Warner, Charles Dudley. *The Gilded Age; a Tale of To-day*. Hartford, Conn.: American Publishing, and Cincinnati, Ohio: Nettleton, 1873.

Twelve Southerners. *I'll Take My Stand: The South and the Agrarian Tradition*. New York: Harper and Brothers, 1930.

Tyler, Royall. *The Contrast*. In *Dramas for the American Theatre 1762–1909*, edited by Richard Moody. Cleveland: World Publishing, 1966. I, 27–59.

Updike, John. *Rabbit, Run*. New York: Alfred A. Knopf, 1960.

Van Nostrand, Albert. *The Denatured Novel*. Indianapolis: Bobbs-Merrill, 1960.

Veblen, Thorstein. *Engineers and the Price System*. New York: B. W. Huebsch, 1921.

Vonnegut, Kurt, Jr. *Between Time and Timbuktu; or, Prometheus-5, A Space Fantasy*. New York: Dell, 1972.

———. *God Bless You, Mr. Rosewater; or, Pearls before Swine*. A Seymour Laurence Book. New York: Delacorte Press, 1965.

———. *Player Piano*. A Seymour Laurence Book. New York: Charles Scribner's Sons, 1952.

———. *Slaughter-House Five; or, The Children's Crusade, a Duty-Dance with Death*. A Seymour Laurence Book. New York: Delacorte Press, 1969.

———. *Wampeters Foma & Granfalloons (Opinions)*. New York: Dell, 1974.

Wadlington, Warwick. *The Confidence Game in American Literature*. Princeton, N.J.: Princeton University Press, 1975.

Wagner, Linda Welshimer. *Hemingway and Faulkner: Inventors/Masters*. Metuchen, N.J.: Scarecrow Press, 1975.

Walzer, Michael. "Puritanism as a Revolutionary Ideology." In *Essays in Colonial American History*, edited by Paul Goodman. New York: Holt, Rinehart and Winston, 1967. Pp. 33–48.

Warner, Charles Dudley. *See* Mark Twain.

Weber, Max. *The Protestant Ethic and the Spirit of Capitalism*. Translated by Talcott Parsons. New York: Charles Scribner's Sons, 1958.

Wertenbaker, Thomas Jefferson. *The Puritan Oligarchy: The Founding of American Civilization*. New York: Grosset and Dunlap, 1947.

Whitman, Walt. *Walt Whitman, Representative Selections*. Edited by Floyd Stovall. New York: Hill and Wang, 1961.

Wigglesworth, Michael. "The Day of Doom." In *Colonial American Writing*, edited by Roy Harvey Pearce. New York: Rinehart, 1950. Pp. 233–97.

Wilson, Charles. "The Other Face of Mercantilism." In *Revisions in Mercantilism*, edited by D. C. Coleman. London: Methuen, 1969. Pp. 118–39.

Wilson, Edmund. Foreword to *The Last Tycoon*, by F. Scott Fitzgerald. New York: Bantam Books, 1976.

———. "Marxism and Literature." In *The Triple Thinker: Twelve Essays on Literary Subjects*. Rev. and enlarged ed. New York: Oxford University Press, 1948.

Wilson, Sloan. *The Man in the Gray Flannel Suit*. New York: Simon and Schuster, 1955.

Winthrop, John. *Winthrop's Journal "History of New England" 1630–1649*. Edited by James Kendall Hosmer. Vols. 7 and 8 of *Original Narratives of Early American History*. New York: Charles Scribner's Sons, 1908.

Wolfe, Tom. *Mauve Gloves & Madmen, Clutter & Vine and Other Stories, Sketches, and Essays*. New York: Bantam Books, 1977.

Ziff, Larzer. *Puritanism in America: New Culture in a New World*. New York: Viking Press, 1973.

INDEX

Aaron, Daniel, 166 (n. 7)
Adams, Henry, 2, 115
Alcott, Bronson, 31
Alger, Horatio, Jr., 55
Algren, Nelson, 80, 92
Anderson, Sherwood, 83, 119–20
Anti-Utopianism, 118–19, 121–23. *See also* Socialism, Utopianism
Aragon, Louis, 94–95
Arnold, Matthew, 83, 115
Arvin, Newton, 42, 48
Astor, John Jacob, 47, 54
Auerbach, Erich, 84

Barlow, Joel, 28, 29, 31
Barlowe, Arthur, 8
Barnum, P. T., 42, 60
Barry, Philip, 65, 67–68
Barth, John, 38, 112, 123
Beard, Charles, 16
Bell, Alexander Graham, 117
Bell, Daniel, 153, 154–55, 158
Bellamy, Edward, 75–76
Bellow, Saul, 84, 112, 125–26, 127, 135, 136
Bercovitch, Sacvan, 19–20, 162 (n. 20)
Blake, Fay M., 166 (n. 7)
Boone, Daniel, 110, 156
Bradford, William, 9–11, 17, 20, 72
Braque, George, 154
Brautigan, Richard, 151

Brooks, Cleanth, 60, 132, 134
Browne, William, 14
Bruccoli, Matthew, 127–28
Bryant, William Cullen, 33, 34

Cabot, John, 8
Cabot, Sebastian, 8
Cahan, Abraham, 77–79
Caldwell, Erskine, 80, 92
Calmer, Alan, 80
Carter, Jimmy, 143
Cather, Willa, 82–83, 88
Chamberlain, John, 2, 6, 77, 152, 161 (n. 5), 162 (n. 16)
Chaplin, Charlie, 116
Cheever, John, 70
Churchill, Lord Randolph, 51
Conrad, Joseph, 153, 158
Confidence Man (con man), 37–44, 45, 51, 56, 59, 101, 151, 164 (n. 5). *See also* Rogue, Yankee Peddler
Connelly, Marc. *See* George S. Kaufman
Cooper, James Fenimore: *Notions of the Americans*, 27; Natty Bumppo, 34, 89, 101, 110, 137, 155, 156
Cotton, John, 12
Cowley, Malcolm, 92
Cummings, E. E., 7, 92, 94–97, 136, 153

Dell, Floyd, 92
Diamond, Sigmund, 161 (n. 5)

Dickens, Charles, 1, 5, 39–40; *A Christ-mas Carol*, 1, 39–40, 99; Ebenezer Scrooge, 1–2, 5, 39–40, 47, 88, 149, 160; *The Life and Adventures of Martin Chuzzlewit*, 40

Dickey, James, 156, 158–59, 160; *Deliverance*, 137, 143–49, 152–53, 154

Diggins, John P., 108

Dos Passos, John, 80, 92, 94, 95, 98–99; *The Big Money*, 68, 99, 120–21; *Midcentury*, 107–9, 110, 127, 132

Dreiser, Theodore, 80, 92, 102; *The Financier*, 4, 58–61, 125; *The Stoic*, 4, 59–61; *The Titan*, 4, 59–61; Frank Cowperwood, 4, 59–61, 62, 63, 64, 80, 81, 89, 101, 125; *An American Tragedy*, 61, 64–65, 80

Dwight, Timothy, 28, 31, 33

Eastman, Max, 97

Edison, Thomas, 117, 122, 123, 124

Edwards, Jonathan, 18, 153, 162 (n. 20)

Eliot, T. S., 92, 128

Elkin, Stanley, 152, 159–60; *The Franchiser*, 137–43, 149, 153, 154, 157–58; *A Bad Man*, 137–43, 149, 157–58

Ellison, Ralph: *Invisible Man*, 38, 114, 126; Invisible Man as tinker, 114, 116, 119, 121, 123–24, 149

Emerson, Ralph Waldo, 6, 43–44, 49; on Napoleon, 20–21; "American Scholar," 27, 52; "Merlin," 30; "Hamatreya," 34–35

Engels, Friedrich, 72, 152

English, Philip, 14

Farrell, James T., 80, 90, 92

Faulkner, William, 33, 90, 92, 102; *The Hamlet*, 39, 60, 131–34, 135; *Absalom, Absalom!*, 68–69; *The Mansion*, 131–34, 135; *The Town*, 131–34, 135

Fearing, Kenneth, 80, 92, 104

Fitzgerald, F. Scott: Jay Gatsby, 14, 61–62, 63, 101; *The Great Gatsby*, 61–62, 65, 125; "Winter Dreams," 63; *The Last Tycoon*, 104–5, 106, 108, 153

Ford, Henry, 114, 117, 138

Frank, Waldo, 16

Franklin, Benjamin, 15, 22–26, 50, 57, 78, 153, 159; attacked by D. H. Lawrence, 16; on the arts, 28–29; as tinker, 114, 116, 123, 124

Freneau, Philip, 28, 29–30, 31

Fuller, Henry Blake, 70–71, 125, 154

Gaddis, William, 7, 63, 109–10, 150, 153

Gardner, John, 3

Gilbert, James Burkhart, 166 (n. 7)

Gold, Michael, 80, 97

Goldwater, Barry, 130

Gordone, Charles, 131, 133, 135

Gould, Jay, 3, 14

Gregory, Horace, 92

Griffith, Sir Percival Joseph, 162 (n. 1)

Haliburton, Thomas Chandler, 39

Hawthorne, Nathaniel, 6, 28, 81, 89; "The Artist of the Beautiful," 45–47, 54, 117; *The Blithedale Romance*, 72; *The Scarlet Letter*, 72, 101, 121; "The Birthmark," 121; "Rappaccini's Daughter," 121

Heller, Joseph, 109, 150, 151

Hemingway, Ernest, 47, 82, 91, 92, 102; *Across the River and into the Trees*, 52; *To Have and Have Not*, 60, 65, 80, 97–98, 99; *The Sun Also Rises*, 84, 85, 89; *For Whom the Bell Tolls*, 98

Herbst, Josephine, 92

Herrick, Robert, 4, 58

Hicks, Granville, 80, 92

Hoar, Victor, Jr., 164 (n. 5)

Hoffman, Daniel, 37, 43, 164 (n. 5.)

Hoffman, Frederick J., 16

Hofstadter, Richard, 6, 20; *Anti-Intellectualism in American Life*, 3, 14, 18, 19, 44, 155, 162 (n. 15)

Hooper, Johnson J., 39

Howe, Florence, 136

Howells, William Dean: *The Rise of Silas Lapham*, 1–3, 5, 56–58, 64, 69; Silas Lapham, 1–3, 56–58, 59, 62, 63, 64, 89, 99, 160; *A Hazard of New Fortunes*, 62–63, 64, 66, 69, 74–75, 76,

89, 125, 131, 133; *A Traveller to Altruria*, 75, 152
Hughes, Langston, 80, 92
Hull, John, 14
Huntington, Henry Edwards, 54

Irving, Washington, 35–37, 40, 51, 56, 60, 70

James, Henry, 2, 27, 81; *The American*, 51–54, 55, 56, 57, 61
James, William, 92
Jefferson, Thomas, 32–33, 34, 41, 58, 114, 117
Jerome, Jenny, 51

Kaufman, George S., 85–86, 104
Keayne, Robert, 12
Kelly, Grace, 51
Kennedy, Jacqueline, 51
Kennedy, John F., 127, 136
Kenner, Hugh, 29
Kesey, Ken, 7; *Sometimes a Great Notion*, 110–13, 137, 141, 149, 152, 154, 156–57, 159; *One Flew Over the Cuckoo's Nest*, 112

Lawrence, D. H., 16, 25
Lewis, R. W. B., 156
Lewis, Sinclair, 92; George Babbitt, 4, 86–90, 104, 126, 144–45, 152, 159; *Babbitt*, 4, 86–90, 122, 153; *Dodsworth*, 53, 159; *Main Street*, 86, 88
Lincoln, Abraham, 49, 105
London, Jack, 4, 80, 92
Longstreet, Augustus B., 38
Lowell, James Russell, 39
Lyons, John O., 167 (n. 12)

MacLeish, Archibald, 80
McTague, Michael J., 165 (n. 5)
Malamud, Bernard, 106–7, 112, 127, 150
Manuel, Frank, 166 (n. 4)
Marquand, John P., 65–66, 126–27
Martin, Wendy, 164 (n. 5)
Marx, Karl, 72, 152. *See also* Socialism

Marx, Leo, 33, 115
Melville, Herman: *Moby-Dick*, 40–41; *White Jacket*, 41; "The Paradise of Bachelors and the Tartarus of Maids," 41, 114; "The Lightning Rod Man," 42; *The Confidence Man*, 42–44; "Bartleby the Scrivener," 47–48
Mencken, H. L., 60–61, 81
Mercantilism, 25, 32
Millay, Edna St. Vincent, 92, 99–101, 153
Miller, Arthur, 39, 90, 106
Moore, Marianne, 31
Morgan, John Pierpont, 54
Murphy, Thomas, 136

Nisbet, Robert A., 169 (n. 10)
Norris, Frank, 58, 103–4, 115
North, Joseph, 8

Oates, Joyce Carol, 134–35
Odets, Clifford, 80, 92
O'Hara, John, 127–28
O'Higgins, Harvey, 16
Olderman, Raymond M., 129
O'Neill, Eugene: *The Hairy Ape*, 67, 79, 131, 133, 152; *Dynamo*, 115–16

Parrington, Vernon L., 14, 16, 19
Patchen, Kenneth, 92
Peters, Paul, 80
Piatt, Mrs. S. M. B., 72–74
Picasso, Pablo, 154
Pilgrims. *See* Puritans
Plath, Sylvia, 135
Pound, Ezra, 81–82, 84, 92
Proletarian literature. *See* Socialism
Puritans, 9–21, 139, 153–54; commonwealth system, 9–13, 20. *See also* Socialism

Raleigh, Sir Walter, 8
Rand, Ayn, 101–2, 104, 108
Ransom, John Crowe, 116
Reed, John, 83, 92
Reed, Peter J., 130
Rice, Elmer, 79, 116

Richardson, Samuel, 28
Rideout, Walter B., 161 (n. 2), 166 (n. 7)
Riding, Laura, 92
Robinson, Edwin Arlington, 58
Rogue, 6, 37–44, 164 (n. 5). *See also* Confidence Man, Yankee Peddler
Roosevelt, Eliot, 128
Roosevelt, Franklin Delano, 93, 94, 128
Roth, Philip, 127, 135
Rourke, Constance, 37
Rukeyser, Muriel, 80, 92

Saint-Gaudens, Augustus, 115
Salzman, Jack, 166 (n. 7)
Sandburg, Carl, 116
Schiff, Bennett, 159–60
Schneider, Isidor, 80
Seelye, John, 164 (n. 14)
Segal, Erich, 127
Sewall, Samuel, 14, 15, 16, 17–18, 22
Shurter, Robert L., 166 (n. 4)
Simpson, Wally, 51
Sinclair, Upton, 2, 6, 76–77, 80, 92
Smith, Adam, 24, 155, 157
Smith, Henry Nash, 3–5, 6, 14–15, 118, 154
Smith, John, 8–9
Smith, Seba, 37
Socialism, 3, 6, 72–80, 86, 112, 155, 166 (n. 7), 168 (n. 8); Marxism, 6, 72–80, 91–92, 97, 99–100, 105, 107, 116, 123, 133–34, 152; Pilgrim commonwealth, 9–11, 72; Puritan commonwealth, 11–13, 20; nineteenth-century communal experiments, 31, 72. *See also* Anti-Utopianism, Utopianism
Spatz, Jonas, 161 (n. 2)
Spencer, Benjamin T., 29
Stein, Gertrude, 7, 151, 153, 156; on Hemingway, 47, 84–85; on money, 91–94, 158
Steinbeck, John, 92, 102

Tawney, R. H., 16, 162 (n. 16)
Taylor, Joshua, 136
Taylor, Walter Fuller, 161 (n. 2), 166 (n. 7)

Thomson, Virgil, 91
Thoreau, Henry David, 44, 89, 114, 152; *Walden*, 41, 144; "Civil Disobedience," 155
Tocqueville, Alexis de, 27, 28, 35, 45
Toklas, Alice B., 91
Trueblood, Valerie, 150–51
Twain, Mark, 38, 117–19, 155; with Warner, *The Gilded Age*, 3, 59
Twelve Southerners, *I'll Take My Stand*, 116
Tyler, Royall, 35

Updike, John, 127, 135
Utopianism, 74–76, 129, 130, 152, 166 (n. 4), 168 (n. 8). *See also* Anti-Utopianism, Socialism

Vanderbilt, Cornelius, 55, 137
Van Nostrand, Albert, 168 (n. 3)
Veblen, Thorstein, 101, 108, 120, 167 (n. 19)
Vonnegut, Kurt, Jr., 7, 28, 168 (n. 8); *Slaughter-House Five*, 63; *Player Piano*, 121–23, 129; *God Bless You, Mr. Rosewater*, 128–31, 135, 150, 159; *Between Time and Timbuktu*, 151

Wadlington, Warwick, 164 (n. 5)
Wagner, Linda, 134
Walzer, Michael, 17, 20
Warner, Charles Dudley. *See* Mark Twain
Wayne, John, 152
Weber, Max, 18, 153, 155, 158, 162 (n. 15); *The Protestant Ethic and the Spirit of Capitalism*, 14–16, 22; theories refuted, 17, 19, 20
Wertenbaker, Thomas Jefferson, 162 (n. 3)
Wharton, Edith, 2
Whitman, Walt, 6, 48–51, 52, 114; "Song of Myself," 48–49; "Democratic Vistas," 49–50, 52; "Passage to India," 50–51
Wigglesworth, Michael, 12–13, 20
Wilson, Edmund, 97, 104, 105
Wilson, Sloan, 90

Windsor, Duke of, 51
Winthrop, John, 11–12
Wolfe, Tom, 168–69 (n. 1)
Wright, Orville and Richard, 117
Wright, Richard, 80, 92

Yankee Peddler, 6, 35–44, 51, 56, 101, 106, 117, 134, 137, 139, 141, 154, 164

(n. 5). *See also* Confidence Man, Rogue
Young, Robert R., 108–9

Ziff, Larzer, 162 (n. 3)

.